THE PATH TO GAY RIGHTS

The Path to Gay Rights

How Activism and Coming Out Changed Public Opinion

Jeremiah J. Garretson

NEW YORK UNIVERSITY PRESS

New York

NEW YORK UNIVERSITY PRESS
New York
www.nyupress.org

Library of Congress Cataloging-in-Publication Data
Names: Garretson, Jeremiah J., author.
Title: The path to gay rights : how activism and coming out changed public opinion / Jeremiah J. Garretson.
Description: New York : New York University Press, [2018] | Includes bibliographical references and index.
Identifiers: LCCN 2017034393 | ISBN 978-1-4798-2213-3 (cl : alk. paper) | ISBN 978-1-4798-5007-5 (pb : alk. paper)
Subjects: LCSH: Gay rights—United States—History. | Gay rights—United States—Public opinion—History. | Gays—United States—Public opinion—History.
Classification: LCC HQ76.8.U5 G3575 2018 | DDC 323.3/2640973—dc23
LC record available at https://lccn.loc.gov/2017034393

New York University Press books are printed on acid-free paper, and their binding materials are chosen for strength and durability. We strive to use environmentally responsible suppliers and materials to the greatest extent possible in publishing our books.

Manufactured in the United States of America

10 9 8 7 6 5 4 3 2 1

Also available as an ebook

CONTENTS

PART I

Introduction

1

A Transformed Society

LGBT Rights in the United States

It is apparent that condemnation of homosexuality is today almost universal. . . . Occasionally one encounters an attitude not so much of tolerance but of actual acceptance, but this is rare. . . . The basic problem is the *hostile spirit* pervading even the more permissive of modern peoples.
—Donald Webster Cory, *The Homosexual in America*, 1951 (emphasis added)

In the late 1980s and early 1990s, a dramatic wave began to form in the waters of public opinion: American attitudes involving homosexuality began to change. The key to understanding why is simple. As the Acquired Immunodeficiency Syndrome (AIDS) decimated the gay community in the late 1980s, lesbian, gay, bisexual, and transgender (LGBT)[1] activists demanded that the media begin to cover AIDS and other issues of importance to them, Then, as the public's fear of AIDS waned and a national dialogue on gay rights emerged in the early 1990s, lesbians and gays across the country began to feel more comfortable living openly. So many people learned of gay family members, friends, and acquaintances that the basic negative reactions that most people had toward lesbians and gays began to evaporate. As this visceral negativity towards homosexuality dissipated in the wake of increased familiarity with lesbians and gays, a marked transformation of the American public's views on gay rights started that has continued to this day.[2]

The transformation of America's response to homosexuality has been—and continues to be—one of the most rapid and sustained shifts in mass attitudes since the start of public polling. As late as 1987, the General Social Survey (GSS)[3] found that 78 percent of the American public thought that same-sex relations were "Always Wrong." A mere twenty-five years later, the same survey found that only 45 percent believed homosexuality was "Always Wrong," with an equal percentage saying same-sex relations were "Not Wrong at All."[4] Put another way, over a third of the American public has changed its view on just this one question. Since the 1990s, change among younger Americans has been so drastic that many pundits and academics have concluded that opposition to gay rights will soon go the way of support for segregated schools and opposition to interracial marriage. Only strong conservatives and the very religious have remained immune to this trend.[5]

How has this change in public opinion occurred? What are its primary causes? Why do we not see attitude change of similar magnitudes on other issues? What makes gay rights different?

The change in Americans' basic reaction to lesbians and gays is much broader than surveys have captured. In the 1960s and 1970s, journalists routinely dismissed gay issues as improper or unseemly for public consumption.[6] Elected officials either ignored lesbians or gays or openly denigrated them.[7] When presented with well-reasoned constitutional arguments for gay rights, federal judges concluded without a second thought that discrimination against lesbians and gays was perfectly legal.

Times have changed. Lesbian and gay issues are now regularly discussed in the national news. Many political figures tend to endorse laws supporting gay rights.[8] Federal judges across the country and a majority of the US Supreme Court now appear persuaded that the equal protection clause of the Fourteenth Amendment renders many anti-gay laws unconstitutional. Lesbian and gay characters are now regularly depicted on American entertainment television,[9] including shows geared toward teenage audiences like *Teen Wolf* and *Glee*. And, most important, a vast majority of the public now reports personally knowing out lesbian and gay relatives, friends, or coworkers.[10]

All of these facets of the nation's growing acceptance of lesbians and gays are interrelated with change in public support for gay rights. In democracies such as the United States, politicians generally respond to public opinion. Judges and television executives do not wish to appear too out-of-step with the public.[11] LGBT people themselves feel more comfortable coming out to those perceived to be more supportive of gay rights.[12]

Although public opinion may encourage these changes, it is often driven by them. The changing stances of politicians, television, and personal experiences with respect to LGBT people have all been shown to cause more liberal attitudes toward lesbians, gays, and their rights.[13] This interrelationship makes understanding the root cause of attitude change difficult. But understanding why and how opinions have changed is central to comprehending why many aspects of American society—entertainment, politics, corporations—appear to be, at least rhetorically, more tolerant of the existence of lesbians and gays. Recognizing the central role that mass attitude change has had in these broader social changes is key to understanding the social revolution regarding sexuality in both the United States and across the globe. This, in turn, leads us to consider the extent to which this process of attitude change may be pertinent to other issue areas.

* * *

The core argument of this book is simple: It is that the most important factor that has allowed for a rapid, significant, and durable transformation in public opinion about lesbians and gays has been the tireless work of LGBT activists, especially during the AIDS crisis. LGBT and anti-AIDS activists reoriented the national dialogue by changing the way the news media approached gay rights issues. As the national media began to discuss gay rights, the lesbian and gay community no longer felt as isolated from society at large. This led to a massive increase in "coming out" and the transformation of American society.

This book is about how the explosion of tolerance for gay rights that Americans are rapidly expressing on surveys has its origins in the ways in which lesbians and gays have fought back against the stigma they have felt from the larger society. As the LGBT movement assaulted this stigma, it unleashed a series of contextual changes in American society that cascaded into further change. The goal of this book is to disentangle these various contextual shifts in media, politics, and society and to explain how LGBT activism eventually caused the metamorphosis of public perceptions of lesbians and gays.

Although LGBT activists started the process of change by pressuring political elites and the national media to pay attention to the AIDS crisis and other gay issues, the eventual responsiveness of these institutions to activist pressure provided another crucial link in causing social change.

The notion that institutional change can bring about shifts in public opinion is hardly a new theory.[14] However, the actual process through which institutions have brought about change in public perceptions of lesbians and gays has been misunderstood. The central problem with preexisting theories of change in mass opinion on gay rights—framing and elite-signaling (explained below and in chapter 2)—is that they tend to operate *directly* through news media. In the media, framing involves the use of phrases and words that cause readers or viewers to apply certain values, like beliefs in equality and fairness, to gay rights, while elite-signaling involves individuals adopting the positions of political leaders on an issue when those positions are communicated through news media.

Such media-led theories are ill-suited as an explanation for the distinctive features of change in support for gay rights. For instance, *not only* has the public become more liberal in its attitudes toward gay rights in time periods of *intense news attention* to gay rights, but it has also grown more tolerant in time periods when *news attention to gay issues has been close to zero*. Furthermore, attitudinal change on gay rights has occurred both among those who follow the news regularly and among those who report *complete inattention to the news*. If attitude change comes directly from news coverage of gay rights, then why is it not most concentrated among those that watch the news?

This book argues that institutional changes in the American media and political system, specifically the start of a prominent national dialogue on lesbian and gay rights, did not act *directly* on the American public as is usually the case when the media causes attitude change on other issues. Instead, rather than causing the distinctive changes that we have seen on gay rights, what these institutional changes did—in reality—*was to encourage lesbians and gays to "come out" en masse*. Thus, institutional change brought about a "'boom'" in public exposure to lesbians and gays—both through media *and interpersonally*. It was this "'boom'" in exposure to lesbians and gays that resulted in all of the distinctive features of change in gay rights and ultimately led tolerance to triumph. Figure 1.1 summarizes this causal sequence of attitude change.

I term this theory—that exposure to lesbians and gays was the defining factor that has caused distinctive change on gay rights attitudes as

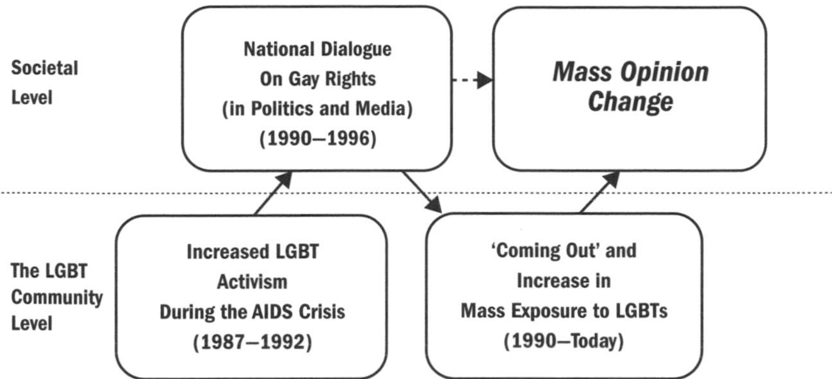

Figure 1.1. The Causal Sequence of Attitude Change. The causal sequence that resulted in durable attitude change on gay and lesbian issues as described in this study is represented in this diagram by the black arrows. Anti-AIDS activism resulted in pro-gay shifts in both national media coverage and among Democratic elected officials in the early 1990s. These were followed by increases in coming out, which led to durable mass attitude change via *affective liberalization*. Preexisting theories of the origin of attitude change, including value-framing and issue evolution, are depicted by the dotted arrow.

compared to other issues—the theory of *affective liberalization*. Evidence in this book demonstrates that exposure to lesbians and gays increased support for gay rights by significantly warming the automatic emotional reactions—positive or negative—that spring to mind when people think about lesbians and gays. While other factors also affect support for gay rights, it is this increased exposure—in the form of interpersonal and mediated contact with lesbians and gays—that has largely defined the most prominent features of opinion change on gay issues: its broadness, its durability, its rapidity, and its concentration among the millennial generation.

The next section outlines change in American attitudes on gay rights over the last forty years. After illustrating these trends, I outline my theory of affective liberalization. One other major feature of this work is also previewed in this chapter: a strong emphasis on the role of the LGBT movement in providing a catalyzing force for change through years of sustained activism. Other academic accounts miss that centrality. A brief outline of the book follows.

A Survey of Changing Views on Lesbian and Gay Rights, 1972–2014

When we survey attitude change on gay rights, we are first struck by the rapidity and scale of the change. However, an equally impressive feature of this change is that it has occurred across nearly every question asked by pollsters regarding lesbians, gays, or homosexuality regularly. From public acceptability of homosexuality to support for allowing gay teachers, we have seen a sustained shift in public support.[15]

Civil Liberties

Without legal support for the rights of minorities to communicate with the public—in the form of speeches, books, rallies, and parades—the public will likely never encounter the viewpoints of minorities.

The first national survey to ask about support for the civil liberties of lesbians and gays was the General Social Survey (GSS) in 1972.[16]

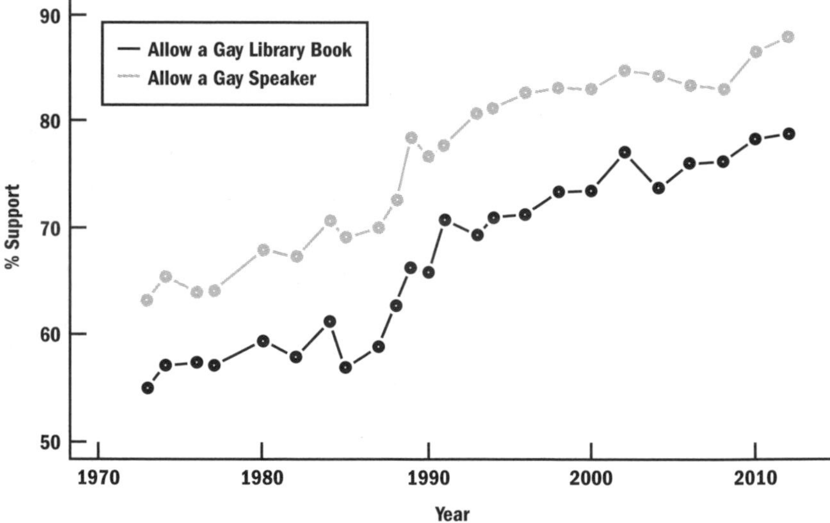

Figure 1.2. Trends in Support for Gay Civil Liberties.
These trends involve the percentage of the public who would allow a library book or a public speech on homosexuality in their community by an "admitted homosexual." The largest shifts take place in the late 1980s as mass attention to AIDS increased.
Source: Smith et al., *General Social Survey, 1972–2016.*

Approximately every two years, this survey asks a different representative sample of the American public an expansive battery of questions during interviews that last well over an hour. Four frequently asked questions involve gay rights. Three questions ask about support for the free speech rights of gays. Of these three, two questions directly involve civil liberties for lesbians and gays: one asks respondents if they believe that homosexuals should be allowed to make a speech in their community; the other asks if it would be proper to have a book favoring homosexuality and written by an "admitted homosexual" removed from a library in a respondent's community.

Figure 1.2 plots the trend in the numbers of respondents that would allow a pro-gay book in the library and allow a pro-gay speaker. In terms of allowing a pro-gay book in a library, there was little overall change until 1988. Before that year, support for allowing such a book hovered around 58 percent on average. Beginning in 1988 and continuing until 1991, support rose rapidly to 70 percent. A steady increase in support then began in the 1990s and 2000s and reached 78 percent in 2012.

A similar trend emerges from the question involving allowing a gay speaker. The only difference is that there does appear to be some more consistent upward trending in support prior to 1988. Support for a gay community speaker rose about 9 percent in the fifteen years from 1972 to 1987. By 1993, the percentage of the public who would allow a gay speaker had risen to 81 percent. Support remained in the low 80s until 2008, before finally rising to 88 percent in 2012. While this represents a much quicker increase in support for gay speakers than for pro-gay books, both questions see similar trends—a rapid increase in support starting in the late 1980s.

Employment Nondiscrimination

No single cluster of issues has been more consistently polled for a longer period of time than the rights of lesbians and gays to hold various forms of employment free from discrimination. Prior to the start of same-sex marriage in 2003, nearly every national battle that occurred over gay rights involved some battle over equal employment opportunities, from California's 1978 vote on Prop 6, which sought to ban lesbian and gay schoolteachers, to the current struggle to pass the Employment Non-Discrimination Act (ENDA) in Congress.

Figure 1.3 shows the trend on responses to four related questions first asked in the 1970s. Many more questions concerned equal employment, though few go back as far in time as those displayed.[17] Plotted here also is the third GSS question from the free speech battery, about allowing a "homosexual" to teach in a college. The other questions plotted are from Gallup, an organization that regularly polls the public on important topics relating to government policy and performance. These questions involve allowing gays to teach in elementary schools and to serve openly in the US Armed Forces, as well as a general question asking about support for nondiscrimination laws in employment practices on the basis of sexual orientation.

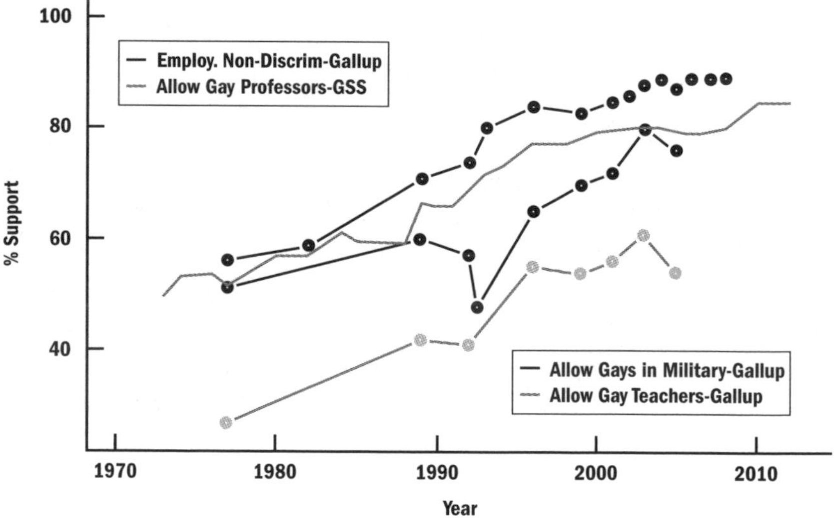

Figure 1.3. Trends in Support for Employment Nondiscrimination and Various Forms of Equal Employment Opportunities for Lesbians and Gays.
Source: Karlyn Bowman and Adam Foster, "Attitudes about Homosexuality and Gay Marriage," *American Enterprise Institute Studies in Public Opinion*, 2008, www.aei.org; Karlyn Bowman, Andrew Rugg, and Jennifer Marsico "Polls on Attitudes on Homosexuality and Gay Marriage," *American Enterprise Institute Studies in Public Opinion*, 2013, www.aei.org; Smith et al., *General Social Surveys, 1972–2016*.

Taken together, the trends reveal a more-or-less even liberalization in support of employment protections from the 1970s onward. The amount of change is fairly consistent across question and decade, although rising support for nondiscrimination may have leveled off in the mid-2000s. Support for allowing gays in the military did decline rapidly in 1992 and 1993. This was at the same time that conservatives in Congress mobilized against a potential executive order by President Bill Clinton allowing lesbians and gays to serve openly, discussed in more detail in chapter 5. That said, support quickly rebounded by 1996.

One thing to note is that support for various forms of employment protections have been consistently high—over 50 percent in the 1970s and between 70 and 80 percent in the 2000s.[18] The one exception in the figure is support for allowing gay elementary school teachers. Support for nondiscrimination in terms of gay doctors, gay salespeople, and gay members of the president's cabinet generally matches the high level of support for nondiscrimination laws in general. Over time only support for gay clergy members has been closer to the generally lower levels of support for gay elementary school teachers.[19]

Legality of Homosexuality

Naturally, the public's stance toward the legality or illegality of homosexuality is important for the lives of lesbians and gays. If laws banning homosexuality are in place, lesbians and gays are—quite literally—criminals. In the past, the existence of such laws has been a major justification for government discrimination in other areas of life.[20] The *Washington Post*, Gallup, and CBS (in conjunction with the *New York Times*) have polled the public regularly on whether or not they believe homosexual activity should be legal or illegal since the late 1970s. Figure 1.4 displays opinion trends on the legality of homosexuality.

One caveat is in order when it comes to the Gallup Poll's question on this topic. In the early 1980s, when Gallup began asking the public about views on the legality of homosexuality, it first asked about support for employment protections for gays or some specific gay right. Egan, Persily, and Wallsten[21] discovered that when such questions preceded the question on the legality of homosexuality, support for legality increased

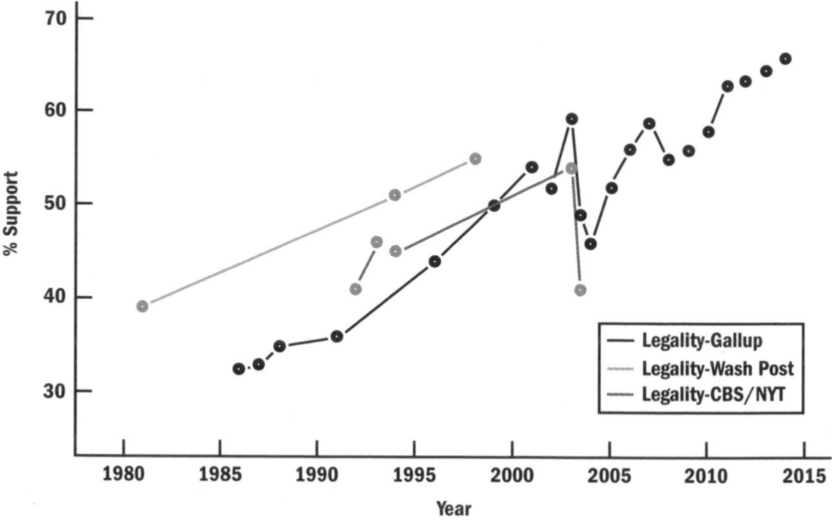

Figure 1.4. Trends in Support for the Legality of Homosexuality.
Source: Bowman and Fostor, "Attitudes about Homosexuality and Gay Marriage"; Bowman, Rugg, and Marsico, "Polls on Attitudes on Homosexuality and Gay Marriage."

by about 12 percent. When it comes to tracking change in opinions, question wording effects like these are problematic. Gallup stopped asking these leading questions on other gay rights policies immediately after the 1986 *Bowers vs. Harwick* Supreme Court decision, which found that state laws banning sodomy, including bans on heterosexual sodomy, were constitutional. This question-order effect on the Gallup Poll may have falsely led to the conclusion that *Bowers* had decreased support for the legality of homosexuality.[22] For the purposes of the trend lines in figure 1.4, I omit polls in years when the legality question was preceded by another gay rights question.

With these responses on the Gallup Poll omitted, the three polling firms that asked the public their support for laws banning homosexuality tell a consistent story. In the 1980s, just 30–40 percent of the public believed that homosexuality should be legal. This changed rapidly in the 1990s. By 2000, legality of homosexuality had majority support. This was just in time for the Supreme Court to reconsider its *Bowers* ruling in 2003, when the court explicitly overturned *Bowers* in its *Lawrence vs. Texas* decision. There was a decline in support for legality after

Lawrence, but that likely had more to do with Massachusetts legalizing same-sex marriage than with *Lawrence*.[23] Since then, support for legality has increased to over 60 percent.

Same-Sex Marriage and Adoption Rights

Since Massachusetts first legalized same-sex marriage in 2003, support for marriage equality for lesbian and gay couples has received more press attention and polling than any other gay rights issue.[24] In marked contrast, the right of gay and lesbian couples to adopt children receives only sparse news coverage.[25] In figure 1.5, the trends on questions asked by *Newsweek* and Pew, another prominent polling organization, involving support for same-sex marriage are displayed alongside questions asked by Gallup and Pew involving support for the adoption rights of same-sex couples. The *Newsweek* question is unique, in that it was first regularly asked in the 1990s, when same-sex marriage was largely off the radar of the other polling firms.

During the 1990s, support for same-sex marriage appears to have been largely flat. That is, while it may have increased slightly during this decade, the question was asked so infrequently that it is hard to tell. Unlike other issues described earlier, few lesbians or gays (or LGBTQ activists) paid any attention to marriage equality in the 1990s.

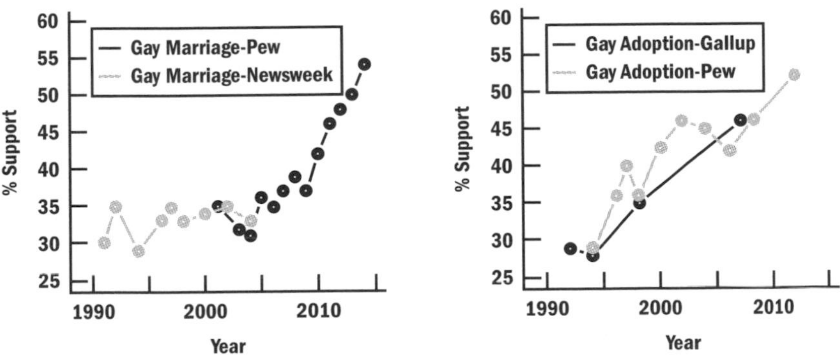

Figure 1.5. Trends in Support for Same-Sex Marriage and Adoption Rights. *Source*: Bowman and Fostor, "Attitudes about Homosexuality and Gay Marriage"; Bowman, Rugg, and Marsico, "Polls on Attitudes on Homosexuality and Gay Marriage."

Nearly all LGBTQ legal activists were more concerned with legal challenges to anti-sodomy statutes, *Bowers*, and other anti-gay laws. Political activists focused their attention on Don't-Ask-Don't-Tell (DADT), hate-crimes legislation, and the Employment Non-Discrimination Act (ENDA). It makes sense, in this context, that with few LGBTQ activists advocating for marriage equality, few members of the public would move in favor of it.

Since 2003, not only has this inattention ended, but marriage equality has become a central focus of movement activity and advocacy. Furthermore, reports of the public becoming more and more supportive of same-sex marriage have dominated the national news. When Barack Obama endorsed marriage equality in 2012, a majority of the public began to support marriage equality for the first time, as shown in the figure.

While this positive movement has been impressive, the rise in support for gay adoption has been of an equal magnitude since the early 1990s. From 1994 to 2002, Pew shows an increase of over 15 percent in public support for adoption rights. Support moved over 50 percent at the very same time that marriage equality began to be backed by a majority. Adoption rights may have received greater media attention than marriage equality in the 1990s,[26] but that press attention has been nowhere near the amount that marriage equality has received in recent years. Yet support for same-sex couples adopting children has increased just as much.

Support for Gay and Lesbian Children

Disapproval of lesbian and gay children is an unspoken crisis. The Williams Institute has estimated that 40 percent of homeless youth are lesbian, gay, bisexual, or transgender.[27] Not every lesbian or gay child with disapproving parents runs away. However, those who stay in homes with disapproving parents are often left both psychologically isolated and saddled with increased levels of stress during their teenage years.[28]

The *Los Angeles Times* and Pew have periodically asked members of the public how they would react if their child told them he or she is gay (see table 1.1). Recent positive changes in responses to this question are

TABLE 1.1. Parents' Reported Emotional Reactions If Their Child Said He or She Is Lesbian or Gay (1983–2014)

<table>
<tr><th></th><th>1983</th><th>1985</th><th>2000</th><th>2004</th><th>2013</th></tr>
<tr><td>Reported Reaction</td><td></td><td></td><td></td><td></td><td></td></tr>
<tr><td>Very Upset</td><td>61%</td><td>63%</td><td>34%</td><td>29%</td><td>19%</td></tr>
<tr><td>Somewhat Upset</td><td>27%</td><td>27%</td><td>38%</td><td>33%</td><td>21%</td></tr>
<tr><td>Not Very Upset</td><td>4%</td><td>4%</td><td>9%</td><td>13%</td><td rowspan="2">55%</td></tr>
<tr><td>Not Upset at All</td><td>5%</td><td>4%</td><td>15%</td><td>20%</td></tr>
<tr><td>Don't Know/Refused</td><td>4%</td><td>5%</td><td>4%</td><td>5%</td><td>5%</td></tr>
<tr><td>N</td><td>1521</td><td>1147</td><td>2071</td><td>1336</td><td>740</td></tr>
<tr><td>Polling Firm</td><td>LA Times</td><td>LA Times</td><td>LA Times</td><td>LA Times</td><td>Pew</td></tr>
</table>

even more unprecedented than change in marriage equality support or change in the legality of homosexuality. In the mid-1980s, over 60 percent of individuals said they would be "Very Upset" if their child confided in them that she or he is gay. In 2013, Pew found only 19 percent still taking this same position—a 40 percent reduction in negativity directed at having gay children. Only 9 percent stated that they would be "Not Very Upset" or "Not Upset at All" in the early 1980s. By 2013, a majority of the public, 55 percent, told Pew they would "Not [be] Upset." This represents a radical transformation of the very nature of the lesbian and gay experience in America.

Acceptability, Approval, and Affective Feelings

For my last set of trends, I wish to show how the public's immediate reactions to lesbians, gays, and their relationships have changed. In figure 1.6, I have plotted responses to a question on the GSS that asks respondents if they approve of same-sex relations. Respondents can pick from one of four categories to express their reactions to these relationships: "Always Wrong," "Almost Always Wrong," "Sometimes Wrong," and "Not Wrong at All." The percentage of respondents who picked "Not Wrong at All" between the early 1970s and the early 2010s is plotted in figure 1.6.

It turns out that people feel very confident about the direction of their response to the same-sex relations question. Very few respondents ever pick the two middle categories: "Almost Always Wrong" or "Sometimes

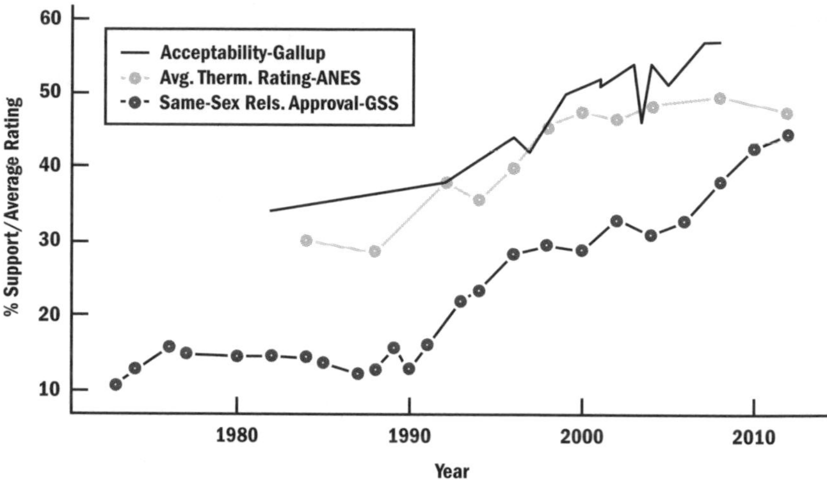

Figure 1.6. Trends in Acceptability, Approval, and Affective Feelings toward Homosexuality, Lesbians, and Gays.
Source: Bowman and Fostor, "Attitudes about Homosexuality and Gay Marriage"; Bowman, Rugg, and Marsico, "Polls on Attitudes on Homosexuality and Gay Marriage." Smith et al., General Social Surveys, 1972–2016; American National Election Studies, and Stanford University, *ANES Times Series Cumulative Data File (1948–2012)*, ICPSR08475-v15, (Ann Arbor, MI: Inter-University Consortium for Political and Social Research [distributor], 2015), doi.org/10.3886/ICPSR08475.v15.

Wrong." This means that nearly everyone picks either "Not Wrong at All" or "Always Wrong."

Displayed alongside the GSS trend are responses to a Gallup Poll question: "Do you feel that homosexuality should be considered an acceptable alternative lifestyle or not?" "Acceptability" tends to be higher than actual "approval" (the GSS question), as shown in figure 1.6.

The last trend in figure 1.6 is the average response on the American National Election Study's (ANES) feeling thermometer of lesbians and gays. Sponsored by the National Science Foundation, the ANES is a well-known poll that asks respondents their views on political issues nearly every two years.[29] In every presidential election year and most midterm election years, the ANES surveys a representative sample of American voters on their political attitudes and engagement with politics. The ANES also periodically conducts panel studies that resurvey the same respondents in order to track how their attitudes change in response to events. Their feeling thermometer question opens with the following prompt:

> We'd like to get your feelings toward some of our political leaders and other people who are in the news these days. We'll show the name of a person and we'd like you to rate that person using something we call the feeling thermometer. Ratings between 50 degrees and 100 degrees mean that you feel favorable and warm toward the person. Ratings between 0 degrees and 50 degrees mean that you don't feel favorable toward the person and that you don't care too much for that person. You would rate the person at the 50 degree mark if you don't feel particularly warm or cold toward the person. If we come to a person whose name you don't recognize, you don't need to rate that person.[30]

To drive the point home, respondents are often shown a picture of an actual thermometer with 0 at cold and 100 at warm. After being asked about their immediate reactions to a number of political figures, like the president or vice president, the respondents are then asked to rate various social groups including "Lesbians and Gays, that is Homosexuals." In figure 1.6, I plot the average ratings of "Lesbians and Gays" since 1984.

The feeling thermometer of the ANES is unique in that it is the best regularly taken measure of people's automatic reactions toward lesbians and gays. Typically, people do not think much about the group in question before picking a response because they must rate some thirty or so social groups and political figures using the thermometer in rapid succession. The feeling thermometer is thus very close to a measure of what people automatically feel, positive or negative, toward the group being rated.

The trends on the GSS's approval of same-sex relations, Gallup's acceptability of homosexuality, and the ANES's feeling thermometer of lesbians and gays are fairly consistent. They show no significant changes until the early 1990s. In the 1990s, all these questions start to trend upward toward greater approval and positivity in a rather consistent fashion. Around the year 2000, the upward trajectory of these trends starts to flatten. In 2003, the Gallup trend in acceptability fluctuates as same-sex marriage first makes the news. When same-sex marriage support began to rise around the end of the 2000s, acceptability and approval started to increase again. The average feeling thermometer score stayed in place.[31]

What does this change in the feeling thermometer actually mean? It is so abstract, it may be hard to wrap our minds around the significance of this change. Because automatic emotional feelings toward lesbians and gays are so central to the public's views on lesbian and gay rights,

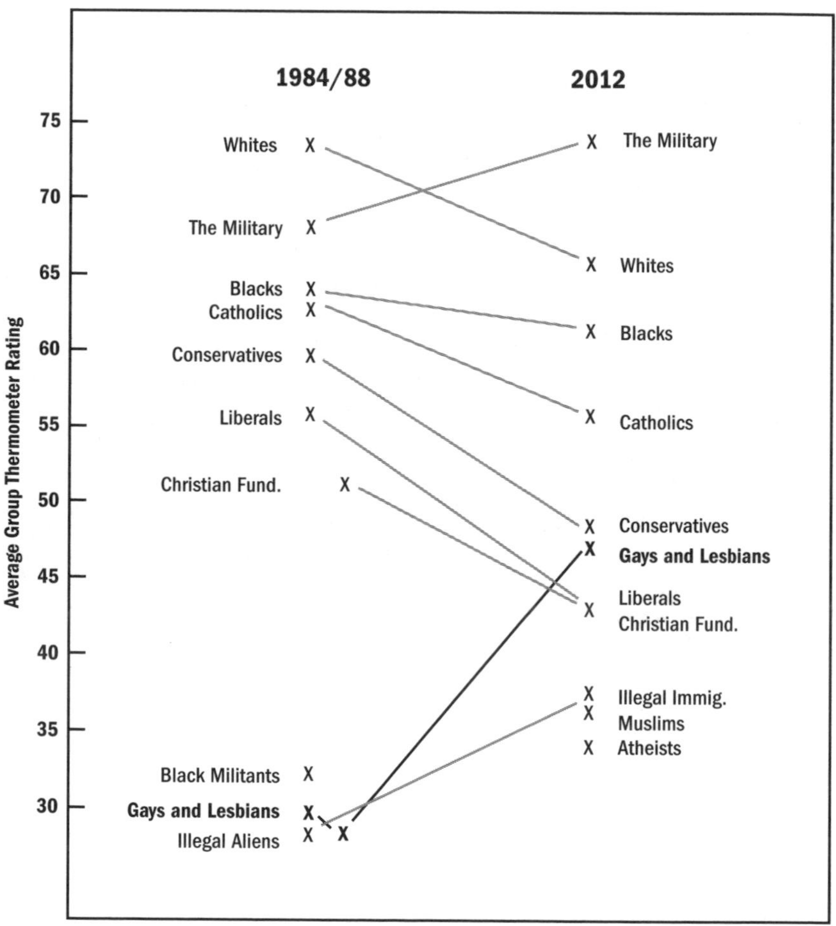

Figure 1.7. Feeling Thermometer Ratings for Various Groups in the 1980s and 2012. *Note*: All of the earlier ratings are from 1984, with the exception of the 1988 average for Christian fundamentalists (who were not rated in the 1984 survey). Both 1984's and 1988's average ratings for lesbians and gays are graphed for purposes of comparison. *Source*: *ANES Times Series Cumulative Data File (1948–2012)*.

and because responses to social groups come so effortlessly to most people, it is necessary to gather more information to determine just what the warming of public reactions shown in figure 1.6 means. Figure 1.7 should help provide some context. It displays the average ratings of several other distinct groups in the mid-1980s and in 2012. In general, emotional reactions to various groups on the feeling thermometer appear to fit into roughly three categories: (1) groups that the public may find threatening (rated below 40 degrees); (2) groups that a vast majority of the public like (rated above 60 degrees); and (3) groups that are disliked by some large segments of the public and liked by other large segments of the public (rated between 40 and 60 degrees). Groups that are heavily active in politics tend to fit into this last "polarizing" group. For better context, I also include in figure 1.7 a few groups in the "threatening" category that are rated only in a single time period.

In the 1980s, gays and lesbians clearly fit into the bottom "threatening" group. Their average rating was similar to that of "black militants" and "illegal aliens." However, by 2012 lesbians and gays had transitioned into the "polarizing" group. In fact, they had become one of the better liked groups in that category. With an average rating over 47 degrees, lesbians and gays were better liked than "liberals" and only slightly less popular than "conservatives." In 2012, they surpassed the average rating of "Christian fundamentalists," the group most often associated with opposition to lesbian and gay rights. Although the relative position of the cluster of "threatening" groups in 2012—"illegal immigrants," "Muslims," and "Atheists"—had also improved as compared to similar groups in the 1980s, their improvement was much more limited as compared to public reactions toward lesbians and gays.

As demonstrated by figure 7.1, the public largely had automatic strong negative feelings toward lesbians and gays in the 1980s. That these negative feelings have dissipated in only two decades is nothing less than staggering. Nothing like that has occurred with any other group. In a broader sense, these reactions encapsulate something much more significant for public opinion than any of the other attitudes mentioned earlier.

Why is this the case? It is because these automatic emotional reactions—the subconscious feelings that spring to mind when a certain group of people is suddenly mentioned—go on to color and shape the experiences of individuals vis-à-vis that group.[32]

When someone learns that a colleague, friend, or family member is lesbian or gay, such emotions spring to mind before any conscious thoughts or memories are mentally accessed. If the instantaneous reaction that a person has when "gay" or "lesbian" is mentioned in conversation is *positive*, then that positive reaction *increases* the possibility that the person will enjoy interacting with lesbian and gay friends, working with lesbian and gay colleagues, or encountering lesbian and gay themes on television. A positive emotional reaction is also likely to increase the chance that a judge would rule in favor of lesbians and gays in a judicial decision, that a politician would endorse gay rights when running for office, or that a survey respondent would support lesbian and gay rights when asked. If these reactions are *negative*, the automatic feelings of dislike will likely have the opposite effect, making it more difficult to ultimately feel positive about encounters with lesbians and gays in ways that would allow for social change.

All of these emotional reactions are very important. When lesbian and gay activists say that social change has occurred—that a positive and meaningful change in the way Americans react to lesbians and gays has happened—they are not necessarily referring to the polling of some policy or abstract right. Rather, they are referring in a deeper sense to the emotional changes they have seen in those with whom they share their lives. The basic, knee-jerk negativity that lesbians and gays experienced as late as the early 1990s—the "hostile spirit" referred to by Donald Webster Cory in the epigraph to this chapter—has dissipated across major parts of the country. That it not to say that resistance to lesbian and gay people is not strong in some areas and among some people. It most certainly is.[33] But this negativity is no longer an ever-present reality for many lesbians and gays. Its absence is real social change.

A Theory of Affective Liberalization

It is around this dissipation of negative reactions to lesbians and gays that I build a theory of the larger causes of attitude change on gay rights. I will explore the full development of the theory in chapter 2, but a short summary will provide a clearer picture of the argument that this book advances regarding both the cause of this dissipation of negative feelings and the cause of the more distinctive features of public opinion change on gay issues: increasing mass exposure to lesbian and gay people. This brief summary will also make clear how this new theory fills in gaps left by prior research.

The Centrality of Automatic Affective Reactions for Gay Rights Support

The first component of the theory of affective liberalization is that change in people's emotional reactions to lesbians and gays has had a major role in swaying the public to favor (or oppose) specific gay rights policies. Many studies on the bases of support for lesbian and gay rights have found that these reactions are indeed a dominant factor.[34] What may have been missing in the prior research, however, is an emphasis on just how central these feelings are for support of gay rights as compared to other considerations or predispositions.

The importance of automatic affective feelings (or implicit attitudes) that people hold toward various groups and political figures has recently become a major focus of the political psychology literature.[35] Specifically, Lodge and Taber, building on dual process theories of decision-making in the work of Kahneman and Tversky, report a plethora of findings conclusively demonstrating that affective reactions emerge nearly instantaneously when individuals are led by some stimulus to think about a particular group or person.[36] Once recalled, these reactions then ease the remembering of affectively congruent considerations from memory. For instance, if someone has a strong negative reaction to George W. Bush, she is more likely to remember specific things about Bush that she does not like. If she were then asked to choose between George W. Bush and another candidate in an election, these recalled negative memories would affect candidate choice over and above any negative effect of the initial emotional reaction, thereby essentially multiplying the ultimate effect of these reactions on decision-making.

While the social science literature on lesbian and gay rights has found this linkage between affective reactions and gay rights support, Lodge and Taber's work suggests a much greater role for these reactions in individuals' support for specific group-based rights of lesbians and gays than previously thought. Because affective reactions are a major predictor of attitudes toward all gay rights,[37] we would expect that if something could warm these affective reactions, then support for the entire constellation of lesbian and gay–related rights—legality of homosexuality, support for employment protections, support for gay adoptions, and so on—would rise without the public ever needing to be exposed to discussions involving the merits of these specific policies. It should be noted that just such a rise in support across all gay rights was directly observed in the public opinion trends described earlier.

The Relationship between Exposure to Lesbians and Gays and Automatic Affective Reactions

Given the likely importance of affective reactions toward lesbians and gays, it is worth asking the question: Just what could have caused such reactions to warm so greatly? This is the more novel and important component of the theory. Based on research in social psychology,[38] there is strong reason to suspect that what has warmed these affective reactions to lesbians and gays is *the marked increase in exposure*—in the United States and elsewhere—*to lesbians and gays themselves*. This exposure has come in two major forms: interpersonal contact with lesbians and gays and portrayals of lesbians and gays in popular culture. As I describe in chapter 6, trends in interpersonal and mediated contact with lesbians and gays show dramatic increases in the 1990s. Not only that, but both trends almost exactly match the changes seen in support for gay rights just described.

According to the theory of affective liberalization, what has ultimately led to the distinctive features of opinion change on lesbian and gay rights is the sharp rise in the number of lesbians and gays willing to share their lives with others. Also important is the increased willingness of those who control the media to allow representations of lesbians, gays, and viewpoints in support of their rights in media. By warming affective reactions, increasing exposure to lesbians and gays led to the rapid increase in support for gay rights in the 1990s. Insofar as affective reactions are a central consideration for support of all gay rights policies, the theory of *affective liberalization* explains why we have seen across-the-board increases in support for all lesbian and gay rights, even on those gay rights issues that receive little press coverage and among individuals who are generally inattentive to news coverage.[39]

Youth Liberalism and the Origin of Cohort Effects

The relationship between affective feelings and gay rights support also leads directly to a theory of one of the most puzzling aspects of attitude change on gay rights from the perspective of the public opinion literature: youth liberalism with regard to homosexuality. Affective reactions have been found to stabilize, or become harder to change, the more individuals learn about a group or person.[40] Similarly, the more information we gain about a group or person, the harder it is to reverse the positivity or negativity of the reaction. For instance, if a liberal has a negative reaction to Bill O'Reilly or Rush Limbaugh, that emotional reaction would be difficult to change, even in the highly unlikely event that he was to repudiate all of his prior political positions, call for massive increases in education and social spending to combat income inequality, and then endorse legal abortion and same-sex marriage. A liberal would still automatically feel a twinge of negativity when seeing images of O'Reilly or Limbaugh on television. An instantaneous negative emotional reaction to the sight of O'Reilly or Limbaugh based on past exposure and experiences would have been stabilized.

To date, no research has found the cause of increasing youth liberalism with respect to gay rights. Some studies have theorized that younger people may be more likely to personally know lesbians and gays and that this may lead to more positive attitudes.[41] But the theoretical explanations tend to end there. Studies that have included year of birth as a predictor of gay rights support and controlling for reported contact with lesbians and gays have still found year of birth to have an independent effect.[42] Thus, there has to be something else also causing youth liberalism vis-a-vis homosexuality. Some have theorized that young people maybe more "open" to new attitudes also,[43] but just why this is the case is seldom explained. Indeed, those who make such a claim never ask why younger people are expected to be more open on gay rights, when on nearly every other issue they adopt attitudes similar to those of their parents.[44]

The central role of affective reactions is directly related to cohort effects on attitudes involving gay rights. Put simply, the first bits of information that a person encounters involving lesbians or gays forms an initial affective reaction for the next time that person encounters lesbians or gays. In earlier time periods, this initial information on homosexuality would likely have involved negative stereotypes of homosexuals as "weird," "deviant," or "perverted." Some may have also formed a negative impression due to stereotypes transmitted through news media. These stereotypes proliferated from Senator McCarthy's "Lavender Scare" in the late 1940s[45] to the early AIDS crisis in the 1980s (see chapter 3).

Thus, effects of exposure to lesbians and gays differ for younger and older people. Past exposure to negative information on homosexuality causes older people to have a negative instantaneous reaction when they meet lesbians and gays and first learn their sexual orientation. Any liberalizing effect of this exposure must then fight against these negative initial reactions for attitude change to occur. Though not insurmountable, the negative emotional reaction stacks the deck against attitude change for older individuals.

For the millennial generation, however, the first exposure to lesbians and gays that likely occurs is when a person either meets lesbians or gays themselves or sees them portrayed on television. Thus, for younger people, meeting a lesbian or gay person (or seeing one on television) *forms* a new (likely) positive reaction for subsequent encounters. In addition to the chance that this initial exposure will have a direct positive effect on gay rights support, it also positively colors future encounters and makes subsequent exposure more likely to result in more pro-gay attitudes. This significantly increases the effectiveness of exposure to lesbians and gays on gay rights attitudes for younger people. Thus, we should see very strong year of birth effects in public opinion on gay rights as compared to nearly every other political issue.

In summary, the theory of affective liberalization posits the following:

1. Interpersonal and mediated exposure to lesbians and gays directly affects the automatic affective reactions people have toward lesbians and gays.
2. Automatic affective reactions then directly affect support for all (or nearly all) specific gay rights policies on surveys.
3. As automatic affective reactions are less stable in younger people, this leads to stronger exposure effects on automatic affective reac-

tions for younger individuals. Ultimately, this results in cohort effects in lesbian and gay rights support in the presence of swift increases in exposure.

One additional feature rounds out the model:

4. Political attention to a specific gay rights policy, transmitted through news, is important in changing attitudes, but mostly only on that specific policy, or on policies the public may closely associate with the specific policy.

The linkage between affective feelings and support for specific gay-rights policies like employment protections or same-sex marriage is key. According to the theory, as these automatic affective feelings warm, support for all gay rights policies should increase as a result. Thus, increased exposure to lesbians and gays is the driving force of rising support for lesbian and gay rights. Accordingly, the major reason for the rapid increase in support for gay rights is that gays and lesbians came out rapidly in the 1990s—both interpersonally and culturally. In chapter 6, I present conclusive evidence that this occurred.

A More Durable Shift in Attitudes

One prominent prediction of the theory is that attitude change, if mediated through affective reactions, will be more durable than other news-based mechanisms of attitude change. First, once people know lesbians and gays, it would be difficult to "unknow" them. This implies that in most situations, it would be difficult for some of the effects of exposure to be undone. However, the very nature of affective reactions means that attitudes that are based on exposure to lesbians and gays will stabilize over time. Therefore, even if gays and lesbians stop coming out and lesbians and gays are removed from television, the effects of prior contact will endure. Unlike change in attitudes caused by news attention, which may quickly decay as news attention fades,[46] change in gay rights support brought about by a warming of affective reactions to lesbians and gays should be longer lasting, given that these affective reactions tend to lead to more durable attitudinal change.

When we think of social change in terms of lesbian and gay rights—its rapidity, its duration, its magnitude, and its concentration among the young—the theory of affective liberalization states that all of these features are, in fact, the downstream effects of increasing interpersonal contact and mediated contact with lesbians and gays. All of these features of attitude change are rarely found with regard to other issues regularly discussed in politics. Thus, while change in public opinion can be caused by political attention or elite messaging, what has produced the more distinctive features of change in attitudes on lesbian and gay issues is, in reality, the "coming out" of lesbians and gays, both interpersonally and culturally.

That said, it would be a mistake to minimize the importance of news attention given to lesbian and gay issues in changing attitudes on gay rights. Changes in the structure of support for gay rights caused by political attention to an issue are important and can occur fairly rapidly. However, the direct effects of these changes can be somewhat short-lived. Examples include those noted earlier concerning support for gays serving openly in the military in 1992 and 1993 and for the legality of homosexuality in 2003. However, in both of these specific cases, support quickly returned to an equilibrium level after press attention to the issue lessened and any information communicated by that press attention was forgotten by the public.

Political and news attention matters in terms of causing lasting opinion change, but in more indirect ways. As I argue in the coming chapters, hard news mattered in encouraging more and more lesbians and gays to come out of the closet. Although the empirical evidence is spotty, the timing of trends presented in this book suggests that media attention to AIDS from 1990 to 1992, Bill Clinton's endorsement of gay rights in 1992, and the 1993 Don't-Ask-Don't-Tell (DADT) controversy may have had a large role in social change by helping to encourage lesbians and gays to come out en masse as described in chapter 6.

The one policy issue that may admittedly be an exception is same-sex marriage. This exception involves how closely it is related to affective feelings over time. In the 1990s, marriage equality was so outside the realm of possibility that even those with positive feelings toward lesbians and gays did not automatically support same-sex marriage. This included many LGBT activists.[47]

Since about 2008, same-sex marriage may have upset the causal order of affective feelings and support for specific gay-rights policies in a different way. Once marriage equality became a possibility starting in 2003, LGBT activists needed to connect the already existing increase in positivity toward lesbians and gays from the 1990s to same-sex marriage specifically in order to raise the level of support for the latter. They have likely done so through the large amount of attention they have brought to the issue in recent years. More recently, subsequent exposure to lesbian and gay couples may have also helped to accomplish this task.

There is some evidence for this hypothesis. In 2008, when California's Prop 8 initiative re-banned same-sex marriage after the California Supreme Court found the state's ban to be in violation of the state constitution, advertisements using so-called "equality" frames, which I will describe more fully in the next chapter, proved to be ineffective.[48] However, advertisements showing real-life same-sex couples in love proved to be more effective in raising support for same-sex marriage during ballot measure campaigns in several states in 2012.[49] These may have worked by subconsciously transferring positive affect created from previous exposure with lesbians and gays to support for same-sex marriage specifically.

So much attention has been given to the issue of marriage equality that many now think of it as being a proxy for support for lesbians and gays in general. Thus, support for same-sex marriage may have transformed in recent years into being a proxy for general approval of lesbians and gays (and perhaps affective feelings) rather than just another specific gay-rights policy. Considering that lesbians and gays are defined by their relationships, this does not seem like a very large stretch. This transformation would mark a complete reversal in the causal relationship of policy views on same-sex marriage and affective reactions and may account for the swift increases in support for same-sex marriage that have occurred since 2003.

The Ultimate Causes of Social Change

To an extent, the theory of affective liberalization by itself is somewhat inadequate if we want to know the complete story of why tolerance has triumphed in the United States and elsewhere. There is much more to the story of what has caused social change. For instance, if the mass "coming out" of lesbians and gays across the country is the root cause of change in support for gay rights in the 1990s, *then why did lesbians and gays suddenly feel comfortable coming out in this time period and not before*? Furthermore, if change in politics and media encouraged lesbians and gays to come out, why did these institutions suddenly reorient themselves on lesbian and gay issues in those years? In addition, how can LGBT activists across the globe convince same-sex attracted people and gender minorities to "come out" and change attitudes in their parts of the world given preexisting stigmas? These questions are of huge importance in those parts of world where lesbians and gays are still legally and socially persecuted and in need of a clear path to follow to achieve social change in their own locales.

The historical sequence of social change in the United States may prove key on this point. There is evidence in the timing of various increases in support for gay rights that suggests the role of LGBT activists in pressuring national institutions to support these rights was the catalyst in unleashing the cascade of other changes that eventually reconstructed national opinion on homosexuality.

The historical evidence suggests that it was only at the end of the 1980s and the beginning of the 1990s, when AIDS dramatically swelled the ranks of LGBT activists, that American national institutions become responsive to the larger lesbian and gay community. These institutions included the news media and the national Democratic Party. As future chapters discuss, both were only intermittently responsive to lesbian and gay constituents prior to 1990, and even then, only in some of the nation's largest cities. Only after these institutions reoriented themselves to support the lesbian and gay community at the national level, in response to intense lobbying by the anti-AIDS LGBT organization ACT-UP and other LGBT activists, did lesbians and gays across the country start to come out in large enough numbers to influence national opinion.

This is important, as the role of LGBT activists in encouraging change in the behavior of influential scientific, political, cultural, and economic elites is often left understated or omitted in some accounts of social change. Elites themselves are often given sole credit for their advocacy of pro-gay positions. This creates an illusion that a widespread social movement, comprised of hundreds or thousands of politically active individuals, may not be necessary for social change to occur. This is not to say that non-LGBT elites, such as elected officials, political candidates, members of the entertainment industry, journalists, or judges, have not contributed to increasing tolerance of lesbians and gays. But more often than not, when looking at the context in which elites are making decisions to potentially support gay rights, we find that a major contributing factor is either the presence of LGBT activists persuading (or pressuring) elites to take pro-gay positions or contextual changes brought about by the existence of LGBT activists or other LGBT people.

For instance, without a tangible increase in the strength and organization of the LGBT movement during the AIDS crisis in the late 1980s, it seems unlikely that Bill Clinton and his 1992 campaign advisors would have perceived any benefits to taking a visible pro-gay position, given the considerable political risks associated with doing so. If Clinton had followed in the footsteps of Michael Dukakis and rejected appeals to support gay rights, coverage of gay rights issues in 1992 and 1993 would have been markedly reduced. This would have likely made lesbians and gays feel less comfortable in coming out. Some credit should be given to elites and other insiders, but one must not miss the backdrop upon which their decisions are forged.

Moreover, consider the de-medicalization of homosexuality by the American Psychiatric Association (APA) in 1974, which is discussed in the final chapter of Zaller's groundbreaking study, *The Nature and Origins of Mass Opinion*.[50] Zaller sees the APA's de-medicalization of homosexuality as an example of scientists creating knowledge according to a supposedly neutral, or empirically objective (and likely scientific), method. In Zaller's model of a society free from elite domination, scientific knowledge then forms the basis of activist, elite, and mass opinion. Zaller speaks specifically about the importance of the research conducted by Dr. Evelyn Hooker and others, who showed that there are no differences in the psychological adjustment of gays and non-gays. According to Zaller: "Hooker's research proved the most influential [of this research, and] used standard scientific research techniques."[51] Later he talks about the effect of this research:

> When homosexuality was considered by virtually all specialists and the press to be a disease, homosexuals largely accepted this mainstream norm by staying, as the phrase goes "in the closet." . . . It was clear that in many cases, the mainstream norm against homosexuality was internalized. But then, offered by some psychiatric authorities a choice of considering themselves sick or merely to have an alternative sexual preference, homosexuals naturally allied themselves with the friendlier view.[52]

No doubt for many lesbians and gays, even ones who would later go on to become lesbian and gay rights activists, this was indeed the case. What Zaller misses, however, is the reason Hooker undertook this line of research in the first place, which he attributes to Hooker's search for neutral and correct knowledge as a scientific elite.

D'Emlio goes into more detail about the origin of Hooker's research in *Sexual Politics, Sexual Communities*,[53] where he details the activities of the Mattachine Society, an early group of gay and lesbian rights activists:

> [The Mattachine Society] arranged a meeting with novelist and screenwriter Christopher Isherwood and with a research psychologist from UCLA, Dr. Evelyn Hooker. Both professed support for what the Mattachine Society leaders were attempting, although they declined to join the board of directors. . . . In 1953 Mattachine provided Hooker with a large pool of gay men for her study of the male homosexual personality. . . . In an interview with the author in Santa Monica on November 4, 1976, Hooker said that her gay friends, all of whom were living proof of the inadequacy of the medical literature on homosexuality, provided the motivation for her subsequent research on the topic.[54]

According to Hooker herself, the origin of her research was inspired by contact with gay men and facilitated by the lesbian and gay activists of the Mattachine Society. This is not to say that free scientific inquiry and the search for knowledge did not have a sizable role in the process. As Zaller states, Hooker's career incentives did encourage her to produce and publish important scientific studies. At the same time, lesbian and gay activists created a context for Hooker to easily complete studies on the psychological adjustment of gay men rather than pursuing other potential lines of research. Positive contact with gay men also predisposed her to move along that path. The incentives of elites and the resources of lesbians and gays in this case formed a mutually beneficial synergistic relationship. Without this positive contact and the resources provided by the Mattachine Society, it seems unlikely that it would have been in Hooker's best interests to study the psychological adjustment of male homosexuals.

At least temporarily, an elite—in this case Dr. Hooker—was encouraged to act in a pro-gay fashion that benefited both Hooker and the gay and lesbian movement. As this book shows, this pattern reoccurs at various points in time, when a myriad of elites find themselves in situations, often created by lesbians, gays, bisexuals, and transgender people, where they benefit directly by advancing lesbian and gay rights or taking some other pro-gay action. Thus, it would be an error to attribute change to the actions of various elites without first understanding how the contexts in which these elites make their decisions have first been affected by activist pressure. This book departs from previous work on elite-led opinion change by pointing out just how the shifting contexts that elites find themselves embedded in have been affected by activists.

A Brief Outline of This Book

Chapter 2 has two purposes. First I situated my theory of affective liberalization in the current political and social psychology literature and discuss how this theory readily explains the distinctive features of gay rights not explained by more popular academic theories of attitude change. I also outline some important empirical considerations that should be taken into account when searching for the root causes of attitudinal change across time. In the last section of this chapter, I briefly examine how affective reactions to lesbians and gays have changed since 1984. For those uninterested in the academic literature or theoretical development, this chapter can be skimmed over or omitted.

After situating the theory, I begin by tracing the political development of the LGBT movement in the United States. Part II of the book focuses on how the LGBT movement became effective at causing *institutional* change. Chapter 3 traces this historical development of the movement up until the AIDS crisis. In 1987 and 1988, government inaction in the face of AIDS shifted the movement into high gear. The most notable event here is the formation of ACT-UP, whose members' relentless activism appears to have caused the national media to pay sustained attention to lesbian and gay issues in the early 1990s. Chapter 4 focuses directly on the ever strengthening relationship between the Democratic Party and the LGBT movement in this period. It was not until the peak of AIDS activism that the LGBT movement became effective at persuading Democrats to support gay rights when they did not already have other constituency-based incentives to do so. The growing influence of the LGBT movement with the Democratic Party then provided a critical impetus for Bill Clinton to run on support for gay rights in 1992, which in turn brought about further news coverage of gay rights.

In part 3, which presents the primary tests of the theory of affective liberalization, the focus moves to the time period after the press and the Democrats became attentive to lesbian and gay issues, when the LGBT movement and gay rights became highly visible in national politics. Chapter 5 specifically examines the independent effects of both the 1992 election and the debate on gays in the military on public support for lesbian and gay rights. The chapter shows that these events contributed to polarizing the public on partisan and ideological grounds in ways consistent with the prior findings of theories of elite-led opinion change. However, the relatively small shifts in mass opinion seen in this time were consistent with elite-led shifts in attitudes observed on other political issues. This suggests that elite-led shifts in attitudes were not the primary cause of the distinctive attributes of change on lesbian and gay rights seen in the 1990s.

Chapter 6 includes the core empirical tests of affective liberalization, which focus directly on determining the origin of cohort effects on gay rights. First, this chapter traces the rise in mass exposure to lesbians and gays starting in the late 1980s. I find that increases in exposure provide a consistent explanation for the magnitude and rapidity of change in attitudes toward lesbian and gay rights and verify that this exposure is much more effective in changing the attitudes of younger individuals in ways that are consistent with affective liberalization.

Chapter 7explains why liberals adopted supportive positions on gay rights much earlier than moderates or conservatives. Building on theories of politically motivated reasoning, I show that instead of having a liberalizing effect, exposure to lesbians and gays tends to cause political polarization in attitudes involving gay rights among strong ideologues. This polarization helps explain why elected Democrats tended to endorse gay rights early and why Republican officials have remained largely opposed to gay rights to this day. This also explains why lesbian and gay rights legislation continues to meet heavy resistance in political arenas where Republicans hold a majority in spite of strong constituent support.

In part 4, I extend my analysis outside of the United States. Increases in tolerance for homosexuality have not just been an American phenomenon. Numerous countries across the globe have witnessed similar or greater changes in their reactions to homosexuality since the 1980s. In chapter 8, I use the cumulative World and European Values Surveys to see if the major factors behind changing views in the United States generalize to other national contexts. I find that nations with free and pervasive media systems—a prerequisite for LGBT visibility and exposure—appear to have undergone similar increases in tolerance of sexual minorities. Limited evidence also shows that the strategic contexts for LGBT activists, as set by a nation's political system, may correspond with the size of the divide between left-leaning and right-leaning individuals vis-à-vis tolerance of homosexuality.

I conclude by outlining the importance of these findings for activists and the academic literature in chapter 9. Knowledge of the causes of attitude change in the American context can be leveraged by activists and others concerned with LGBT rights in order to encourage social change. Based on my findings, I also outline what the future has in store for LGBT rights in the United States—and in the rest of the world.

2

Understanding Affective Liberalization

The prejudiced mind, and that is what we are fighting, is not penetrated by information and is not educable. This has been shown in a number of studies. . . . Communication of facts is generally ineffectual against predispositions. . . .

The prejudice against homosexuality is primarily one of an emotional commitment, not an intellectual one; and appeals based upon fact and reason will, for the most part, not be effective.

—Dr. Franklin Kameny, *Civil Liberties: A Progress Report*, 1964

What has caused social change in the public's support of lesbian and gay rights? The trends provided in the previous chapter provide some clues. We know that the period of the late 1980s and early 1990s is crucial. Yet these trends hardly suggest a firm and comprehensive framework for moving forward.

In this chapter, I will survey some of the more prominent findings of the academic literature on attitude change involving lesbian and gay rights. These are (1) theories of elite-led attitude change, including issue evolution;[1] (2) theories involving changing media "frames" of lesbian and gay rights and people's closely held fundamental values;[2] (3) theories of attitude change that implicate increases in the belief that homosexuality is due to biological causes;[3] and (4) theories that describe some change as caused by policy advances on gay rights.[4]

While these theories explain change, they cannot account for the distinctive features of attitude change on lesbian and gay rights discussed in the first chapter. After summarizing these alternative theories, this chapter reviews the research findings on interpersonal, mediated, and imagined contact with lesbians and gays and then discusses other prominent theoretical developments in the political psychology literature, particularly dual process models of political decision-making. When integrated with intergroup contact theories (interpersonal, mediated, and so on), these recent developments suggest a new theoretical framework that can predict all the distinctive features of social change involving public responses to homosexuality—affective liberalization.

Since this book focuses specifically on attitude change, this chapter concludes by outlining a few considerations that motivate the empirical analyses in subsequent chapters. My empirical analyses depart from mere cross-sectional analyses used in most studies. An emphasis must be placed on the factors causing social change that are themselves either changing in society from one time to another or that are increasing or decreasing in their ability to predict support for gay rights. To illustrate, I perform a quick analysis of change in the demographic predictors of more positive affective feelings toward lesbians and gays among the American public *across time*. The findings of this analysis further show the early 1990s to have been a crucial period for the reconstruction of the American public's emotional responses to homosexuality. These initial findings also set the stage for the next two chapters' focus on gay and lesbian political development in the 1980s and prior.

The Correlates of Support for Gay Rights and Their Theoretical Causes

The Demographics of Tolerance

If we were to survey the academic literature on public support for lesbian and gay rights, we would discover a plethora of important findings regarding the demographic groups more likely and less likely to support these rights. These findings are often treated as the "effect" of certain demographics—for instance age or party identification—on lesbian and gay rights attitudes. When I use the word "effect," I mean something akin to the size of the gap in lesbian and gay rights support between the various social groups mentioned. For instance, the effect of gender on gay rights support is, more or less, the size of the gap in support for lesbian and gay rights between men and women, controlling for various other quantities of interest that may also affect support. Of course, gaps can only exist between two values of a variable, which is why I say that the effect of a variable is only akin to a gap in opinions, but effects are often expressions of relationships between variables that can take on more than two values like year of birth or income. They are roughly akin to the difference between the highest and lowest level of the explanatory variables—in this case the demographics of the respondents. Most of these findings of "effects" are remarkably consistent both across time and in terms of specific lesbian and gay rights policies like employment protections or same-sex marriage.

I go over these demographic effects somewhat quickly now, not because they are unimportant, but because many of these demographic gaps have not changed much since the mid-1980s, or have changed only in a very minor fashion. For instance, education is a major predictor of lesbian and gay rights today.[5] But it was also a major predictor prior to the start of the large bulk of attitude change in the 1990s, and the size of the relationship (the effect or gap) has generally remained the same.[6] There are a few exceptions to a general rule of stability in the size of these demographic effects, and I mostly describe demographic gaps that have changed over time. These involve differences in levels of support for gay rights by ideology, party, year of birth, and (occasionally) factors relating to religion. My ultimate reasons for focusing on these demographics will become clearer in the last few sections of this chapter.

The findings on demographic differences in support for gay rights are quite clear. Specifically, women support lesbian and gay rights more than men,[7] while on some issues such as same-sex marriage, whites and Latinos/as support lesbian and gay rights more than African Americans.[8] Latino/a support may have become stronger in more recent years, but it is difficult to tell as many older studies lumped Latinos/as in with other racial groups. People with more years of formal education support lesbian and gay rights more than those with fewer years of education.[9] Republicans, for most of the period in which lesbian and gay rights have been polled regularly (that is, since 1992), are less likely to support lesbian and gay rights than Democrats,[10] And there is some evidence that this gap has increased. Liberals support lesbian and gay rights more than conservatives.[11] Likewise, this gap in ideology has also increased over time.[12] Those living in urban areas tend to support lesbian and gay rights more than those in rural areas.[13]

The relationship between support for lesbian and gay rights, religious denomination, and religiosity is fairly important and a key focus of academic studies of LGBTQ rights support. But while religion and religiosity are major factors that correlate with lower levels of support for lesbian and gay rights,[14] they are not a major focus of this book. This omission should not be interpreted as a signal that religion and religiosity are not important. Far from it. But because the primary focus of this book is on the factors leading to increased support for lesbian and gay rights, I spend more time discussing those factors than religion and religiosity, which tend to be correlated with lower support for lesbian and gay rights. To be sure religious convictions can form the basis for increased support for lesbian and gay rights, especially among those with progressive religious beliefs that emphasize fairness, forgiveness, and equal treatment of all people, as will be shown by several analyses throughout this book, but on the whole, studies have consistently found that religion and religious intensity are associated with lower support for lesbian and gay rights.[15] Those who identify as born-again or evangelical Christians, those who attend church regularly, or those who believe in a literal interpretation of the Bible all tend to be less likely to support gay rights. The specific questions used to measure religion or religiosity tend to vary by survey or analysis. Almost universally though, there will be some positive relationship found between hostility toward lesbian and gay rights and religious intensity.

"Replacement" Effects and Birth Cohort

One aspect of attitudes about lesbian and gay rights is worth additional discussion due to its ubiquity: younger people strongly support lesbian and gay rights *more* than older people.[16] Regarding this finding, the first thing to note is that many studies using data from the 1980s and the early 1990s contradict it. That is, while controlling for other factors, many such studies found *higher support* for laws banning discrimination based on sexual orientation among *older individuals* than among younger individuals.[17] This suggests that year of birth effects (or cohort effects) have reversed on some gay rights issues, and since then, also grown stronger over time. Indeed, it is not until after the mid-1990s that studies started to *consistently* show that younger people support nearly all lesbian and gay rights at higher levels.

Although most people believe that younger people are automatically more tolerant than previous generations, the more one thinks about this proposition, the less satisfying it becomes as an explanation for social change. In addition to the inconsistency in cohort effects prior to the mid-1990s, one vexing question one may ask from reading through the academic literature is just *why* one generation of people should be more tolerant than a generation born a few years before it. Surely, there must be something specific to that time in which the younger generation was born that led them to be more tolerant. By just stating that younger generations are more tolerant, in the absence of any explanation for why that may be so, we have come no closer to explaining the root causes of social change.

Cohort effects are also problematic because the data does not conclusively support that every generation is automatically more liberal. We could hypothesize that living through the sexual revolution in the 1960s should have made the generation that came of age in that time more tolerant of homosexuality. However, this was not that case. Only a marginal and inconsistent effect of coming of age in the late 1960s carries over into attitudes regarding gay rights.[18] So just being born in a younger, more sexually permissive cohort has little to do with expanding support for gay rights. There is something specific about younger people who came of age *in the early 1990s* and after that made their generation the first to be overwhelmingly pro-gay, as will be further discussed in chapter 6. In addition, studies are quite clear that just being younger, in and of itself, has nothing to do with attitudes toward gay rights. Only younger people born more recently are more pro-gay.[19]

Other than the theoretical problems with the generational argument, there is the further problem that the rate of attitude change that generational replacement can deliver is only half of that which has been observed on gay rights.[20] We know that individuals have become more pro-gay, and that these "conversion" effects, where people switch from being against gay rights to being supportive of gay right, must explain about half of the change observed. Thus, generational replacement cannot come close to providing a full explanation for the scale of social change observed on gay rights since the 1980s.

Why do we see differences in attitudes on lesbian and gay rights in various demographic groups and in birth cohorts? The most prominent theories of demographic differences involve two potential causes: the first involves signals from elites and opinion leaders either in support of or opposition to, lesbian and gay rights. The second involves differences in the fundamental values held by various demographic groups and changes in how reporters construct stories on lesbian and gay issues in the news media.

Theories of Elite-Led Change and "Issue Evolution"

Theories of elite-led attitude change provide some theoretical explanation of why we see differences among various demographic groups in attitudes toward lesbian and gay rights. Studies of public opinion consistently find that individuals tend to trust the judgment of political or social elites who share their ideological or partisan identity. This is especially the case for issues that are difficult to understand, like support for a complex changes in the tax code, issues that the public knows little about, like whether the United States should intervene and depose the leader of Slovenia, or issues that the public cares very little about, like trade policy with the country of Nepal. Across these types of issues, members of the public have little desire to research the pros and cons of a specific policy. It makes sense for them to take shortcuts when forming an attitude, and some of the easiest shortcuts often involve adopting the policy judgment of a trusted leader or politician. Because lesbian and gay rights falls consistently into the last category, issues the public cares little about, theories of elite-led change have been applied to understand change in attitudes on lesbian and gay rights.

Bailey, Sigelman, and Wilcox have found that Democrats and liberals tended to become more pro-gay during the 1993 DADT controversy.[21] This controversy is discussed in detail in chapter 5. This is because Bill Clinton's pro-gay positions were communicated to the public through media reports that year. Because Democrats and other liberals in the public had favorable views of Clinton, they tended to trust his views and moved in a pro-gay direction, widening the gap between parties vis-à-vis support for lesbian and gay rights.

When this type of elite-driven opinion change takes place in a sustained fashion, in which the positions of divergent groups of large numbers of elites become clarified and then polarize the public over the course of years or decades, we call it *issue evolution*.[22] The most noted instances of issue evolutions have been on race and gender issues.[23]

In general terms, Democratic and Republican presidential candidates and members of Congress became polarized on an issue like race in the 1960s, as seen in their roll-call voting on legislation in Congress. As these positions were communicated to the public through media, Democratic and Republican identifiers in the electorate also diverged in their attitudes on the issue.

Some have argued that attitudes toward sexual orientation have also undergone an issue evolution. The evidence on this is mixed, however. Lindaman and Haider-Markel found that the expansion in the gap in lesbian and gay rights support based on political party lagged polarization in congressional voting on lesbian and gay rights too much to fit the classical definition of an issue evolution.[24] A modified theory of issue evolution that brings in media attention may still prove explanatory. I will return to the prospects of an issue evolution on lesbian and gay rights in chapters 4, 5 and 7.

In addition to party identification and ideology, religion and religious intensity also influence views on lesbian and gay rights. A lot of very thorough research in the last decade has examined communications from the leaders of more conservative faiths, including evangelical and born-again Christian groups, and has found anti-gay themes rife with negative stereotypes of lesbians and gays to be prominent.[25] As the "Culture War" narrative makes clear, anti-lesbian and gay voices started becoming more vocal as lesbians and gays started winning policy victories in the 1970s and especially since the 1990s. As leaders and other members of these religious groups have disseminated their negative views on homosexuality, their communications have likely either reinforced anti-gay stereotypes among the very religious or countered any factors from the larger culture contributing to increased support for lesbian and gay rights.

"Framing," Values, and Attitude Change

In addition to theories of elite-led change, basic differences in closely held fundamental values among certain demographic groups have provided a second major theoretical explanation for why we have witnessed attitude change on lesbian and gay rights. To an extent, this theory reinforces the predictions of theories of elite-led change. The most intense differences in fundamental values according to these theories should be felt across the lines of religious, ideological, and political differences.

Support for two sets of fundamental values has been found to undergird support for lesbians and gay rights in the political science literature: egalitarian values and values involving moral traditionalism. Both of these are highly associated with holding either liberal or conservative views, respectively. Egalitarianism is commonly measured by asking respondents a set of questions involving support for the equal treatment of various social groups. For instance, respondents are more egalitarian if they agree with the statement: "One of the big problems in this country is that we don't give everyone an equal chance." Moral traditionalism, on the other hand, tends to be correlated with respondents disagreeing with statements like "The world is changing and we should adjust our views of moral behavior to those changes" or agreeing with statements such as "The newer lifestyles are contributing to the breakdown of society."

Differences in these underlying values, as well as other values not measured by egalitarianism or moral traditionalism, are thought to contribute to differences in degrees of support for gay and lesbian rights among some demographic groups. For instance, women's tendency to be more egalitarian contributes to strong gender differences in support for lesbian and gay rights. On race, African Americans tend to support both egalitarian values and have greater levels of moral traditionalism, which explains both their greater *support* for nondiscrimination laws based on sexual orientation among blacks and their greater *opposition* to same-sex marriage and adoption as compared to whites.

These fundamental values shift little over time, however. What we need to consider is not only cross-sectional support for lesbian and gay rights, but also dynamic change in support for lesbian and gay rights. Something has to reinforce the relationship between the fundamental values held by individuals and support for lesbian and gay rights, in order to explain change in support over time.

A theory of just what this might be was provided by Brewer.[26] Brewer examined the American National Election Study (ANES) from 1992 to 2004, the years when egalitarianism and moral traditionalism were measured, and, controlling for a host of other variables, he found that these variables exhibited different effects in different years.[27] That is, they corresponded to statistically larger or smaller gaps in public support. He attributed this strengthening relationship to another factor: change in various media frames used in news stories involving lesbian and gay rights in the 1990s.

The way issues involving gays and lesbians are framed in the media may have an effect on public attitudes as suggested by Brewer.[28] Specifically, "framing" refers to the ways in which certain aspects of a story are emphasized and thereby influence the conclusion the audience reaches about the issue in question.[29] According to Brewer, news stories that emphasize equality and equal rights for lesbians and gays tend to resonate with those holding egalitarian views and lead to greater gay rights support. News stories that emphasize "tradition," "morality," "sin," or biblical interpretations reinforce preexisting levels of moral traditionalism and bring greater opposition to gay rights. In an experimental setting consistent with the statements mentioned earlier in this chapter, Brewer finds evidence that different media frames can push respondents to be more pro-gay or more anti-gay.[30]

Thus, according to framing theory, frames work to remind individuals of their closely held values and suggest these values are key considerations in making a decision on a particular issue. For instance, the phrase "gay right activists want equality" in a news story can remind readers of their general egalitarian values and thereby encourage them to see lesbian and gay rights in those terms, which they already favor.

Brewer also showed that "equality" and "moral-traditionalist" frames were common in media coverage of lesbian and gay rights in the early and mid-1990s. As the media covered lesbian and gay issues little before this time, it then stands to reason that egalitarians in the public would encounter these frames for the first time in this period and become more supportive of lesbian and gay rights. Those who held moral traditionalist values either became less supportive of lesbian and gay rights when they encountered moral traditionalist frames or became inoculated from other factors that may have encouraged them to become more supportive.

Framing theories fit well with theories of elite-led change. Political and religious leaders, when giving reasons for support or opposition to lesbian and gay rights, can easily fall back on these frames when needing to justify their positions. Phrases like "I support gay rights because everyone should be treated equally under the law" or "I oppose gay marriage because the Bible says that homosexuality is immoral" can be recalled from memory easily when a position needs to be defended.

All is not well with framing theory, however. No doubt differences in frames do affect support for lesbian and gay rights. But while framing has been demonstrated to have similar effects in increasing or decreasing support for civil liberties, abortion, healthcare, and so on, [31] on none of these issues have we seen the sheer scale of change in attitudes that we have seen toward homosexuality. Elites and frames do move attitudes on lesbian and gay rights, but likely by causing short-term changes in support or opposition to gay rights. It seems unlikely that frames would have such a huge and disproportionately large effect on attitudes involving homosexuality, while at the same time having more limited effects on a whole host of other issues. Theories of elite-led attitude change and framing theories both depend on the news as a medium to transmit considerations on lesbian and gay rights to the public. Individuals learn the positions of their leaders through the news. They also encounter "equality" and "moral traditionalist" frames through the news. Therefore, if these factors are significant causes of attitude change, that change should be concentrated in individuals who consume the most news. Addressing just this proposition, the American National Election Study (ANES) has asked about both lesbian and gay rights and television news consumption in election years since 1988. Specifically, it has asked about levels of support for laws banning discrimination based on sexual orientation and about frequency of watching evening news on television. Using this data, table 2.1 breaks down support for employment protections by the number of days respondents on the ANES reported watching the news in 1988, 1996, and 2008.

The results are disappointing for theories of elite-led change and value-framing. It turns out that the group that changed its attitudes the most from 1988 to 2008 was the one that *did not watch the evening news at all*. Similar results are found if we examine change in affective feelings toward lesbians or gays or break-downs of respondents by how much they know about politics.[32]

Thus, other factors specific to lesbian and gay issues have to be operating on attitudes toward lesbians and gays (on top of any change caused by elites or media frames) to explain the pattern in table 2.1, as well as the rapid and drastic change in attitude toward lesbian and gay issues.

TABLE 2.1. Support for Employment Protections and TV News Viewing (ANES, 1988, 1996, 2008)

In 1988				
Days Watched	0	1–4	5–7	Diff.
Oppose, Strongly	24.8%	27.5%	24.9%	0.1%
Oppose, Weakly	14.3%	13.7%	14.8%	0.5%
Depends/Don't Know	15.3%	10.7%	11.9%	–3.4%
Favor, Weakly	22.1%	26.1%	23.9%	1.8%
Favor, Strongly	23.6%	22.0%	24.5%	0.9%
In 1996				
Days Watched	0	1–4	5–7	Diff.
Oppose, Strongly	22.0%	22.0%	21.8%	–0.2%
Oppose, Weakly	12.4%	11.6%	13.8%	1.8%
Favor, Weakly	21.5%	22.9%	24.3%	2.8%
Favor, Strongly	38.2%	40.4%	34.7%	–3.5%
Don't Know	5.9%	3.0%	5.4%	0.5%
In 2008				
Days Watched	0	1–4	5–7	Diff.
Oppose, Strongly	16.0%	15.3%	19.4%	3.4%
Oppose, Weakly	9.9%	13.4%	10.9%	1.0%
Favor, Weakly	18.0%	18.0%	21.9%	3.9%
Favor, Strongly	53.6%	51.0%	45.8%	–7.6%
Don't Know	2.5%	2.3%	1.9%	0.6%

Policy Advances, the Courts, and Anti-Gay "Backlash"

In the early 2000s, there was a palpable fear on the part of the Left that advances in gay rights would lead to public backlash. Political observers saw that gay rights laws adopted by city councils had been frequently repealed at the ballot box from the early 1970s to the 2000s, that the lengthy debate on gays in the military may have been partly to blame for losses for Bill Clinton and the Democrats in the 1994 midterm elections, and that the 1999 decision of the Vermont legislature to legalize civil unions for same-sex couples had aided the Republican takeover of the Vermont House of Representatives the following year. The perception that advances in LGBTQ rights—whether put in place by a city council, state legislation, Congress, mayor, governor, or a court—could trigger backlash among the public and thus result in a less positive legal climate for lesbians and gays has likely prevented supportive officials from advocating and advancing pro-gay policies. Some academic literature has supported this account.[33]

However, those who have looked for the results of such "backlash" in public opinion have been fairly conclusive: it does not exist.[34] Experimental and observational studies have asked individuals to read about policy advances on gay rights initiated by legislatures, the courts, and ballot measures and have found no consistent decline in support for gay rights when individuals read of such advances.[35] Policy advances may mobilize conservative activists to push against LGBTQ rights and those with preexisting negative attitudes to vote down ballot measures, but they have little to no direct effect on public support for LGBTQ rights.

In fact, other observational studies have found that when states adopt pro-gay policies, public opinion in those states shifts to become slightly more supportive of those pro-gay policies. There is firm and persuasive evidence that legalizing same-sex marriage in localities moves public opinion on gay rights in a pro-gay direction both at the individual[36] and mass level.[37] It does not matter whether policy is made by the courts, state legislatures, or ballot measures. Although the implication is that citizens are learning about these policies from news reports and updating their attitudes accordingly, such an avenue of influence has not been *directly* explored.

Born that Way? Attribution Theory and Attitude Change

One other prominent theory as to the cause of attitude change on homosexuality involves the increasingly common belief that individuals are born with an orientation toward being lesbian or gay and that they cannot change it[38] The percentage of individuals who say they believe that homosexuality is due to biological or genetic causes began to increase substantially in the early 1990s[39]— at the same time that positive attitudes toward gay rights gained more broad support.

Just why might this increase affect support for lesbian and gay rights specifically? Attribution theory from social psychology suggests that this understanding of homosexuality and support for gay rights may indeed be connected. That is, attribution theory states that those who attribute homosexuality to genetics, biology, or to other causes outside of someone's control are less likely to believe that lesbians and gays are "to blame" for their orientation. If lesbians and gays have little choice in the matter, then it makes sense that they should have equal rights and legal protections based on sexual orientation, just as others do based on sex and race. However, if lesbians and gays are gay by choice (or can change their orientation at will), then any harassment or discrimination that lesbians and gays receive from society is partially thought to be their own fault. In that case, the onus is on lesbians and gays to change, rather than on society to protect lesbians and gays as a class.

A very strong correlation between believing that lesbians and gays cannot change their orientation, or that lesbians and gays are "born that way," and support for lesbian and gay rights does exist, suggesting that change in attributions may be the cause of more liberal attitudes.[40]

At this point though, this argument also starts to falter. While attributions of innate tendencies to homosexuality can cause support for lesbian and gay rights, it is equally likely that increasing support for lesbian and gay rights can lead individuals to adopt the belief that lesbians and gays are "born that way," especially since supporting this belief has been framed as being pro-gay in the media. It turns out that most of the large increases in support for biological attributions of homosexuality have been driven by political liberals adopting that attitude.[41] That they did so at the same time as the 1992 presidential campaign and the 1993 DADT controversy suggests that liberals were responding to political factors. That, however, does not explain the degree and extent of attitude change any more than attribution theory, which means that we should look elsewhere for a theory that can explain the distinctiveness of change in public opinion on lesbian and gay issues.

Toward a Theory of Affective Liberalization

What of the assertions of lesbian, gay, bisexual, and transgender leaders who have stated that what is really necessary to change the public's mind on lesbian and gay rights is for LGBT people themselves to come out and be visible to the public? Has this assertion been tested in the academic literature? The answer is, of course, yes. But as I explain, certain factors have prevented a more thorough analysis of the effect of "coming out" as compared to many of the other factors discussed above.

Contact Theories and Attitude Change

The theory that contact with members of various social out-groups tends to improve attitudes toward those out-groups has a long history. The *social contact hypothesis*, as it is known in the academic literature, was first suggested by Allport in his classic study *The Nature of Prejudice.*[42] Allport suspected that four factors increased the possibility that interactions with members of out-groups result in improved attitudes toward those out-groups: if the individuals interacting are of equal social status; if the interaction is not superficial and is sustained; if the interaction is not opposed by authority figures; and if the individuals interacting are attempting to achieve common goals. Allport originally thought that all of these factors may be necessary in order for contact to be effective in attitude change, but more recent meta-analyses have found that, while these factors increase the possibility of efficacious contact, none of them is strictly necessary.[43]

The most common way of assessing if contact with a lesbian or gay person has an effect on support for lesbian and gay rights has been to test for a significantly sized correlation between reported interpersonal contact with lesbians and gays and some reported attitude in support of lesbian and gay rights. Typically, reported interpersonal contact is constructed from one of a variety of survey questions asking whether the respondent has acquaintances, co-workers, friends, or family members who are lesbian and gay. A few questions from the 1980s even asked if individuals knew anyone whom they *suspected* were lesbian or gay.

The most expansive study of this relationship found that the effect of self-reported contact with lesbians and gays on support for lesbian and gay rights increased the likelihood of support by about 10 percent.[44] This study also found that effects were consistent across various lesbian and gay rights policies, survived controls for various demographics, were consistently positive across different demographic groups, and were roughly the same in size across time. The findings also showed that contact effects were statistically weaker among conservatives and evangelical Protestants. Contact effects were also weaker among highly educated people and older cohorts, but not in a statistically significant fashion. This means the differences were not large enough to rule out the possibility that they were due to random differences due to survey sampling. Various other studies have found similar results. Contact may be less effective for the very religious, for conservatives, or for Republicans in more recent years.[45]

The area where social contact theory has traditionally run into problems involves the direction of the causal relationship between contact and support for lesbian and gay rights. Although contact theory suggests that meeting lesbians and gays will lead to more positive attitudes, some have suggested that the strong relationship found between the two may be due more to the fact that LGBT people may feel more comfortable coming out to individuals who are already supportive of lesbian and gay rights. This critique is one of the reasons why theories of elite-led attitude change and framing theories have dominated the political science literature.

In recent years, however, a number of tests have found that interpersonal contact does, in fact, lead to improved support for gay rights. As contact is effective for other groups that cannot easily hide their identities, such as racial groups or the elderly, this should hardly come as a surprise.[46]

First, as I will show in later chapters, the sheer number of people reporting interpersonal contact, including those who are religious and politically conservative, suggests that lesbians and gays are not assessing support for lesbian and gay rights when deciding to come out to the degree that they may have done so in the past. For instance, it is not uncommon in recent years to find 70 to 80 percent of respondents on surveys indicating that they know someone who is lesbian or gay, a percentage that usually surpasses support for most gay rights policies. As I point out in chapter 6, this includes 60 percent or more of political conservatives. Furthermore, the size of increases in reported contact between political groups has been roughly consistent across ideological groups, while the increase in gay rights support has not. At the very least, this shows that any "selection effects"[47] for those who report contact with lesbians and gays have declined considerably and much more quickly than support for gay rights has risen (in percentage terms).

Likewise, Egan and Sherrill have shown that having family members who are lesbian or gay leads to greater support for same-sex marriage, when compared to the effect of other forms of contact.[48] This is important because, as the oft-quoted saying goes, "You can choose your friends, but not your family." We would expect larger effects of contact on support for gay rights for other types of relationships if the relationship were due to selection effects since LGBTs cannot pick their family members based on prior support for gay rights to the extent they can with friends. Lewis does generally find smaller effects of reported contact for those who cite family members versus friends who are lesbians and gays, but concludes that the diminished effect may be due to the smaller number of people who report such a form of contact.

The strongest evidence of an effect of interpersonal contact on support for lesbian and gay rights comes from experimental studies. One of the most interesting of these was performed in the 1980s by Bob Altemeyer, a social psychologist who studies the origins of prejudice and authoritarianism.[49] At the end of a semester of teaching, Altemeyer (who is heterosexual) decided to test the contact hypothesis by coming out as gay to one of his introductory psychology classes and to compare the attitudes of this group with an identical "control" class where he made no such statement of sexual identity.[50] Immediately after this, he gave both classes end-of-semester questionnaires that involved rating him in terms of his teaching as well as asking students about their attitudes involving lesbians and gays. He found that in the class he came out to, attitudes toward lesbians and gays tended to be more positive, in a manner that was consistent with the contact hypothesis.[51]

This all suggests that increased contact could have a significant role in improving attitudes toward lesbians and gays, even allowing for a small "selection effect." The evidence gets even stronger when we start to look at just how powerful contact with LGBTs can be. In fact, it is so powerful that *direct interpersonal contact with LGBTs is not necessary* for contact to result in attitude change.

Scholars in social psychology and communication have extended Allport's original hypothesis to consider contact with LGBTs through media. Such "parasocial," "vicarious," "imagined," or "virtual" contact, as it is variously termed, works the same way as interpersonal contact, except that exposure to lesbians and gays comes in the form of books, plays, films, or television. What is necessary for parasocial contact to work is the development of a *parasocial relationship* with an LGBT individual portrayed through one of these forms of media rather than a face-to-face interaction.

For those who do not have interpersonal contact with lesbians and gays, parasocial contact with lesbians and gays can act in nearly identical ways to improve attitudes. For instance, Schiappa, Gregg, and Hewes found that those who report viewing *Will and Grace*, a comedic television show on ABC that premiered in 1998 and featured two gay lead characters, generally had more positive views toward lesbians and gays than those who did not, but only among respondents who reported no direct contact with lesbians and gays.[52]

Generally, it is not easy to do an experimental study involving a direct interaction with a LGBT person. Experimental research designs are the preferred method for assessing causal effects directly, but it can be difficult to reproduce an interpersonal interaction exactly across different subjects. On the other hand, it is much easier to show LGBT people to individuals though television or other media in an experimental context. Riggle, Ellis, and Crawford, for instance, showed a group of students the film *The Times of Harvey Milk* (1984), a documentary of the life and assassination of California's first gay elected official, and generally found a reduction in prejudice toward lesbians and gays.[53]

While mediated contact can replace direct contact, it turns out that even mediated contact is not a prerequisite for contact to result in changed attitudes. Just *imagining* contact with lesbians and gays can result in attitude change. For example, in a recent study of Hong Kong residents, Lau, Lau, and Looper asked individuals who did not report contact with lesbians and gays to *imagine* they were having such contact using the following vignette:

> Please imagine that you are at a restaurant and are seated next to a family consisting of two middle-aged [women/men] and an elderly couple. You overhear that family's conversations. You learn that the two [women's/men's] names are [Irene and Mary/Anthony and Michael]. They are a same-sex couple who have been living together for 15 years and they are having a meal at the restaurant with [Mary's/ Michael's] parents. Six

> months ago, [Mary/Michael] was struck by a reckless car driver and severely injured. As a result, [Mary/Michael] has had to stop working. Since the accident, [Irene/Anthony] has been financially supporting [Mary/Michael] and [Mary's/Michael's] parents. [Mary's/Michael's] parents are very grateful and consider [Irene/Anthony] to be like a [daughter/son].[54]

The authors found that, having read this vignette and imaged such an encounter, respondents agreed less with statements that homosexuals were immoral, had more positive attitudes toward homosexuals, and had higher support for nondiscrimination laws based on sexual orientation.

Just how might increases in contact or exposure to lesbians and gays work to improve attitudes? Several mechanisms have been brought forth as possibilities. Exposure to lesbians and gays may trigger feelings of empathy and increase positive emotions toward lesbians and gays as a group.[55] How empathic a person is may also have a role in the effects of intergroup contact, since empathy allows individuals to put themselves in the position of an out-group member. When empathy is present, those interacting with members of out-groups feel the stigma they feel.[56] Seeing aspects of oneself in others fosters empathy and opens others up to persuasion.[57] While interacting with members of an out-group, people may also start to "project," or associate, things they generally like about themselves with the out-group members they are interacting with, causing them to like the out-group members more.[58] This, in turn, allows those positive emotions to be transferred to the entire out-group. Positive interactions also reduce negative anxiety toward out-groups by reducing any anxiety that may be felt involving an uncertainty surrounding how future interactions with out-group members may go.[59]

The theme of these findings has been summed up in a concise fashion by Hewstone and Swart, who write that "more generally, contact exerts its effects on prejudice by both reducing negative affect (e.g., inter-group anxiety) and by inducing positive affective processes (e.g., empathy and perspective taking)."[60] Thus contact has been shown to act through mechanisms that implicate affect itself. It is to other recent findings in the political psychology literature concerning in the role of affect in decision-making that I know turn.

John. Q. Public, Dual Process Models of Decision-Making, and Automatic Affective Feelings

The role of affect in political decision-making has become considerably more prominent in the last few years thanks to the development of the John Q. Public (JQP) model by Milton Lodge and Charles S. Taber.[61] The basic premise of the JQP model is that our subconscious reactions to various individuals or social groups come more easily to mind than any conscious considerations or factual information relating to these people or groups.[62]

The easiest way to illustrate this is in a candidate election. For the sake of this illustration, let's say you were in a coma for the year before a presidential election. You wake up on the day of an election for president having no idea who is on the ballot. You go to your local polling place to vote. When you arrive, you look down at your ballot and see, for the first time, two names: Hillary Clinton and Rick Santorum. According to the JQP model, the most important mental processes in your decision involving who to vote for occurs in a fraction of a second after reading those names. Before any other information is recalled from your memory, your affective feelings toward Clinton and Santorum, the warmness or coolness you feel toward them individually, pop into your head. If one of these is overwhelmingly positive, while the other overwhelmingly negative, then your decision is effectively made in that instant. Affective feelings, positive or negative, rather than facts or issue positions, are the driving forces in vote decisions when candidates are generally as well known as Clinton or Santorum in the JQP model.

The roots of the JQP model rest in dual process models of decision-making from cognitive psychology. These models were developed in order to explain how people engage in decision-making across various contexts. The best characterization of the two different decision-making processes common in these models has been given by Kahneman in his book *Thinking Fast and Slow*.[63] Kahneman calls these processes System 1 and System 2:

> System 1 operates automatically and quickly, with little or no effort and no sense of voluntary control. System 2 allocates attention to the effortful mental activities that demand it, including complex computations. The operations of System 2 are often associated with the subjective experience

> of agency, choice, and concentration. . . . Although System 2 believes itself to be where the action is, the automatic System 1 is the Hero . . . [System 1 is] effortlessly originating impressions and feelings that are the main source of the explicit beliefs and deliberate choices of System 2.[64]

System 1 works through shortcuts, such as affective feelings that pop into a person's head when making a quick decision. When we feel the answer to the decision *implicitly* before thinking, this is System 1 in operation. Kahneman's point is that System 1 can often arrive at an objectively correct decision with little cognitive effort. That is why it is the "hero." But when it comes to complex political and social issues, it can just as easily lead us astray. System 1 can be biased and prejudiced when it comes to social decision-making. System 1 is also very bad at logic, math, and statistics, unlike System 2. When we get a feeling that a certain answer is better than another on a math test, that feeling is just as often wrong as right.

A lot of people feel uncomfortable with these dual process models when they first encounter them. Most people are very comforted in the belief that when they engage in decision-making, they behave in a wholly rational manner. The suggestion that people do not engage the rational System 2 when making decisions, including important decisions such as whom to vote for in a presidential election, can be unnerving. But often System 1 does indeed guide us in making our decisions. Thus, the suggestion that much of what we do is driven by subconscious forces can be jarring for some people.

The driving force of political decision-making in the JQP model is something akin to Kahneman's System 1. A "*likeability heuristic* stored as an implicit attitude" is the driving force here.[65] This is the affect, positive or negative, attached to a person or social group that springs to mind when that person or group is encountered or is involved in a decision.

There are other features of the JQP model that are relevant for attitudes involving social groups like lesbians and gays. One is that items in memory that are affectively congruent are more easily recalled from memory. For instance, if you have positive affective feelings toward lesbians and gays, this makes it easier to remember something positive involving lesbian and gay rights or lesbians and gays specifically. It may be easier to think of a funny joke by Ellen DeGeneres or an article describing the joy of same-sex couples marrying when a state begins to allow same-sex marriage if you have a positive reaction to lesbians and gays in general rather than a negative reaction. If these instantaneous affective feelings are negative, then negatively laden affective recollections, such as those associating lesbians and gays with child molestation, tend to be called up instead.

System 1 can thus have a double effect in the creation of political attitudes. For instance, assume a person is asked his or her opinion on laws that protect gays and lesbians from discrimination on a survey. If the initial affective reaction, positive or negative, does not drive the response to the survey, and the person stops to think about the questions and engages System 2, considerations affectively congruent with the initial affect toward lesbians and gays will be more likely to be recalled. These negative or positive bits of information will then bias the logical System 2 into making a decision identical to the outcome of System 1 processing. Lodge and Taber term this *affective contagion*.[66] For instance, someone who has a negative emotional response to lesbians and gays is more likely to remember a previously encountered opinion *against* gay rights, whether this opinion came from interpretation of a biblical passage or phrases from a speech by a political leader against gay rights. That person is less likely to remember any pro-gay information that may have been previously encountered, like for instance a positive portrayal of a lesbian or gay character seen on television.

In explaining the process by which affective reactions are formed, Lodge and Taber note that "people form impressions of others automatically, anchor on these early impressions, and adjust insufficiently to later information."[67] Earlier information has a much stronger effect on the affective feeling of a person or social group than later information. This is because the earlier information pushes the affective consideration in a positive or negative direction. Once formed, the affect is automatically felt when new information on the person or social group is encountered. This affect then biases the processing of that information in ways congruent with the direction of the affect.

A New Synthesis: Affective Liberalization

We are now ready to form a new theory of the major causes of the distinctive features of attitude change with respect to lesbian and gay rights.

These features include the rapidity, magnitude, and durability of change, as well as the specific year of birth effects. Drawing from axioms summarized in chapter 1 and concepts discussed in this chapter, we can say that

1. Contact with (or exposure to) lesbians and gays, in its various forms, tends to warm people's automatically recalled affect toward lesbians and gays, consistent with the findings of various theories of social contact.
2. Automatically recalled affect toward lesbians and gays is a dominant consideration in determining support for all lesbian and gay rights (that are minimally discussed in the media) in a manner that is consistent with the JQP model of political decision-making.

Thus, an affective measure, like the feeling thermometer discussed in the previous chapter, contains within it the stored affective history of the respondent's past encounters with lesbians and gays (to an extent).

Notice I am assuming that exposure to lesbians and gays is *positive* and conducive to social change in a manner consistent with the social psychological findings on social contact. Lesbians and gays seem to exist in all or most parts of the country in nearly all social roles and in all forms of employment. One of the mediating factors facilitating contact (though not discussed earlier) involves a basic similarity between the two people interacting. Assuming most negative stereotypes involving differences between lesbians, gays, bisexuals, and heterosexuals are false, and that lesbians and gays are similar to heterosexuals in terms of interests, hobbies, employment, or any other factors that two people might potentially share, regardless of any differences in sexual orientation, lesbians and gays should thus be well positioned for efficacious contact.[68]

Because of the primacy effects of earlier information in the development of the affective response, cohort effects will develop on all lesbian and gay rights issues, but only if a sharp increase in exposure to lesbians and gays takes place after a long period when most information on homosexuality was generally negative. Older people will start to liberalize after such an increase, but only very slowly, as new exposure to lesbians and gays has to work against previously created negative affect. After the shift in media content, younger people without such negative affect should form pro-lesbian and gay attitudes quickly, form positive affect, and bias the processing of new information in a pro-gay direction.

Thus, to continue:

3. Because automatically recalled affect is less stable in younger people, exposure effects on them are stronger. Thus, a marked increase in positive, intergroup contact across a society in a short period of time leads to cohort effects in support of lesbian and gay rights.

If a marked increase in exposure took place in the late 1980s and 1990s, then affective liberalization explains why the direction of cohort effects on lesbian and gay rights became more consistent and remarkable after the mid-1990s.

The durability of attitudinal shifts on lesbian and gay rights also follows from the role that affective feelings hold in the System 1 process, which in turn, has some influence on System 2 processes in the JQP model. Since affect, once stabilized, biases the processing of new information in the direction of the affect, pro-gay or anti-gay attitudes should be continually reinforced as new information is encountered involving lesbians and gays. It would take a strong headwind of either very pro-gay or very anti-gay information to reorient this affect once formed. The basic conclusion is that attitudes caused by affective responses toward lesbians and gays, as well as attitude change caused by change in these affective evaluations, should be theoretically stronger and more durable than attitude change induced by other mechanisms like framing or elite-led change.

Elite-led change and framing still do affect attitudes on lesbian and gay rights under the theory of affective liberalization. However, the scale and durability of any aggregate attitudinal change caused by these elites or frames may be short lived. A good analogy comes from the various factors that affect whether it is warm or cold outdoors: on one day, the amount of cloud cover may affect the temperature; on the next, the clouds may pass and temperatures rise. Framing and elite-led theories are like cloud cover, affecting lesbian and gay rights support in the short term, while not contributing much to the long-term trend. Changes in automatic affective feelings, caused by exposure to out-groups, are more like climate change. They affect the long-term average of support in an enduring fashion, but can go unnoticed as causes of increased support on a day-to-day or month-to-month basis. This explains why in periods of considerable attention to specific gay rights issues, such as 1992–1993, when it was gays in the military, and 2003, when it was the legality of homosexuality, attitudes shifted quickly. The effects of framing and elite-led views were temporarily taking over as the dominant factors in attitudinal change. But when the attention ended, these frames and elite position were forgotten, except when they reinforced the direction of affect, and support returned to the level dictated by affective liberalization.

This theory of affective liberalization also explains why adoption of pro-gay policies results in attitude change.[69] Specifically, advances in pro-gay policies make LGBTQ individuals feel more comfortable coming out to others. If LGBTQ individuals feel more comfortable in coming out in locations where their rights are protected, after a legislature, executive, or court put in place such policies, this increased contact could be responsible for any increase in gay rights support that occurs. Evidence of a time lag in the effects of policy change on public opinion seems to validate this explanation.[70] For example, Kreitzer, Hamilton, and Tolbert[71] found that when the Iowa Supreme Court legalized same-sex marriage, little opinion change occurred instantaneously; instead, shifts in attitudes occurred in the years after the decision, as would be the case if LGBTQ individuals felt more comfortable coming out to their neighbors after the decision.

Summing up the last key implication of affective liberalization:

4. Political attention to an issue, transmitted through news, is important in changing attitudes, but mostly only on that specific issue, or on issues the public may closely associate with it.

In a sense, then, affective liberalization is also a *pre-political* theory of attitude change. That is, it takes into account the role of nonpolitical affective feelings, formed by nonpolitical interactions, in changing views on political issues and policies. Absent a recognition of the nature and effect of such preconditions, political scientists have lacked the tools necessary to explain attitudinal changes on the scale seen vis-à-vis lesbian and gay rights. Most interactions with lesbians and gays do not involve explicit appeals for individuals to support specific policies like gay adoption or employment nondiscrimination. Life is more mundane. Affective liberalization, by working through ostensibly non-political affect involving lesbians and gays, and without being filtered through news coverage of political events, can thus act equally on political sophisticates and a-politicals alike; hence, we also have an explanation for the pattern in table 2–1. This is not to say that affective liberalization does not interact with politics. Chapter 7 will make clear that it does. But it can bypass politics and have an effect on those who don't care about politics in a manner that other theories of the causes of mass opinion change cannot match.

Empirical Considerations in the Search for the Causes of Change

The Search for the Causes of Change

Because my emphasis here is on examining change *explicitly*, this book departs from the basic cross-sectional framework used in much of the prior research on gay rights support.[72]

An example should make some of my reasons for doing this clear. Let's assume that in one year, 20 percent of the population supports the legality of homosexuality. Five years later, this has risen to 40 percent. If someone analyzes a poll (perhaps using a tool like regression analysis, which estimates various effects allowing for control variables), and finds that liberalism is the only major predictor of support for the legality of homosexuality in the later period, does this mean that liberalism is the cause of this attitude change?

Maybe, but there is not enough information to say conclusively. One of two things would need to be true. Assuming the relationship between liberalism and support for gay rights did not change between the two surveys, liberalism could be responsible if the proportion of liberals in the public increased significantly from the first poll to the second five years later. Let's say that this is not the case. The proportion of liberals is found to be exactly the same in both years. Liberalism *could* still be responsible for the increase in support under some circumstances. For instance, let's say a prominent liberal politician endorsed lesbian and gay rights between the two polls. This might increase the effect of liberalism—essentially increasing the gap in support between liberals and conservatives on gay rights—and this greater support among liberals may be causing the increased support for gay rights in response to the endorsement.

But to test this, we need to determine if, in a statistical sense, the effect of liberalism on support for lesbian and gay rights actually increased significantly from the first poll to the second poll in a manner not due to chance given the selection of the two different polling samples. Thus, we need to analyze *both* polls to make sure any rise in the *effect* of liberalism is larger than what chance can account for. The take away here is that the original study, which showed that liberals were more likely to support gay rights in the later time period, neither shows that the number of liberals increased or demonstrates that the effect of liberalism (or the gap between liberals and conservatives) increased between the two time periods. Thus, we cannot be sure that liberalism is related to the increase in support unless we look at both polls, even though the original study found an effect of liberalism in the second.

Mindful of this, I take the following approach when examining change in public opinion: Rather than using cross-sectional studies, which analyze a poll in a single time period, I use multiple polls taken at multiple times to validate my findings. For instance, I use the American National Election Study from 1984 to 2012, the General Social Survey from 1972 to 2012, and the World and European Values Studies from 1981 to 2009.[73] I also construct an additional dataset of polls from American news media outlets that ask respondents if they know lesbians and gays and if they support lesbian and gay rights and use demographic variables to see just how the relations between demographics and other factors, like exposure to lesbians and gays, differs across time in terms of their importance for predicting attitudes toward lesbian and gay rights.

Shifts in Which Groups Are "Persuadable"

Next, we should not assume that the same factors that predict lesbian and gay rights support at one time necessarily predict lesbian and gay rights support (or change in that support) at another. Even if we do see increasing or decreasing effect sizes of some demographic variables, things may be changing in ways that are not quite as straight forward as they at first appear. This is because different groups of people may be persuadable on lesbian and gay rights at different time periods. And these varying groups of people may be susceptible to change due to different causes.

Take for example, the prominent finding in the academic literature that those exposed to "equality frames" in the context of a debate on lesbian and gay rights will become more supportive of lesbian and gay rights if they also tend to value equal treatment of people and social groups. Additional experiments undertaken in the late 1990s support this finding: exposure to equality frames does increase support for gay rights, at least temporarily. As mentioned earlier, lesbian and gay rights groups then began incorporating these "equality" frames in their messaging. This was especially the case during Prop 8 in 2008 and other anti-gay ballot initiative campaigns. The purpose of doing so was to sway public opinion. But these pro–same-sex marriage campaigns largely failed; if anything, the state electorates tended to become less supportive of same-sex marriage during the course of these campaigns.

Does this mean the original findings were invalid? Hardly. What had changed was the population that was open to persuasion on lesbian and gay rights through these equality frames. In the 1990s, the people being persuaded to support gay rights for the first time were likely liberals and others holding strong egalitarian values, like the highly educated. They needed a bit of a push to support gay rights, in the context of other changes taking place in the 1990s, and an equality frame in a news story would have likely accomplished this job, just as these experimental studies showed.

By 2008, however, most of the more tolerant individuals susceptible to equality frames and other themes of equal treatment were already somewhat firmly in support of lesbian and gay rights. "Equality" frames would not have been raising support for same-sex marriage among these more tolerant individuals, as they had already expressed high levels of support. By 2008, the universe of individuals open to persuasion on marriage equality was likely comprised of political moderates and individuals with intermediate amounts of education who may have known LGBT people, but not very well. These individuals were less egalitarian than liberals, and thus less likely to react to an equality frame when compared to more liberal people in the 1990s. Although the academic findings were very clear that these frames worked in the 1990s, those needing persuasion during the Prop 8 campaign were very different from those for whom these frames were found to be effective in 1990s studies, and there was little change in mass attitudes when the "No on Prop 8" campaign aired.

A Preliminary Roadmap: Change in the Basis of Affective Feelings toward Gays

For further clues as to how affective evaluations of gay rights issues have changed, I model the affective feelings that people have toward lesbians and gays as measured by the American National Elections Study's (ANES) feeling thermometer. Recall that the ANES is a set of nationally representative surveys of the US population generally taken in election years. While the ANES usually surveys different respondents in each year, the surveyors occasionally resurvey the same respondents in a "panel" study.

The model depicted in table A2.2 in the appendix predicts these feelings as a function of some of the major demographics variables found to affect support for lesbian and gay rights in prior research: party, ideology, gender, race, religion, education, and year of birth. This is also the first example in this book of a 'regression analysis' and I will attempt to explain clearly what the results mean and why they are important. The ultimate goal is to take a preliminary look at whose affective evaluations have changed specifically, and in what times these social and political groups are shifting in terms of their attitudes. If we see a rapid change in one-time period, among one group of people, it merits a close examination of the historical contexts that are leading that group to change in that time. The analysis is a little technical, so I take it a bit slow.

The exact wording of the ANES's feeling thermometer was described in the first chapter. The scale of affective feelings, again, is measured from 0 to 100, with 0 being "cold" toward the group and 100 being "warm." I model these feelings as a function of differing levels of respondent religiosity, political party identification, ideological identification, gender, race, education, and year of birth. Coding for these variables is discussed in the data appendix at the end of the book.

Since the focus of this study is change, it is important to understand how demographic effects may weaken or strengthen over time in response to increasing exposure or other factors. To see if the effects of these demographics change in various years, affect toward gays and lesbians (the feeling thermometer score given by individual respondents) is modeled by created a set of variables that take on the value 1 for each specific year and 0 for all other years. One variable was created for *each year* in the survey, with the exception of 1984, the first year. Each of these annual "dummy" variables was then multiplied times each of the 7 demographic variables and all of these were used as predictors in an ordinary least squares (OLS) regression analysis predicting affective feelings toward lesbians and gays for a total of 70 different predictors (7 demographics, 9 dummy variables indicating years, and 54 demographic X year interactions). The results of the analysis are in appendix table A2.1.

This type of analysis is performed for a very specific reason. In such an analysis, the effect of the direct effect reported on each of the demographics' variables becomes the common effect of that variable in the first year, 1984. This "effect" can be thought of as something very similar to the *gap* in feelings on the thermometer between the highest and lowest value of the demographic controlling for all the other factors in the model (or the 0 and 1 on that specific variable specified). For instance, the effect of party affiliation in 1984 is 5.48. This means the difference in the average affective evaluation between a strong Democrat and strong Republican in the fitted model of attitudes would be 5.48 degrees, controlling for the other demographics. The "intercept" effect is just the average value for that year when all of the other demographic variables are 0.

The "interaction effects," or the values in the model for the year variables multiplied times the demographic variables, signify the difference in the effect, or gap, between the 1984 common value of the effect and the effect, or gap, in the year specified. To find the effect of a demographic variable in any given year, just follow the year indicated in the row across to the demographic of interest and add that value to the value for 1984 in the first row. For instance, the difference in the party effect between 1984 and 1992 is 4.98 degrees because that is the estimated interaction effect between the 1992 variable and the party variable. This means the gap between strong Democrats (the 0 for party) and strong Republicans (the 1 for party) found by the model in 1992, controlling for the other demographics included, is 10.46 degrees (= 4.98 degrees + 5.48 degrees).

Any symbol (@) or stars (*) in a model represent various levels of statistical significance depending on the type or number of times the symbol is repeated. Because a random sample of people was selected for the surveys in various years, we may have found a relationship by randomly selecting an unrepresentative sample by chance. These indicators of statistical significance, generally, tell us that the effect (or gap) is larger than what we would have expected from chance, given that we have drawn a random sample of people. If things are not starred in a model, it doesn't necessarily mean an effect isn't there, or that one variable isn't directly causing another variable, but merely that the variable may be too closely related (or correlated) to the other demographics to distinguish the effect from chance, or that the sample size of the poll may not be large enough to accurately do so.

What I have found is that few of the effects of the demographics weaken from 1984 onward (see appendix 2 for more detail). Only race appears to be a consistently unimportant factor when it comes to affective feelings toward lesbians and gays. Religiosity is consistently associated with a gap of about 10 points, but this gap does not change much over time. Education was more important in 1988 than in 1984, but its strength immediately dropped back down to 1984 levels in the next year. Gender became a stronger predictor in 1998, and possible 2008, but there appears to be little consistency in the pattern of change in its effects. The more important findings involve change in the effects of party, ideology, and year of birth. Although it is only weakly statistically significant, party was more important in 1992, when Bill Clinton was first elected to the presidency. Ideology is consistently the largest predictor in terms of the gap in affective feelings. In 1984, ideology predicted nearly a 21-degree gap. In 1994, after the debate on gays in the military, the estimated gap between liberals and conservatives ballooned to over 35 degrees and remained significantly higher until 1998. Year of birth is typically associated with a 10-degree gap in feelings. Although many of the deviations from 1984 are not significant statistically, and thus may be due to chance variations in the sample of people selected, they are still substantial. The gap in year of birth closed completely in 1988, but clearly reopened by 1994. It exploded in 2008, becoming statistically larger than in 1984, at 33 points total.

It should be noted that just because the increase in the 1994 gap between liberals and conservatives closed in 2000, liberals were not necessarily going back to their old attitudes. Figure 2.1 plots the trends in average affective evaluations separately for liberals, moderates and conservatives. Note the increase in the gap between liberals and conservatives from 1988 to 1994. However, that gap later closes, not due to declining affective feelings among liberals, but due to increases in affective feelings among conservatives. Liberals appear to have been warming to lesbians and gays earlier than conservatives.

This change in liberals merits special attention, as they may be responding to either elite signals from liberal leaders or "equality" frames in the media rather than increased exposure to lesbians and gays. However, as I show in chapter 7, these differing shifts can be explained by affective liberalization when the theory of *motivated reasoning* is applied

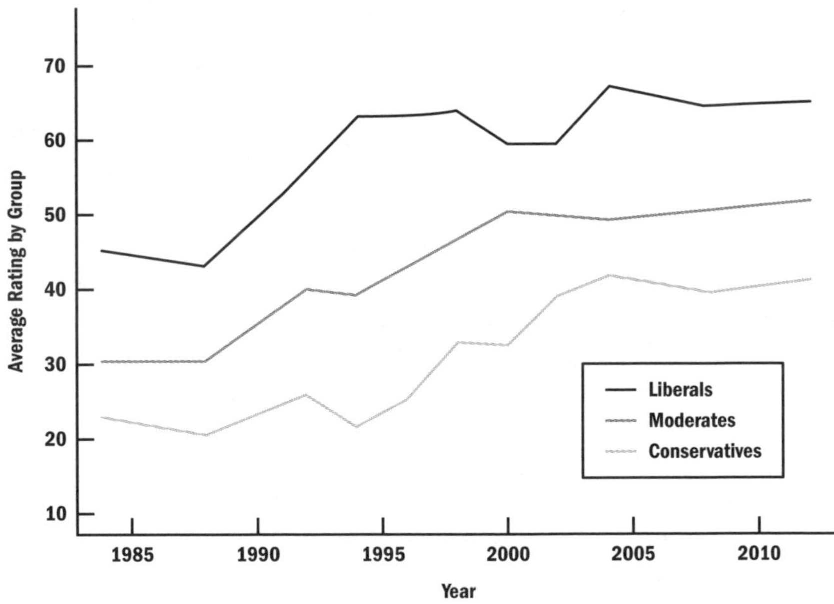

Figure 2.1. Average Thermometer Rating of Lesbians and Gays by Ideological Group. *Source*: Compilation by author from *ANES Times Series Cumulative Data File (1948–2012)*.

to exposure to lesbians and gays. Still, the late 1980s and early 1990s appear again to be a key time period as affective evaluations are shifting first among Democrats and liberals, then later among moderates and conservatives.

Conclusion

The dominant existing theories of attitudinal change on lesbian and gay issues have stated that changes in television news coverage of lesbian and gay rights are the major drivers of social change in public opinion. However, when examined under a critical lens, these theories do not hold up. Pro-LGBTQ frames employed in coverage of LGBTQ issues do not appear to concentrate change among those most likely to have watched television news and do not seem to move attitudes in a pro-gay direction at the times they occur on television the most.

Given the flaws in these existing theories, the theory of *affective liberalization* is derived from an integration of intergroup contact theory and dual process models of political decision-making. The core features of the theory are that positive interpersonal and mediated intergroup contact with lesbians and gays has a long-lasting effect on peoples' subconscious or implicit views on lesbians and gays. These implicit attitudes are particularly moveable in the young. Once intergroup contact has shifted a person's implicit attitudes, these implicit attitudes then form the primary basis in determining support for any individual lesbian or gay rights policy that may be asked about on a survey. Several other findings on causes of attitude change, such as findings that pro-gay policy advancements cause mass gay rights support,[74] can be incorporated into the theory by suggesting that increasing rates of intergroup contact act as a crucial mediator in the process of attitudinal change.

In the next part of the book, I provide crucial background for understanding the contextual changes leading up to and encouraging public opinion change. It is not enough to show that increases in "coming out" are central to increasing gay rights support, if those increases themselves were due to political or media elites rather than the LGBTQ movement. Thus, the following chapters trace the history of the lesbian and gay community up to the AIDS crisis and its gradual political integration into the Democratic Party. These two events dominated news coverage of lesbian and gay issues in the early 1990s, the same time that an increase in coming out must be observed for affective liberalization to be correct. As I will show, these contextual changes, which contributed to increased comfort levels in coming out among LGBTQs had their roots in the changing experiences of lesbians and gays and their activism from the origins of the LGBT movement to the peak of anti-AIDS activism in the early 1990s, rather than in the generosity of supportive elites.

PART II

A Prelude to Change

LGBT Movement Development and Political Integration

When they ushered us out [of the Stonewall Inn on the night of the riots], they very nicely put you out the door. Then you're standing across the street in Sheridan Square Park. But why? Everybody's looking at each other, "Why do we have to keep putting up with this?"
—Ray "Sylvia Lee" Rivera

How can an unpopular social group end the animus the public feels toward it? The factors discussed in chapter 2—positive exposure, endorsements from political leaders, or positive frames in the media—may all be effective at changing attitudes. But any social group seeking social change on a large scale will immediately run into intense resistance when it tries to secure any of these.

Figuring out how to trigger the mechanisms that change minds is not easy. Persuading the press and elected officials to support their struggle initially provided an almost insurmountable task for activists in the 1960s and 1970s. The fact that only a small number of individuals devoted themselves to the movement prior to the 1980s also hindered advancement. Before social change could occur, ways to change the basic negative responses of the media and elected officials to lesbian and gay issues would have to be found.

Part 2 traces the process by which the behavior of these decision-makers was changed. In chapter 3, I trace the origin of the American LGBT movement up to the peak of AIDS activism in the early 1990s. The AIDS crisis, while decimating large sectors of the LGBT community, motivated a period of intense activism that swelled the movement starting in 1987 and continuing through the 1992 presidential election. Without the AIDS crisis to motivate an increase in LGBT activism, it remains uncertain if the social changes we have seen would have occurred as rapidly, particularly considering the resistance of the press to covering lesbian and gay issues extensively before 1992.

Chapter 4 focuses on political change. Although liberal Democrats, somewhat begrudgingly, started endorsing gay rights in the 1970s, it was only after the start of AIDS activism that political party became a consistent predictor of lesbian and gay rights support in Congress, rather than the education levels of a member's district and whether or not it was in an urban area. These two chapters describe the origins of contextual changes that took place in the national press and the political arena which would make possible the more profound changes that occurred in public opinion in the 1990s. In doing so, they reflect the contributions of LGBT activists in setting up the necessary conditions for later social changes.

3

The Spread and Intensification of Gay and Lesbian Identities

Putting a label [homosexual] on myself was a big step forward. . . . Once I said, "Yes, that's me, that's what I am," I was able to work with it.
—Barbara Gittings, interview, 1974

To begin a chronicle of the American LGBT movement, one needs to look rather far afield, to Germany in 1871, when paragraph 175, a law criminalizing consensual sex between men, was passed.[1] While laws banning homosexuality had existed before, the debate over the adoption of paragraph 175 was different.[2] No longer did it turn on morality or religion. Instead, the emphasis fell on an assertion that those who tended to engage in same-sex relations were chronically diseased. For the first time, it was not sin or morality that motivated legal action against homosexuality, but the state's role in protecting the health of its citizenry from homosexuality.

The origins of this shift, its relation to the industrial revolution and urbanization, and its precise timing, have been much debated in the lesbian and gay studies literature.[3] The rise of the medical community and enlightenment notions of sickness and the treatment of disease are major causes.[4] Havelock Ellis, in *Sexual Inversion*, describes the most prominent theory of the day, that of Richard von Krafft-Ebing, who called homosexuality "sexual inversion":[5]

> At the outset . . . [Krafft-Ebing] considered inversion to be a functional sign of degeneration, a partial manifestation of a neuropathic and psychopathic state which is in most cases hereditary. This perverse sexuality appears spontaneously with the developing sexual life, without external causes . . . and must then be regarded as congenital; or it develops as a result of special injurious influences working on a sexuality acquired.[6]

Over the centuries, homosexual behavior had been considered, for the most part, a sinful act. A same-sex tryst was probably something on par with an extramarital affair. But with the rise of the medical community and the concept of treatable congenital disease, justifications for laws against homosexuality shifted accordingly. The emphasis was now on those who engaged in that act rather than the act itself.[7] And, in the name of public health, people who engaged in same-sex relations would need to be brought under the purview of government scrutiny.

Scholars have named such theories that state that sexual relations are not just acts between people, but rather a mark of a long-term characteristic of an individual who engages in such acts, "essentialist." This shift marked the beginning of an essentialist theory of homosexuality that would come to be dominant the West. A homosexual act, which had been considered a short-term moral lapse, had now morphed conceptually into evidence of a "homosexual" identity. An important aspect of this essentialist theory was that the identity had also been decoupled conceptually from the act of sodomy. An individual could be completely celibate, but still be considered a homosexual. This disjunction marks the birth of the modern notion of homosexuality: homosexuality as identity.

In this chapter, I outline concisely the effects that this new understanding of those that tended to engage in same-sex relations would have in the twentieth century. From the Progressive Era through World War II, the opinion that those that who engaged in same-sex relations had an illness spread from the scientific medical literature to virtually all educated political leaders and progressive elites in the United States and other industrialized nations. Regarding homosexuality as an illness that threatened society became official government policy. From this time until the 1960s, this new understanding spread beyond governmental and bureaucratic channels to the mass public through public health campaigns, military enlistment interviews, and attempts to cure "moral degeneracy." Homophobia as social policy reached its zenith as homosexuality and communism became linked during the 1950s.

After a brief recap of these developments, this chapter turns to a retelling of the first stirrings of an organized LGBTQ movement in the United States. Although it consisted of only a handful of people at first, the creation of an LGBTQ subculture caused more same-sex attracted individuals in the early 1970s to coalesce into a constellation of large, visible communities in the nation's urban centers. These communities could weld some political power locally in the 1970s and 1980s, but were too numerically small to affect national politics. The final factor that caused these communities to form into a movement capably of affecting politics and society on a grand scale was AIDS. AIDS provided the impetus for formerly apolitical LGBTQs to engage in sophisticated political and media activism, which spread the LGBTQ subculture outside of the nation's urban centers and unleased further political and social changes that later chapters examine.

US Government Action against Homosexuality up to the Lavender Scare

The position that homosexual behavior was the mark of chronic mental illness quickly spread to the United States. While laws against sodomy, seldom enforced, were common from the colonial period, the development of the medical and mental health professions in the late 1800s and early 1900s provided a new, "rational" basis for the existence of anti-homosexuality statutes. This led to a general strengthening of the government's regulation of homosexuality as the modern welfare state developed in the first half of the twentieth century.[8] According to Canaday, "Progressive era reformers used the word homosexuality somewhat interchangeably with 'pervert', 'degenerate', 'pederast', and 'sodomite' in their campaigns to improve public health."[9] Gradually, such notions took hold even among those who had little interaction with the medical or mental health fields, such as the working class.[10]

As new medical notions of the homosexual as a distinct type of person started to take root in the public mind, they became connected to previous notions of homosexuality as sinful and immoral. Although many in the medical profession believed homosexuals were ill and thus in need of treatment, not sinners in need of punishment, the majority of the public came to believe that a whole class of individuals who were inherently degenerate or immoral existed. In the early 1900s, this both paralleled, and perhaps reinforced, "essentialist" theories of inherent differences between racial groups that had also been "scientifically proven" in that time period.[11]

Over the course of the first half of the twentieth century, in a progressively more intense fashion, homosexuals became more and more excluded from government programs in order to make sure that those benefiting from these programs were not degenerates. Homosexuals were banned from legal immigration for having "immoral purposes," screened from the armed services during the end of World War I and all of World War II for reasons of being unfit (though many lied in order to enlist), ejected from New Deal relief programs for fear that impressionable others would learn "perversion," and later denied earned benefits under the G.I. Bill.[12]

By the end of the 1940s, government panic over homosexuals came to a head. In the 1950s, its role in discouraging and stigmatizing homosexuality reached a peak. Homosexuality, communism, espionage, and political scandal became tightly interwoven in the public mind in what has been termed the "Lavender Scare" by historians. The origins of the scare were in the Truman administration, in February of 1950, when the US Secretary of State at the time, Dean Acheson, was testifying about dismissals from the State Department over security risks.[13] Under questioning, one of Acheson's undersecretaries admitted that ninety-one people had been under investigation and dismissed for "moral weaknesses" in the "shady category" of homosexuality.[14]

Congressional Republicans and other opponents of Truman were quick to seize on these dismissals, which buttressed assertions by Senator Joseph McCarthy (R-WI) that the state department employed "Communists and Queers."[15] Of course, it mattered little for McCarthy that these dismissals were exclusively in the second of these two categories. News of the dismissals quickly garnered press attention and left the Truman administration deeply embarrassed. "The issue of homosexuals in government, observed columnist John O'Donnell, constituted "a new type of political weapon—never used in this republic."[16]

Thus, homosexuality, communism, and security risks were all associated in the minds of the 1950s public. After all, both communists and homosexuals had secrets to hide. In the shadows, both associated discretely with others of their kind. Both were out of step with the 1950s American ethos. Although there was little firm evidence of it ever occurring, homosexuals could conceivably be blackmailed by communists into selling state secrets. In effect, then, these two perceived threats, a communist threat to the nation and a homosexual threat to the health of the traditional family, started to blend together during this period. The public could easily draw the conclusion that permissiveness toward homosexuality could lead to a communist victory in the Cold War. Issues of national security and immorality were now solidly linked.

Although McCarthy shifted his own rhetorical focus to potential communist infiltration of the government, rather than "moral degenerates," both Democratic and Republican administrations became highly motivated to take a tough stance in policing the sexuality of civil servants in order to avoid a similar political embarrassment. For Truman, much of the damage from the revelation of homosexuals in the State Department could not be undone. That did not stop other high-ranking administration officials from attempting a complete purge of homosexuals from the civil service in order to fight back against accusations from political opponents of "subversives" being employed by the federal government. Republicans attempted to gain the upper hand after accusing the Democrats of being lax on homosexuality, when President Eisenhower issued executive order 10450 upon taking office in 1953. The order declared that "sexual perversion" rendered a person wholly unfit for government service.

The Development of the Lesbian and Gay Movement to 1960

Before the Lavender Scare, enclaves of homosexuals had developed in urban areas. While the population of the country had relocated to cities during the industrial revolution of the late 1800s, in the early twentieth century, immigration caused the nation's urban areas to swell in size, and as urban population density increased, interpersonal contact between homosexuals occurred more frequently. Some homosexuals discovered that they shared a common sexual orientation distinct from that of the majority.[17]

As time passed, a few of the places where homosexuals choose to live developed reputations as bohemian enclaves. In turn, this association caused more homosexuals to gradually settle there. Friendship networks grew and developed. According to D'Emilio, "a small but stable group life was forming"[18] for those living in these urban enclaves.

Somewhat counterintuitively, World War II sped up this whole process. Traditional American gender roles were transformed in the 1940s as males left for overseas and women were mobilized to work in industry.

The same-sex environment was freeing for many, both in the military and on the home front. Lasting friendships and relationships survived hostilities during the war years,[19] and the social webs that persisted led to the origins of a distinct lesbian and gay movement.[20] However, the reinforcing notions of the time, that homosexuals were either immoral, sick, or threats, strongly encouraged most to keep their heads down and their mouths closed when talking to those from outside these nascent communities.

Nonetheless, many homosexuals resisted and denied the validity of the ubiquitous views of homosexuality as degenerate and diseased. Based on their own personal experiences, they found it self-evident that these notions were obviously incorrect. As Kay Lahusen writes of her experience as a lesbian around 1950, "I finally brought it to a head within myself. I just decided that I was right and the world was wrong and that there couldn't be anything wrong with this kind of love."[21] Similarly, according to Dr. Evelyn Hooker (mentioned in chapter 1), not only did her interactions with gay men lead her to personally doubt the validity of the scientific consensus of the day, but her gay friends actively solicited her to challenge that consensus scientifically. "I don't remember a time when Sammy or George said, 'We're Gay.' They just let down their hair and became very good friends of ours. . . . Sammy turned to me and said, 'We have let you see us as we are, and now it is your scientific duty to make a study of people like us.' Imagine that."[22]

Others openly critiqued the validity of the dominant scientific research. Frank Kameny, a prominent gay rights activist, openly attacked the scientific underpinnings of the consensus. "A reading of the so-called authorities on the matter [of homosexuality as illness] shows an appalling incidence of loose reasoning, or poor research, of supposedly generally applicable conclusions being derived from an examination of non-representative samples, of conclusions being incorporated into initial assumptions, and vise-versa, with the consequent circular reasoning."[23]

New forms of biological research, which were quite distinct from the medical and psychiatric research on the "disease" of homosexuality, also started to undermine the dominant justification of laws criminalizing same-sex relations, that homosexuality was the mark of illness. In 1948, zoologist Alfred C. Kinsey, with Wardell B. Pomeroy and Clyde E. Martin, published the widely read *Sexual Behavior in the Human Male*.[24] It was based on 12,000 interviews performed by the authors. A volume on women soon followed.[25] The original study argued that the percentage of the public with a homosexual predisposition was close to 10 percent, a figure much greater than previously thought. Although the study had severe methodological flaws, and modern surveys have placed the percentage identifying as gay or lesbian closer to 3–5 percent,[26] that number became greatly significant to the homosexual community in the United States. Even as it was used by opponents of lesbians and gays to justify the magnitude of the "homosexual menace," it signified to those who would form the first enduring lesbian and gay organizations that they had a potentially large group of compatriots. To some, 10 percent may seem small, but it was similar in size to that of the US Jewish or Latino communities in the 1950s. As of 2017, the US LGBT community is about twice the size of the US Jewish community and only slightly smaller than the Asian-American community.

The distinctive feature of the Kinsey study was not necessarily in the data, however, but in the tone of the chapter discussing same-sex behavior. Kinsey, who grew to become bisexual over the course of his research, made a clear normative break from the older medical and psychiatric literature. The opinion that homosexual activity, in and of itself, was evidence of a psychopathic personality, was materially challenged by Kinsey's interpretation of his incidence and frequency data on homosexual acts:

> Of the 40 or 50 percent of the male population which has homosexual experiences, certainly a high proportion would not be considered psychopathic personalities on the basis of anything else in their histories. . . . Psychiatrists and clinicians in general might very well re-examine their justification for demanding that all persons conform to particular patterns of behavior. As a matter of fact, there is an increasing proportion of the most skilled psychiatrists who make no attempt to re-direct behavior, but who devote their attention to helping an individual accept himself.[27]

He concludes the chapter entitled "Homosexual Outlet" with the following paragraph:

> If all persons with any trace of homosexual history, or those who were predominantly homosexual, were eliminated from the population today,

> there is no reason for believing that the incidence of the homosexual in the next generation would be materially reduced. The homosexual has been a significant part of human activity ever since the dawn of history, primarily because it is an expression of capacities that are basic in the human animal.[28]

Although Kinsey's work was scientifically flawed, it affected both the medical establishment, where some individuals began to reevaluate the notion of homosexuals as having psychopathic tendencies, as well as a large number of homosexuals into the 1950s. As Chuck Rowland, who would later become a gay rights activist, put it, "As soon as I read that there were millions of us, I said to myself, 'Well it's perfectly obvious that what we have to do is organize.'"[29]

Not long after the Kinsey Report was released, the first formal lesbian and gay organizations began forming on the West Coast. This first wave of lesbian and gay advocacy groups became known as the homophile movement. It began when a former member of the Communist Party, Harry Hay, met with a group of his homosexual friends specifically about creating a political organization for homosexuals.[30] Although Hay was no longer active in the Communist Party, he drew from both his knowledge of the theoretical arguments of Marxism and the organizational skills he had learned while in the party. Society was divided into opposing classes by sexual orientation. Heterosexuals functioned largely as the bourgeois had for Marx. For Hay, "Liberation" for homosexuals would come only from concerted action by the oppressed—that is, themselves. This first LGBT organization, named the Mattachine Society by Hay, initially believed in educating homosexuals to think of themselves as an oppressed minority.[31] This conceptual innovation, adopted from Marxist philosophy, cannot be understated. It is very similar to the consciousness raising of the women's movement in the 1960s and 1970s.

Not only did Hay borrow from Marxist theory, but his society also developed as an underground structure modeled on the Communist Party model. Members would join a cell, and when one cell got too large, it would splinter into two.[32] For an unpopular minority that could blend into society easily, this model proved extremely effective as an organizing tool. Although the organization was predominantly male, women were included in the original Mattachine Society. A separate organization eventually formed in San Francisco for lesbians called the Daughters of Bilitis.[33] At that point, the homophile movement largely sex segregated as difficulties in dealing with gender differences were not handled effectively by its leadership, thereby causing women in leave the organization.[34]

Growing throughout much of Southern California, the Mattachine Society eventually spread to the Bay Area and then to other major population centers like Chicago and New York City. Membership ballooned into the thousands.[35] More important than the new members' geographic locations were the different backgrounds and demographics of those who joined the thriving organization. Although the early members had been leftists—and hence already outside the political mainstream—the newer members were much more diverse in their political views and professions (if not their race and gender). This created a schism among Mattachine's large Southern California membership. The original members favored more radical social change using the oppressed minority model. The newer members believed more or less in the preexisting 1950s social order with the exception of the inferior place of homosexuals within that order.

A series of changes started to take place within the organization, foreshadowing its decline. First, it went above ground and radically changed its structure in the process at the insistence of the more conservative newcomers. There was a palpable fear that an underground organization of homosexuals would play into the hand of those who conflated homosexuals with communist subversion. Instead of separate cells, the organization voted to shift to a structure that conformed to the social clubs of the day. It adopted a constitution, elected an executive committee, and held regularly scheduled meetings like other traditional 1950s social organizations.[36]

The major divergence in outlook between the newcomers and older members revolved around what the proper role of the homosexual should be. Should the organization try to articulate a political and social identity for the homosexual distinct from mainstream society? With values and goals such as radical social change, sexual liberalization, nontraditional gender roles, a more equal society for all individuals, and a broad advocacy for social justice? Or should the Mattachine Society try to advocate the idea that homosexuals were no different from other members of society except for their choice of sexual partners? The older and more leftist members tended to take the former position, while the newcomers and more conservative members (in the context of homosexual politics) tended to believe in the later.[37] In the end, perhaps because of the conservative nature of the 1950s and the society's political need to distance itself from its communist origins, the latter members won out. This being 1953, a time when homosexuals were still being accused of aiding communists, such a move may have helped the organization survive into the late 1960s.[38]

As an above-ground and traditionally minded advocacy organization, however, the Mattachine Society proved to be less successful with membership retention and recruitment than in its earlier period. Without a clear message of liberation from oppression and an affirmative identity and life to advocate for, the Mattachine Society stagnated. It would take interaction with a much broader network of social movements after the conservative climate of the 1950s had waned to rekindle the potential of a nationwide lesbian and gay identity.

The 1960s and the Creation of the Modern Lesbian and Gay Identity

The members of the Mattachine Society in the 1950s and 1960s could not claim a single national elected official who was openly supportive of their rights. By the late 1960s,, the chance of an elected official voicing support for lesbian and gay rights remained close to zero. Something obviously needed to change for the movement to become more effective at lobbying elites who were largely socialized in a time when homosexuals were considered degenerates.

While the 1950s was a conservative decade, inhibiting the lesbian and gay movement, the end of the 1960s saw a widespread surge in movement development. One of the chief factors causing this was the adoption of tactics from the civil rights movement and the women's movement,[39] both of which had grown into a network of organizations capable of engaging in the collective lobbying of leaders and other influential elites. The liberalization in the sexual attitudes of American youth in the 1960s was also important. Although this did not affect social mores toward homosexuality, it provided a link between freedom, a value supported by all Americans on an abstract level, and sexuality.

The tactics used by the civil rights movement, the women's movement, and later, the Black Power movement, which had proven successful, spread to the LGBTQ movement. At the very end of the 1960s and the start of the 1970s, a set of new and more radical lesbian and gay organizations formed, and quickly adopted these other movements' more radical playbooks.

It started modestly enough. In Washington, DC, in the 1960s, members of one of the more activist branches of Mattachine under the leadership of Dr. Franklin Kameny picketed the White House to lobby for an end to discrimination in the civil service based on sexual orientation.[40] Picketing may seem like a relatively conservative activity, but for those fearful of being fired for their sexual orientation, it was a much more radical act in that it publicly identified participants as gay or lesbian. However radical picketing may have been to those activists who came of age in the 1950s, it did little to quell a more intense desire for change among the young. As younger LGBTQ people immersed in the anti–Vietnam War movement started joining the older 1950s-style homophile organizations, they were immediately shocked by their timidity. Having grown up with the student movement and the protests it inspired, mere picketing of the government seemed dangerously quant to a generation that came of age in an era of widespread social and political upheaval. Instantly, more radical organizations started to form and outflank the older homophile organizations on the Left. One of the more important of these was the Gay Activists Alliance (GAA), which formed in New York in 1969. The GAA used civil disobedience tactics called "zaps" to push elected officials to support lesbian and gay rights.[41] One of these zaps included a sit-in at the offices of the New York City council person who represented Greenwich Village and had refused to back a gay rights ordinance. This echoed similar actions at lunch counters across the American South.

Although the adoption of civil disobedience tactics was important, the key innovation that defined this newer wave of activism in the late 1960s and early 1970s was a devotion to asserting *a collective, shared identity* that was different from the mainstream. This is the very thing that the Mattachine Society did at its start when under the control of the more radical Harry Hay, but then stopped encouraging as the more conservative members took control. The development and spread of a lesbian and gay identity marked a turning point in the struggle for LGBTQ rights.

Collective Identity and Movement Development

The collective identity that these lesbian and gay organizations started to emphasize around 1969 was key to the creation of an LGBTQ community that was starting to become self-conscious enough to engage in limited collective action. For organizations and movements that wish to be successful in establishing a large, enduring presence necessary to create social change, fostering such a shared identity is, among other things, psychologically rewarding. And identity-based organizations do succeed, for reasons explained by *social identity theory*.

Social identity theory was developed by social psychologists Tajfel and Turner to explain the interplay between collective (or group) identities and our own, individualized identities.[42] They sought to understand why individuals sometimes act as "an interchangeable member of a social group," like soldiers in an army, fans of a sports team, or members of a political party, and sometimes as individuals distinct from any group membership. For instance, if a person thinks of himself as a police officer, a group-based identity, he will likely feel it appropriate to intervene if a street fight breaks out, whether or not he is on duty. But if that group identity is not as important to him when off duty, he will presumably act according to his own personal preferences, which may be to avoid conflict and thus not intervene.

Feminist, black, Native American, lesbian, disabled, Latino/a, Baptist, Irish, or any other category that can have social or political meaning can form the basis of an identity movement. However, an identity needs to be made salient (or meaningful for a person) for it to inspire change in a person's behavior. For instance, as the Black Power movement developed, the slogan "Black is Beautiful" asserted both that African American identity had value in society and should be respected and that being African American and *being proud* of being African American were good for a person. Those advocating this position would likely argue that abandoning black subculture for mainstream American culture would be harmful to an individual, because in mainstream culture, black identities are subordinate and disrespected, rather than esteemed.

According to *social identity theory*, as developed by Taijfal and Turner, it is the desire to hold *positive* group-based identities—ones that have prestige and are esteemed—that encourages individuals to think of themselves as group members and to engage in behaviors associated with their groups, including collective action.[43] Key to social identity theory is that holding esteemed social group identities provides a basis for self-esteem for their members. Taijfal and Turner also outline a number of strategies that those in groups perceived as being in a negative social category or social group tend to engage in when holding an identity that the mainstream regards as negative: individual mobility (trying to leave the group in question), social creativity (making positive social comparisons with the dominant group on an alternative dimension of values), and social competition (engaging in strategies to change the subordinate social position of the group).[44]

It is the drive for positive self-esteem that explains why gay-themed organizations were so successful. By emphasizing that gays and lesbians have a significant shared social and political identity—and a positive one at that—gay liberation organizations and gay-themed organizations that developed in the late 1960s and early 1970s were able to raise the self-esteem of their members, which in turn fueled the expansion of a lesbian and gay subculture starting in the late 1960s and continuing throughout much of the 1970s.

According to social psychologist Marilynn Brewer, once identification with a group has occurred, individuals are more likely to transfer positive feelings about themselves to their group as a whole.[45] This fosters a sense of community and belonging, necessary to all humans.[46] In other words, group-based identification processes can lead to increased individual self-esteem, which in turn can strengthen the individual's identification with the group and result in a greater devotion to the shared culture that the new group is in the process of developing.

This all took place, briefly, at the start of the Mattachine Society. Once a positive identity was established and reinforced in small social groups, it spread in a rapid fashion during the society's early period in Southern California. Later, the drive for positive self-esteem among same-sex attracted and gender nonconforming people in major urban centers such as San Francisco, Manhattan, and West Los Angeles led to a similar boom in LGBT organizations in the late 1960s and early 1970s.

When organizations like the GAA started making a positive gay identity salient to individuals, and as this identity started to increase the self-esteem of movement participants, they became encouraged to participate in LGBTQ organizations more and more. Gay activists even developed a similar slogan to "Black is Beautiful" in the late 1960s: "Gay is Good." Likewise the words "lesbian" and "gay" became popularized in a developing lesbian and gay subculture to articulate identities and express affirmation. For those participating in the movement, homosexuality was no longer associated with sickness or criminality; rather, it became associated with activism, a common community, and being genuine to oneself. Unlike the conservative message that the later Mattachine adopted—namely, that there was no difference between homosexuals and heterosexuals—identity articulation meant embracing differences and affirming that the identity is a net positive for a person. In short, these new organizations, stated *directly and unequivocally* that being lesbian or gay is a good thing for individuals. The homophile organizations simple did not do this on a large scale and were often beset by debates over whether affirming the lesbian and gay identity was a good movement strategy. In fact, many members of the later Mattachine Society argued that the dominant views of homosexuality as sickness should be considered alongside the notion that being a homosexual was healthy solely because these views of sickness were held by many respected psychiatric experts, a farcical position for younger LGBTQ activists.[47]

* * *

The Stonewall Riots in Manhattan, which took place on June 28, 1969, and have been mythologized as a cause of this new collective consciousness of lesbians and gays, were in fact an outpouring of this new consciousness.[48] These riots are not significant for any material changes that occurred directly in the social and political lives of LGBTQ people. Rather, because the riots roughly divide a period in time when a large mass of LGBTQ people in urban areas thought of themselves as a distinct social group from a prior time when they did not, they have a pivotal role and a symbolic importance in the development of this consciousness as the LGBTQ subculture was solidifying.

The rioters, who identified as lesbians and gays and who demanded an end to the police harassment of LGBTQ people, could not have done so without having a collective positive identity and a sense that it was shared by a massive number of individuals. When lesbian and gay movement leaders described the rioters fighting back against the police, they echoed and reinforced the minority model of oppression first advocated for in the early days of the Mattachine but later cast aside. Other cultural symbols relating to the gay and lesbian movement date to this period in the 1970s, including the rainbow flag created by Gilbert Baker.

This new militancy was not to last, however. Nearly all of the militantly political gay liberation organizations formed after the Stonewall Riots folded by the end of the 1970s. Although they, like the homophile organizations preceding them, provided a payoff for their members in terms of fostering positive identities and building communities, the extensive political involvement they required of their members was not sustainable. Many simply burned out on politics. Yet the distinct gay and lesbian identities that the gay liberation organizations helped to shape did not go away. On the contrary, affirmative lesbian and gay identities were furthered by "gay and lesbian-themed" organizations that followed in the wake of the collapse of the gay liberation movement.

Some examples of such organizations from the 1970s include the San Francisco Tsunami Gay/Lesbian Swim Club, Presbyterians for Lesbian and Gay Concerns, Bay Area Gay and Lesbian Bands, and the Gay Medical and Dental Referral Service.[49] Although these organizations did not share much in common specifically, they all provided social, religious, commercial, and networking opportunities expressly for lesbians and gays. In doing so, they strengthened individuals' psychological connection to the gay and lesbian community and encouraged this identity to become more salient to people with same-sex attraction than it would have been otherwise. They also had an advantage over the gay liberation organizations in that the latter required a *much more active* membership devoted to a wider range of social justice issues than just the articulation of a lesbian or gay identity to operate. Paradoxically, in focusing more narrowly on gay and lesbian identities, the themed organizations developed a greater ability to effect change. And as their numbers grew during the 1980s—San Francisco alone had several hundred, and a similar trend developed in Manhattan and Los Angeles, creating a much wider basis for collective action in the decades that followed.[50]

Although these organizations drew on random personal interests,[51] one feature common to them, which survived from the political gay liberation movement, was an explicit emphasis on acknowledging one's homosexuality, taking pride in it, and coming out to others. This not only reduced the stress felt by those who feel compelled to hide their sexual identity, but could also potentially humanize those who engaged in homosexuality to heterosexuals.

Three weeks before his assassination in 1978, openly gay San Francisco City Supervisor Harvey Milk encapsulated the strategy of the LGBT movement for political change:

> Every gay person must come out. As difficult as it is, you must tell your immediate family. You must tell your relatives. You must tell your friends if indeed they are your friends. You must tell the people you work with. You must tell the people in the stores you shop in. Once they realize that we are indeed their children, that we are indeed everywhere, every myth, every lie, every innuendo will be destroyed once and for all. And once you do, you will feel so much better.[52]

The Establishment of the Lesbian and Gay Community

These gay-themed organizations proved so successful that lesbian and gay subcultures developed almost overnight in major urban centers in the early 1970s. Homosexuals interacting in these places was nothing new. However, what had been a collection of underground and informal social and sexual networks transformed into something larger. This strengthened identity would lead to additional gay-themed organizations, which would, in turn, strengthen the identities of more individuals. This cycle started to reinforce itself until nearly all homosexuals not completely predisposed against thinking of themselves as lesbian or gay for religious or "moral" reasons had adopted a lesbian or gay identity in San Francisco, Manhattan, and West Los Angeles. It is in these urban areas that the LGBTQ community first pushed back against a heterosexist politics.

This represents a rather profound shift. In the 1960s and prior, lesbians and gays had lived in urban enclaves (most prominently Lower Manhattan, Northeast and Central San Francisco, West Los Angeles, and so on). Their existence was well known to many, yet these communities were largely underground. As such, they were generally either ignored by policymakers or harassed by police. But in the 1970s, these communities suddenly became visible as more and more gay organizations developed and the (largely nonpolitical mass of) lesbians and gays in these areas started to move outside of the closet. This reduced the stigma of such identities in these geographically bounded areas and dramatically lowered the costs in terms of esteem for more individuals to come out.

Furthermore, whereas in the past, lesbian and gay activists had trouble parlaying their numbers into political action due to a lack of a collective identity, now, although the larger lesbian and gay community remained politically inactive, lesbian and gay activists could leverage the size of their community into political power (discussed in more detail in the next chapter). Although I characterize the larger lesbian and gay community that developed in the urban enclaves in the 1970s as nonpolitical, I mean this only in comparison with the highly active cohort of lesbian and gay–rights activists who had existed since the Mattachine Society. The lesbian and gay community, like most people, still voted in elections and occasionally volunteered and gave money to candidates. But now, like other ethnic or racial communities in urban centers, their voting, volunteering, and donating could be an expression of support from their specific group: lesbians and gays. Likewise, politically active lesbian and gay activists could communicate with the larger lesbian and gay community to direct the limited political activity of the larger community to supportive officials in the same fashion that ethnic and racial groups often did.

The 1970s were thus the first time when LGBT activists were first able to achieve some success in affecting change through the political system. Most prominently, they could persuade a few local municipalities to pass nondiscrimination ordinances. Other major successes involved the election of the first out-lesbian and out-gay officials, including Elaine Noble in Boston and Harvey Milk in San Francisco.

The American Psychiatric Association removed homosexuality from its list of disorders in 1973, but only under intense pressure from lesbian and gay political activists. This is not to suggest that scientific research—like that of Evelyn Hooker—was not important in its removal as other accounts attest,[53] but that LGBT activists had a much bigger role than these other accounts admit. As other medical and mental health organizations followed suit, the scientific and medical justifications for the stigma attached to homosexuality and for anti-gay government policies were removed. The only remaining legitimate objection to homosexuality concerned its "immorality"—a judgment inherently religious and subjective in nature.

This was not without influence. In the 1970s and 1980s, evangelical Christians entered politics largely in response to early policy gains by the women's movement of the 1960s and the victories of the early lesbian and gay movement. Thus, former Miss Florida Anita Bryant, who was also a Christian singer, led a campaign to overturn an ordinance passed in Miami-Dade County in Florida by ballot initiative. When Bryant's Miami campaign proved successful, similar anti-gay initiatives spread to other municipalities across the country including Wichita, Kansas, St. Paul, Minnesota, and Eugene, Oregon. These anti-gay initiatives all passed with large majorities. The tide didn't start to turn until California's Proposition 6, a ban on lesbian and gay teachers, was defeated in November of 1977. Later that month, in a development that shocked the country, Harvey Milk and San Francisco Mayor George Moscone were assassinated by San Francisco Supervisor Dan White.

The AIDS Crisis and the "Third Wave" of LGBT Activism

Apart from voting, most lesbians and gays did not engage in much political activity in the late 1970s, although some may have been pulled into political activism locally by people like Milk. The most egregious acts of police harassment of lesbians and gays, such as organized raids on bars, largely declined as local lesbian and gay community leaders negotiated with elected officials and police chiefs. A quiescence started to settle among the large mass of lesbians and gays living in the enclaves.

This is not to say that political activity in a coordinated fashion did not occur. Boycotts of Florida oranges in response to Anita Bryant's anti-gay campaigns and fundraising at gay bars did happen, and the LGBTQ taskforce did lobby for gay rights bills (see chapter 4). But nationally this political activity in the 1970s was limited in scope to a handful of activist networks or consisted of ad hoc responses to better organized anti-gay campaigns.

Over the course of the 1980s, however, AIDS would shatter that state of inactiveness for many, although it would take time for some to realize just how profound the role of the government's inadequate response was in prolonging and intensifying this crisis in the lesbian and gay community. Immediate reports of the role of sex in transmitting the plague were resisted by many. The scale of the problem and its high concentration in the gay community remained unknown until 1981, when the *New York Times* published an article describing the first symptoms of what would be called AIDS entitled "Rare Cancer Seen in 41 Homosexuals."[54]

At the immediate beginning of the epidemic, it was difficult for lesbian and gay leaders to decide on a unified response. Those advocating for preserving sexual freedom often clashed with those advocating for modest regulations of sexual activity in the name of saving lives. According to Randy Shilts, a reporter for the *San Francisco Chronicle*, "Everybody was . . . thinking that AIDS was media hype and they weren't releasing this information."[55] According to Larry Kramer, some "took the position that sexual promiscuity was the one freedom that we had and that we had to fight to maintain it—even if it killed us. And it did kill us."[56] As diagnosed AIDS cases started to grow from hundreds in 1981 to nearly 20,000 in 1986, new organizations formed to combat AIDS and care for those affected by it. The most prominent among them was Gay Men's Health Crisis in New York.

Heterosexual fears over contracting AIDS led to an increasingly hostile climate toward lesbians and gays nationally. Although AIDS was seldom discussed in the media in the early years of the crisis, this did not mean that the public was not reacting negatively to the small amount of information that was broadcast through the media, regardless of the accuracy of that information. This intensified after the death of film star Rock Hudson in 1985, which was the first time many in the public realized the scale of the epidemic. "No One Is Safe from AIDS," announced a *Life* magazine cover. Unfounded fears about AIDS transmission reemerged, as they had following an erroneous American Medical Association report about casual contact in 1983; a *Newsweek* poll that summer found that 62 percent believed it was "very likely" or "somewhat likely" that AIDS would spread to heterosexuals.[57]

The breaking point shattering the quiescence for many LGBT individuals was the *Bowers v. Hardwick* Supreme Court decision in 1986. In it, the Supreme Court held that laws banning consensual sodomy between individuals were constitutional. Although many were surprised by the ruling, the hostile tone of the opinion toward lesbians and gays from the nation's highest court was more shocking. The concurring opinion by Chief Justice Burger read: "To hold that the act of homosexual sodomy is somehow protected as a fundamental right would be to cast aside millennia of moral teaching." This decision, for many in the LGBT community, validated the notion that they were second-class citizens with few legal rights and that this was not going to change anytime soon.

Five years into the crisis, a new wave of LGBT activism started with the founding of ACT-UP. Taking a more militant and political stance in fighting AIDS compared to earlier anti-AIDS organizations, ACT-UP also focused specifically on gaining visibility for the anti-AIDS movement by confronting recalcitrant officials directly. Other organizations such as the Lesbian Avengers and Queers Nation formed, but ACT-UP was the most active and best known, particularly for the work of its original New York City branch.

The most intense period of activism for ACT-UP was from 1987 until the election of Bill Clinton in 1992. According to sociologist Deborah Gould, AIDS activism *before 1986* was driven primarily by a few emotional responses to the crisis: sorrow over those lost, pride in the LGBT community's response, and despair over the magnitude of the deaths.[58] But in 1986 and 1987, the stark reality that the government was doing little to combat the crisis as it entered its sixth year became clear. *After the 1986 Bowers* decision, the emotions felt by many in the LGBT community shifted from despair to rage. *Bowers* became in effect the LGBTQ movement's "shot in the dark," mobilizing it in much the same way that *Roe v. Wade* mobilized Pro-Life activists.[59] ACT-UP helped to frame this rage and to give it an appropriate target: media leaders and government officials who either minimized or outright ignored the crisis.[60]

Some of the more prominent activities of ACT-UP included demonstrations at the New York Stock Exchange to demand greater access for experimental drugs, at the Food and Drug Administration over the length of time it took to approve AIDS medications, and at the Centers for Disease Control over their failure to define AIDS in such a way that the definition included women with the disease, as well as a massive protest in New York City at St. Patrick's Cathedral over Cardinal John O'Connor's stand against safe sex education at the height of the epidemic.

Because ACT-UP was largely an unstructured organization, it could pursue multiple strategies to its advantage. According to Larry Kramer, some activists employed an insider strategy, persuading decision-makers to take actions supported by ACT-UP through meetings and discussion, while others tried to pressure or harass these same decision-makers through either protest activities or negative media attention. As Kramer writes,

> The bad cops were all the kids on the floor, and the good cops were all the people inside doing the negotiating. In the end, that's what it boiled down to. And that I learned in the movie business. That's how every successful company of any kind really works. And that's basically what I think I was trying to steer ACT UP towards. . . . What destroyed ACT UP was when Treatment and Data picked up their marbles and went somewhere else, leaving only the bad guys, so to speak.[61]

ACT-UP was also very deliberate in pursuing media attention in order to shine a spotlight on those whose lives had been lost and the inadequacy of the Reagan and Bush administrations' anti-AIDS efforts. As Michelangelo Signorile recalls, when he joined the ACT-UP media committee,

> Bob Rafsky was there. Vito Russo was—I believe—I don't know who was chairing the committee at that time. . . . Their strategy was to use whatever the group was doing—whether it was actions and protests that were going on to get a lot of attention, or people in the Treatment and Data Committee, who were uncovering information that needed to be put out there. That wouldn't be about some spectacular protest. That would be

> about trying to work *New York Times* reporters—get the news out that way. Their strategy was to work on several fronts. Publicize the demonstrations, but also work on editors and reporters to get the information out there that wasn't being written about. . . . The Media Committee of ACT-UP was starting to get a better relationship with the *New York Times* and with reporters there than the rest of the group. It sort of became a good cop/bad cop scenario. The rest of the group might protest the *Times*, but we would be on the phone with those reporters, sort of in a more neutral position. . . . Even though we knew a lot of these reporters were terrible . . . we had to educate them.[62]

Signorile stresses that until the early 1990s, when the executive editor of the *New York Times*, Abe Rosenthal, lost power, the group had trouble with the paper. "Abe Rosenthal had just grade-A anti-gay, homophobic sentiments." It was not until Rosenthal retired that usage of the words "gay" and "lesbian" replaced "homosexual" in *Times* coverage.[63]

In some cases, journalists would aid ACT-UP in its publicity goals if doing so matched with their own self-interest in drawing readers or viewers. Signorile notes that

> Brian Williams . . . before he was with NBC, he was with local CBS News here. And I remember, we were doing a protest at City Hall, and it was a die-in, outside of City Hall, and he asked us if we could time the die-in for exactly at six o'clock, for when he went live, so that he would have great television. . . . And we were fine with it, and he was fine with it. I don't think he'd want many people to know about that now, but they were clearly—whether it was because they were helpful with our agenda, or knew they wanted good TV, working with us in that way.[64]

One final thing to note is that a much larger proportion of the lesbian and gay community devoted themselves to political activism during the height of the AIDS crisis than in previous years and since then. These people brought with them a much broader skill set than older generations of political activists, particularly when it came to knowledge of the national media. For instance, Bob Rafsky of ACT-UP's media committee was a public relations executive before he joined ACT-UP. Kramer estimates that ACT-UP had thousands willing to engage in collective action at its peak.[65] It is unlikely that many of these individuals would have given up so much of their time to single-mindedly focus on activism in the absence of AIDS.

The Rise of National Attention to LGBT Rights

What did the mass public experience as all this was going on? So many of these historical events lacked media coverage, did any of LGBTQ history penetrate to be seen by the American people? Media coverage of an event is a prerequisite for that event to influence those both separated from the event and without contact with those who directly participated in it. Both in traditional theories of media effects on public opinion and in terms of the theory of *affective liberalization*, coverage is a necessary prerequisite for attitude change, in terms of its effect on the public and its effect in encouraging lesbians and gays to identify as LGBTQ and to reveal that identity to others. In this last section of the chapter, I track coverage of LGBTQ issues in the news to determine what, outside of the urban centers, the majority of the American people, both LGBTQ and non-LGBTQ, were seeing about those issues. This will inform our discussion of the effects of that media coverage through the rest of the book.

Although ACT-UP is known for its help in encouraging the government to increase AIDS funding and changing the process by which the FDA approves drugs, the rise of national media attention to AIDS may have had a more profound impact on social change. In figure 3.1, I report the number of evening news stories on the big three networks (ABC, NBC, and CBS) devoted to lesbian and gay rights in gray from 1969 to 2005. I also plot the number of evening news stories on the same networks that mention AIDS from 1984 to 2000 (in black).[66] Both of these time-series were created from a search of the Vanderbilt Television News Archive's abstracts.[67] The major stories are shown above the more intense times of coverage. This is what the mass public was seeing regarding lesbians, gays, and AIDS when they turned on the news during that time.

As an alternative measure of attention, figure 3.2 depicts the word usage rates of "gay" or "lesbian," "AIDS," and "homosexual" in written American English over a similar period. These series were constructed from the Google Ngrams Viewer, which samples a very large number of nonfiction books in every year in order to gauge usage rates. The viewer

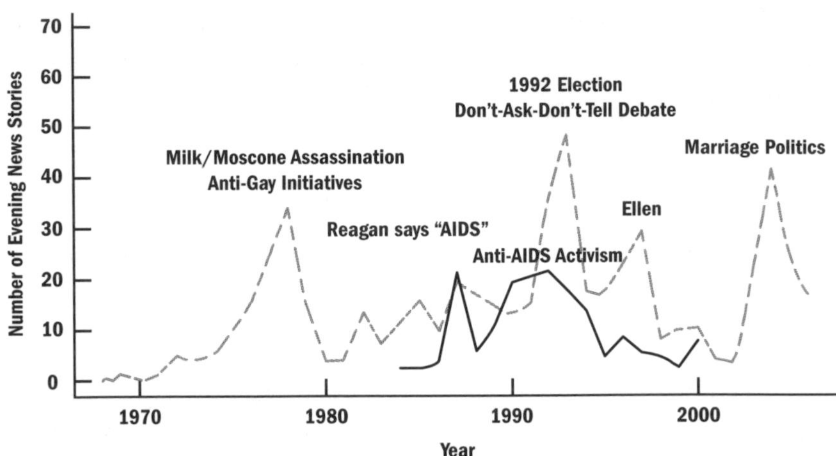

Figure 3.1. Lesbian and Gay Rights and AIDS on the national evening news, 1969–2006. The number of evening news stories on the "Big 3" nightly news broadcasts (ABC, NBC, and CBS) devoted to either gay or lesbian issues (in gray) or AIDS (in black). The major topics of the coverage are written over the time periods where news attention was most intense. *Note*: These series were constructed from the Vanderbilt Television News Archive's story abstracts. See Althaus, *Collective Preferences in Democratic Politics*, for additional details.

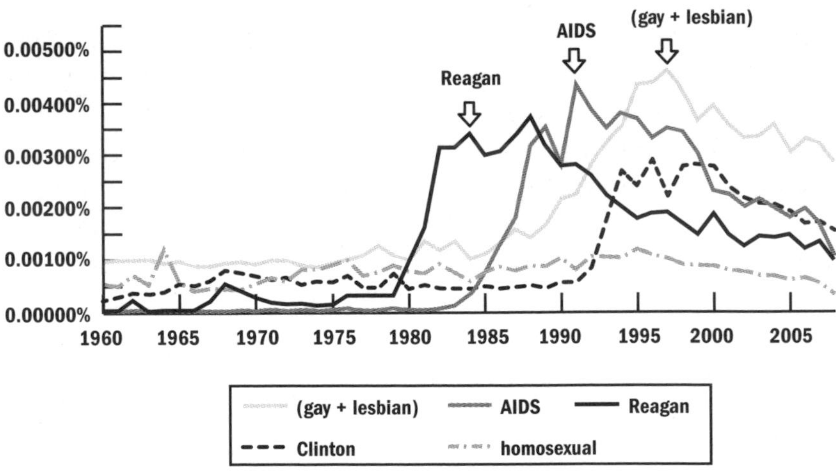

Figure 3.2. Relative Word Usage Rates from Google's NGram Viewer, 1960–2007.

essentially reveals what people are writing about in any given year. Also included are the word usage rates for "Reagan" and "Clinton," which may provide some proxy of the relative quantity of writing devoted to politics to provide a sense of scale.

Turing to the TV evening news series in figure 3.1, it is apparent that there was considerable news coverage in 1977 and 1978 surrounding the first anti-gay ballot initiatives and the assassinations of George Moscone and Harvey Milk. However, attention to these developments was not met with any corresponding increase in the use of the words "lesbian" or "gay." This suggests that these stories had little to no enduring effect on the public, or, at the very least, that they had little to no effect on members of the public who were writing books as indicated in figure 3.2. Little coverage of lesbian and gay issues on TV news occurred in the 1980s. Coverage of AIDS spiked in 1987, when Reagan finally gave a speech on the subject, but declined quickly thereafter.

However, beginning in 1990, evening news coverage of AIDS suddenly increased to nineteen stories in that year. Many of these stories also mentioned ACT-UP. Usage of the word "AIDS" actually increased slightly earlier. Although it was little used in 1982 and 1983, usage started increasing slowly in 1984, and from 1987 to 1988, it effectively doubled. Somewhat ironically, "AIDS" became more common in nonfiction books written in 1988 than "Reagan." News attention to AIDS declined in 1993 and 1994, the same time that ACT-UP's activity declined, yet prior to the 1995 introduction of protease inhibitor drugs, which caused a steep decline in the progression of HIV to AIDS.[68]

While attention to AIDS declined in 1993, it was in 1992 and 1993 that a large and sustained amount of *national* media coverage was devoted to lesbian and gay issues. Much of that coverage surrounded the gays-in-the-military issue in 1993, but 1992 witnessed the largest number of news stories devoted to lesbian and gay rights on record. Furthermore, there was no major external event to trigger this coverage.

What, then, did? Although little quantitative data exists from the time, the broader normalization of news coverage on the lesbian and gay community in the national press that we see beginning in 1992 may well have been related to ACT-UP's intense focus on cultivating the national media based in New York and its efforts to extend coverage of AIDS. Once reporters started regularly covering the LGBT communities in the context of AIDS, continuing coverage of issues important to the lesbian and gay community seemed less unthinkable. The multiyear campaign by ACT-UP and other organizations to force the national media to cover the lesbian and gay communities had finally come to fruition in the early 1990s.

The research of Edward Alwood validates this perspective.[69] Several newspapers, at the request of reporters who either were gay or had AIDS, or at request of people who had friends who had died of AIDS, began covering the crisis in the late 1980s. Alwood reports that eventually their AIDS coverage shifted to a "gay beat." Later, gay and lesbian issues were integrated into their more mainstream coverage.[70] Alwood also provides evidence that many news organizations were unaware of lesbian and gay employees in their midst until AIDS forced them out into the open. "As journalists began to contract it, AIDS became increasingly difficult for the media to ignore."[71]

At the same time as use of the word "AIDS" was reaching its peak, use of the words "lesbian" and "gay" began to increase steadily. Media coverage of lesbian and gay issues in 1992 and 1993 appears to signal an increase in public attention to lesbian and gay issues when compared to the spike in coverage of such issues in the late 1970s. In 1995, use of the words "lesbian" and "gay" exceeded use of the word "AIDS" for the first time. Even more impressive, over the entire course of the Clinton presidency, a larger number of people were writing about lesbians and gays than they were writing about the president of United States.

This spike in attention to lesbian and gay issues in the late 1980s and early 1990s is also important for the lesbian and gay identity in the United States. The primary mechanism through which that identity was spread, gay-themed organizations, was highly concentrated in the urban enclaves prior to the rise in press attention in the early 1990s. With little attention to lesbians and gays in the mass media, people with same-sex attraction living outside of cities with LGBTQ enclaves had a much lower probability of encountering any mechanism that would encourage the development of an LGBTQ identity.

When the mass media started to discuss lesbian and gay issues in the late 1980s and early 1990s, it began to convey the existence of this identity and its basic parameters to a much larger segment of the public. Same-sex attracted individuals, without direct exposure to lesbians and gays, could see this coverage and come to identify as lesbian and gay themselves. What had happened in the 1970s in the urban enclaves was now, to a much greater extent, happening nationwide.

There is evidence for this among people in their teenage years. The average age of "coming out" was nineteen to twenty-three in the 1970s and early 1980s. This dropped to fourteen to fifteen in 1999.[72]

Conclusion

The collective consciousness of the LGBT movement developed as a response to the state's interest in homosexuals as imagined threats to public health and national security. The later development and intensification of lesbian and gay identities, along with their associated political activity, was a first step in reorienting government policy and changing the animus that the public felt toward lesbians and gays.[73] However, the development of lesbian and gay communities based around a shared identity in the nation's urban areas was not enough to begin a national dialogue on lesbian and gay issues. It took the AIDS crisis, which threatened the very existence of these communities, to motivate a period of activism intense enough to cause contextual changes that would make further advancement possible. AIDS activists carefully targeted the national media, heavily concentrated in New York City, with the goal of disrupting a journalistic culture in which reporting on the problems of lesbians and gays was a non-starter. The timing of increases in attention to lesbian and gay issues in the national media suggests that, in achieving this goal, AIDS activists may also have disrupted the media's neglect of lesbian and gay issues by regularizing coverage of issues important to lesbians and gays.

Developing in parallel to these trends, and pausing only during the AIDS crisis, was also a sustained campaign by mainstream LGBT political activists to garner vocal support for their rights from elected officials. Although lesbian and gay political activists constituted a much smaller group of people than ACT-UP did at its peak, these activists had been slowly cultivating connections with political leaders since well before the Stonewall Riots. As we will see in the next chapter, they met with limited success until attention to AIDS and LGBT issues rose in prominence in the 1980s and 1990s.

4

The Capture of the Democratic Party and the Clinton Victory

Gays comprise one of the largest minorities in America. They are capable of getting the representation they need, but can only do so, it seems, by public confrontations that make politicians face and respond to issues they otherwise avoid. Right now, that part of the gay movement that's forcing the system to respond is fighting its way up the liberals.
—Marty Robinson, 1971

The development of a gay and lesbian community that took considerable pride in its identity, rather than hiding itself, led directly to a growing interrelation between LGBT activists and the Democratic Party. As mentioned in chapter 2, a growing polarization between Democrats and Republicans on lesbian and gay rights is a key component of models of elite-led change in support for lesbian and gay rights. However, any study that attempts to understand change in attitudes toward lesbians and gays caused by elite polarization should first step back and ask why political elites, given public hostility toward lesbians and gays, suddenly decided to start supporting gay rights?

No doubt politicians justify these shifts in terms of fundamental values like equality, justice, and fairness toward all groups. However, changes in the electoral context within which elected officials are embedded, caused by LGBT activists, provide a more compelling explanation for these sudden changes of heart. As the gay- and lesbian–identified community grew into a sizable constituency in the post-Stonewall era, it began to exert greater influence on local politics in the gay enclaves of New York City, San Francisco, and Los Angeles. The shared lesbian and gay identity could now be used as a basis for solving the collective action problem inherent in coordinating political activity. As this identity strengthened with the spread of local gay and lesbian–themed organizations in the 1970s, its concentration in the urban enclaves could be exploited by a new wave of liberal political candidates, working in concert with mainstream LGBT activists. Some of the first politicians to work with these activists eventually advocated for lesbian and gay rights. In return they were provided with votes, volunteers, and donations from LGBT people. Once elected, these urban politicians formed a small cohort of members of the US House in the 1970s who were supportive of lesbian and gay rights. Others members of Congress who were affiliated with the civil rights movement, like members of the Congressional Black Caucus, quickly joined them in support of LGBT rights. Finally, a very small group of ideologically liberal and libertarian Republicans rounded out the early sources of 1970s congressional support for gay rights.

The slow process of building support for lesbian and gay rights accelerated as Washington-based gay rights interest groups began to develop. The Human Rights Campaign (HRC) and the National Gay and Lesbian Task Force (NGLTF) date to the late 1970s and early 1980s. Both organizations were founded in order to advocate for LGBTQ rights at the federal level in the absence of any formal LGBTQ interest groups in DC. However, public fear of AIDS may have countered the efforts of these organizations to develop support for lesbian and gay rights among national leaders. After the advent of AIDS, endorsements of lesbian and gay rights did not pick up significantly until 1991, when AIDS activism hit its peak.

By far the most important political development at this time was the 1992 presidential campaign and election of Bill Clinton. This is evidenced by the spike in media attention to LGBT issues in 1992 shown in figure 3.1, although that spike itself would later be dwarfed by media attention to the Don't-Ask-Don't-Tell debate the very next year. While Clinton's pro-gay platform drew substantial lesbian and gay support, his incentives for adopting this platform may have involved more self-interest and less principle than most realize.

Political elites were almost universally opposed to LGBTQ rights in the early 1960s. In this chapter, I explore the process through which the lesbian and gay community confronted and ultimately changed the political system by transforming the Democratic Party into the relatively LGBTQ-supportive group that it is currently. One factor was the new visibility of the LGBTQ movement in the nation's urban centers in the

1970s, which provided younger, liberal candidates with an opportunity to garner votes and political resources in exchange for support for lesbian and gay rights legislation that older politicians were reluctant to capitalize on. By the 1980s, the nexus of LGBTQ political activism was shifting from a loosely connected network of local activists to DC-based interest groups like the Human Rights Campaign. However, additional progress on converting rural and suburban Democratic members of Congress to support gay rights did not occur until ACT-UP successfully broke down the national media's resistance to covering LGBTQ people and the AIDS crisis from 1990 to 1992. Media depictions of this activism appear to have communicated to Democratic office holders that the LGBTQ community could now provide campaign resources at a national level beyond the nation's urban centers, and the party's support for LGBTQ rights quickly began to broaden outside of its urban and liberal wings. The most visible example of this was Bill Clinton's early support for lesbian and gay rights in 1992. Still, many Democrats resisted this trend into the late 1990s, and I find that the party did not become uniform in its support for LGBTQ rights until the early 2000s.

Subconstituency Politics and Party Position Change

The core finding of the last chapter, regarding the development of a lesbian and gay community and an increase in lesbian and gay activism after the *Bowers* Supreme Court decision, is key to understanding why elected officials began to slowly embrace gay rights in the 1970s. In a democracy, most assume that the primary factor that determines the support of elected officials is constituent opinion. However, the reality of democratic politics is more complicated. Politicians must not only reflect public opinion to get elected; they must also gather campaign resources and reflect the positions of activists who vote in primaries in order to make it to, and compete successfully, in the general election. This creates situations where candidates have incentives to instead cater to subconstituencies who care intensely about specific policies and to deviate away from what the majority of their constituents prefer under certain circumstances.

This insight—that intensely interested minorities can have their preferences supported by elected officials, rather than that of a disinterested majority—forms the basis of the *subconstituency politics theory of representation.*[1] Although this theory seems self-evident in the era of the Tea Party movement and the "alt-right," the notion that a majority of constituents' attitudes sway their representatives still dominates much political science research on representation.

Social identities, like the lesbian and gay identities discussed in the last chapter, are the core theoretical building blocks of the subconstituency politics theory of representation, as developed by Benjamin Bishin,[2] who points to ways that candidates can use social identities to advance their goals of election and reelection.

> [Social identity] groups provide resources to politicians. They are easier to activate than individuals and provide disproportionate benefits. In addition to voting, they may provide money, time, contacts, prestige, and information that aids candidates in their drive to get reelected. In addition, they are often geographically concentrated, and this amplifies their relevance. . . . While activating a shared identity may not dictate an individual's behavior, it should serve to reduce the cost to candidates who are trying to tap that identity, especially when compared with the costs of attempting to motivate the behavior of a typical, apathetic individual.[3]

Subconsituency politics suggests that, even in the absence of majority support for a position, a minority based around a social identity can have its viewpoints' represented by elected officials. Such an identity was spread in the late 1960s and early 1970s in the nation's urban centers by gay militants and later gay-themed organizations. Subsequently, the rise of press attention to AIDS and lesbian and gay issues in the early 1990s likely shifted the spread of LGBTQ identities from urban-situated organizations to the national media starting in the early 1990s. If this sequence describing the spread of these social identities is correct, the subconstituency politics theory of representation would predict that different candidates could exploit an expanding lesbian and gay identity in different geographic locations in different times. This opportunity would first become an option to urban politicians in the 1970s, and later to national politicians starting in the early 1990s.

There is, however, one drawback to the subconstituency politics theory—namely, that empirical tests of the theory are not dynamic.

When applied to LGBTQ issues, many of the key tests have been across various districts and constituencies rather than over years and decades. Thus, what has not been tested is whether *change* in social identities in a constituency directly translates into change in candidate activity.

Here, David Karol's *Party Position Change in American Politics* is helpful in explaining why and how political parties, which are largely thought of as rigid institutions resistant to change, sometimes switch sides on certain issues.[4] Of the processes he describes, the most relevant for LGBTQ issues is *coalition group incorporation*:

> Party leaders shift positions to attract a particular constituency. A formerly cross-cutting issue becomes partisan. Parties change positions more slowly in such cases than in [other] instances . . . and elite replacement may matter more. . . . The slower pace and greater role of elite replacement in such cases stem from the fact that these issues require politicians to redefine their coalitions. . . . Yet as a new [social] group enters a party, it gains leverage over the party's elected officials, leading them to increasingly reflect the group's preferences *rather than overall sentiment in a state or district*. This shift further stimulates more group members to support the party. This process is iterative and may occur over many years.[5]

Hence, the defining features of coalition group incorporation are gradual change, elite replacement (more supportive officials replacing older, less supportive officials), and an increasing interconnectivity between the new social group and the political party over time. Both in the subconstituency politics theory and in Karol's theory of party position change, new groups can cause officials to take positions unpopular among voters, but only if those issues (like LGBTQ rights in general) are not particularly salient to the public. Karol has also examined party position change on gay rights specifically and found change on gay rights to be due to a mix of gradual replacement and conversion among elected democratic officials consistent with political group incorporation.[6]

Both theories provide some insight into how the extension of the lesbian and gay identity should affect both individual politicians (subconstituency politics) and the political parties (coalition group incorporation). One thing to keep in mind in the rest of this chapter is the timing of attitudinal change on gay rights described in chapter 1, wherein little change occurred before the early 1990s, and mass changes started becoming undeniable only in the mid-1990s. Accordingly, any movement in the behavior of politicians to court the gay vote before the mid-1990s is unlikely to be due to change in constituency opinion. Thus, it is safe to conclude that the spread of LGBTQ identities and/or the intensification of LGBTQ activism are key to explain any elite behavioral change prior to the mid-1990s and not changes in constituent opinion.

The Electoral Connection and the Shifting Incentives of Urban Politicians

The shift in focus by lesbian and gay activists to an identity-based movement built on the examples of the civil rights movement and the women's movement resulted in the creation of a lesbian and gay subculture now self-aware of its subordinate status. Throughout the 1970s, the consequences of the extension of this identity became more and more apparent, as lesbian and gay activists worked with liberal political candidates running for office within cities with the largest lesbian and gay enclaves—namely, New York and San Francisco.

To be clear, although some political leaders became supportive of lesbian and gay issues in the 1970s, the broader public's attitudes toward lesbians and gays had not yet begun to liberalize. Even politicians in San Francisco and Manhattan would have been taking a risk if they came out in favor of lesbian and gay rights, since support for such rights was a potential political liability. Moreover, even if such support resulted in winning a local election, it could come back to haunt a politician who desired to run for statewide office as intense opposition from voters in more suburban and rural areas could spell certain electoral doom.

Times were changing, however. It first began in San Francisco, where local lesbian and gay leaders had been trying to affect local politics since the middle of the 1960s with limited success.[7] Because of the group's unpopularity, many in the San Francisco lesbian and gay community were surprised when Diane Feinstein showed up at a candidate's night in 1969 at the Society for Individuals Rights (SIR), a gay political organization, and affirmed her support for the equal rights of lesbians and gays. Feinstein was running for the board of supervisors of San Francisco,[8] the city's city council. Later, in lower Manhattan, Bella Abzug, a women's rights advocate, went so far as to campaign in gay bathhouses during a run for New York's nineteenth congressional district in 1970.[9] This marked the start of a strong and growing relationship between the lesbian and gay community and liberal candidates for political office. Both Feinstein and Abzug were ultimately successful in winning elected office. It is probably not a coincidence that the two ran in the two geographic areas most associated with the lesbian and gay community.

Something had obviously changed in Manhattan and San Francisco by the early 1970s as officials were winning election by actively supporting gay rights. A collective identity among gays and lesbians now allowed politicians to target appeals specifically to this emerging identity group by promising support for lesbian and gay rights. In order to do so effectively, they needed to seek endorsements from local lesbian and gay political organizations like SIR in San Francisco. Because of the shift to an identity-based politics in the lesbian and gay community and the development of a social identity that could form the basis for voting behavior, politicians would receive a bloc of votes in return. This was simply not possible before the shift toward a movement that emphasized out gay and lesbian identities in these areas. Before that occurred, seeking the support of gays and lesbians would have been interpreted (even by some homosexuals) as akin to campaigning for the votes of felons or psychopaths. The concentration of same-sex attracted people in New York City and the Bay Area of California—in combination with the shift to an identity-based social movement—drastically expanded the number of local elected officials and members of Congress susceptible to electoral pressure from lesbian and gay constituencies.

Although West Los Angeles also had a large number of LGBTQs and a spike in movement activity in the 1970s, the geographical vastness of the city of Los Angeles may have diluted the impact of potential lesbian and gay votes.[10] This may explain the lack of a candidate like Feinstein or Abzug in Los Angeles, in spite of the formation there of a successful political action committee supporting lesbian and gay–friendly candidates by 1977. San Francisco and Manhattan, in contrast to Los Angeles and Chicago, are bordered on three sides by bodies of water. Geographic concentration in these two cites led to a greater per capita density of gays and lesbians and magnified the impact of LGBTQ votes.

To be completely clear, rhetorical support for lesbian and gay rights and endorsements from lesbian and gay political organizations did not always result in support for lesbian and gay rights after Election Day. Although Abzug largely followed through, Feinstein backtracked in her strong support for the lesbian and gay community. By the mid-1970s, she had become the leader of the moderate/corporate Democratic bloc on the city's board of supervisors. When Feinstein became mayor after the assassinations of Harvey Milk and Mayor George Moscone, she vetoed domestic partner benefits for the lesbian and gay employees of the city of San Francisco.

The Growth of Congressional Support for Gay Rights: 1975–1992

From New York and the Bay Area, political support for lesbian and gay rights spread. In 1975, Abzug introduced the first gay rights bill largely on her own initiative. In doing so, she caught lesbian and gay activists off guard, as they were not consulted in the drafting of the legislation. The introduction itself was primarily symbolic, though. All knowledgeable political observers knew that gay rights were not popular enough to survive a House roll-call vote.[11]

The original bill had twenty-three co-sponsors. The distinguishing feature of the list of co-sponsors was a lack of geographic diversity: ten hailed from New York City and six from the San Francisco Bay Area. Of the others, one was from Minneapolis, two were from Massachusetts (including Representative Gerry Studds, who would later be the first openly gay member of the US House), one was from West Los Angeles, one from Denver, and one from Philadelphia. Having a highly urban district, likely a proxy for a large community of out lesbians and gays, seems to have dominated early support for Abzug's gay rights bill.[12] This also explains why the gay rights bill found little support in the rural-dominated U. S. Senate.

For the next decade, the only legislation involving lesbian and gay rights in the House was the gay rights bill. It was introduced in every Congress until 1993 in a nearly identical form.[13] Other members of Congress took over the task of introducing the bill when Abzug left to run for the US Senate.

Figure 4.1 displays the co-sponsorship rates for every Congress the bill was introduced until its last introduction during the 102nd

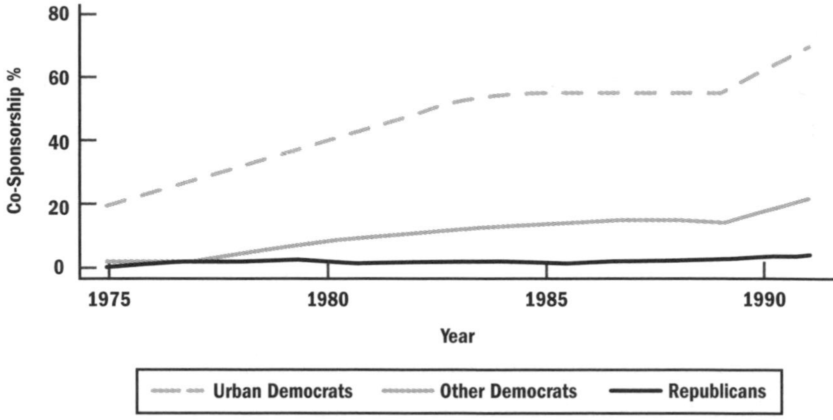

Figure 4.1. Co-Sponsorship Rates for the Gay Rights Bill in Congress, 1975–1992.

Congress (1991–1992). The co-sponsorship rates are displayed for three groups: (1) Democrats representing districts in which over 85 percent of the district population was classified as urban according to the US Census; (2) Democrats representing districts where less than 85 percent of the population was classified as urban; and (3) Republicans.

Support over the entire period from 1975 to 1992 was heavily concentrated among Democrats representing urban districts. In fact, all the initial supporters of the bill hailed from these districts. Initially, 20 percent of the members from these urban districts supported the bill in 1975 and 1976. Support in this group increased to 50 percent in 1983, remained flat over the rest of the 1980s, and rose again to over 60 percent in the 102nd Congress, whose members were elected during the peak years of attention to AIDS in the media during the 1990 midterm elections.

Democrats from less urban districts did not start to support the legislation until 1979. Their support never broke 20 percent. Still, in the last Congress it was introduced (1991–1992), support for the gay rights bill broadened considerably. Democrats from six southern states, as well as Colorado, Iowa, Ohio, and Utah, went on record in support of the legislation.[14] Nearly all of these members added their names as co-sponsors well before Bill Clinton had clinched the party's nomination in April of 1992, which indicates that these decisions were independent of Clinton's.

Few Republicans ever co-sponsored the bill. Some liberal Republicans like Pete McCloskey (R-CA) and Jim Jeffords (R-VT) signed on, as did a few libertarian-inclined senators like Barry Goldwater (R-AZ) and John Tower (R-TX).[15] Still little widespread support from the Republican Party was manifest at any point.[16]

Although these trends are suggestive, a more thorough analysis is warranted. Could some factors other than the presence of an urban gay enclave, like the education levels of a district, actually be responsible for this relationship? Could the factors that caused a member to co-sponsor the gay rights bill have changed over time? For each Congress from 1975 to 1992, I estimated a logistic regression analysis of co-sponsorship of the bill, incorporating various demographic characteristics (see appendix 1 for additional details on methodology).Because these are the first statistical models in this book that depart from a typical linear regression (such as the one examined at the end of chapter 2), I have included a short primer on the interpretation of such models, for readers who have not encountered them before (see the methodological appendix).

While district urbanicity is likely causing legislators to co-sponsor the gay rights bill due to the presence of LGBTQ urban enclaves based on the trends in 4.1, other factors may ultimately be driving this relationship, especially in later years. I include controls for district characteristics: district education as measured by the percentage with a college degree and district median income. I also control for membership in the Congressional Black Caucus, which is more concerned with civil rights issues than other groups in Congress, and a measure of civil rights support of members of Congress more generally. Although black members of the public have historically been less supportive of same-sex marriage and other specific gay rights, prior research has demonstrated that this is not the case for black political leaders, who generally hold more consistent positions in favor of minority civil rights including LGBT rights.[17] Two variables that I also include are of interest in gauging the changing role that political parties may have in support for the gay rights bill. The "party" variable is coded as a "1" for Democrats and a "0" for Republicans. Alternatively, I include a measure of "district partisanship": the percentage of the two-party vote won by the Democratic presidential candidate in the most recent election. If these two variables start to become important in various years, it suggests that Democrats in general are trying to moderate on gay rights, rather than just members who represent urban, educated districts with a large group of out, LGBTQ constituents. I estimated a different analysis for each Congress from the 94th (1975–1976) to the 102nd (1991–1992), the last time the omnibus gay rights bill was introduced in that form before being subdivided into many separate bills by activists and supportive members of Congress in 1993.

The big story is the change in the effect of the two *partisan* variables on support for the gay rights bill across time. In figure 4.2, I plot the difference in the predicted probability of co-sponsorship of the gay rights bill between members who hail from districts that voted 40 percent for the Democratic presidential nominee and 60 percent for the Democratic presidential nominee for every year. Also plotted is the difference in the predicted probability of support among Democrats and Republicans and the joint difference in predicted probability due to both district and member partisanship.[18] The effect of district urbanicity and Black Caucus membership on support for the gay rights bill declined almost monotonically until the 101st Congress. The percentage of the constituents in a district with a college education is an important predictor of co-sponsorship. However, except for a momentary decline in the late 1970s, the effect was relatively consistent across time. The effects on these variables are similar to those found in previous studies of voting on gay rights in Congress.[19]

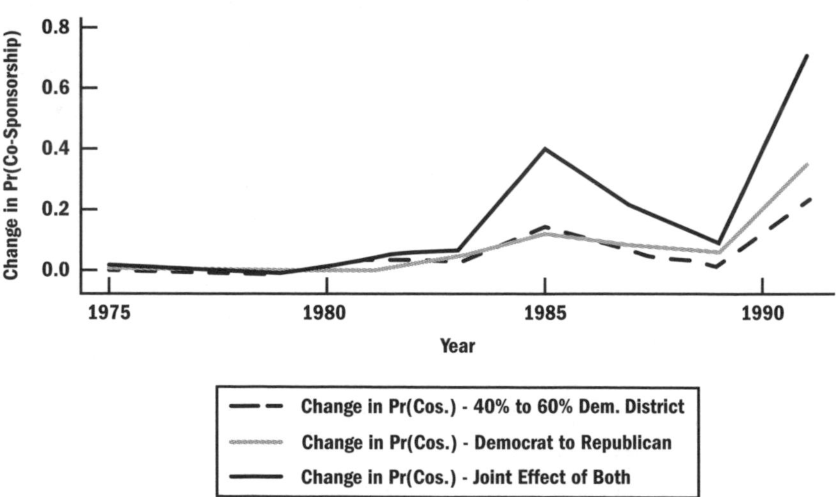

Figure 4.2. Change in the Effect of Party on Probability of Support for the Gay Rights Bill in Congress, 1975–1992.

As figure 4.2 shows, partisanship had nearly no effect on co-sponsorship in the 1970s. The multivariate analysis reveals that district differences were driving the partisan differences in figure 4.1 before the 1980s. Then, partisanship increased as an independent effect on support for the gay rights bill in the early 1980s until 1985 and 1986. As the AIDS crisis heated up from 1987 to 1990, Democrats from districts demographically predisposed against gay rights support remained unsupportive. However, the effect of party increased significantly in the era when AIDS activism was portrayed in the news media. The Congress elected in 1990, which served from 1991 to 1992, was the first one in which differences emerged between Democrats and Republicans in support of the gay rights bill regardless of district demographics. In that year, Democrats holding solidly Democratic districts were roughly 70 percent more likely to co-sponsor the gay rights bill than Republicans with solidly Republican districts (controlling for the demographic characteristics of those districts).

What does this tell us about the origin of Democratic Party support for LGBTQ issues? That the sharp increase occurred at the same time that ACT-UP was having its greatest successes in normalizing coverage of AIDS and LGBTQ issues suggests that increased coverage was the crucial factor shifting support for gay rights from local and urban constituencies to national and partisan ones. This dramatic change in partisan congressional support has been generally missed in past studies.[20] Since the increase in Democratic Party support clearly took place earlier than change in public opinion as a cause, subconsituency politics appears to have been at work here.[21] Beyond that, the exact causal mechanism seems difficult to disentangle completely. Did Democratic politicians see the coverage of ACT-UP and other organizations and detect a potential subconstituency that could contribute to their campaigns? Or did the coverage increase the number of individuals who identified as LGBTQ outside of the urban enclaves and who then formed new suburban and rural subconstituencies? There is some support for the latter hypothesis in the academic literature, as some studies of more recent time periods have found a link between the size of the LGBTQ population in states and districts and pro-gay voting.[22] Or could both causes have been operating at the same time? Without additional data, it remains unclear how activism and the increased news coverage brought about Democratic officials' endorsements of gay rights, but it is clear that LGBTQ activism inspired by AIDS was the root cause.

One other major development that could have encouraged this shift was also underway. This was the institutionalization of lesbian and gay interest groups in Washington, DC, which may have allowed the LGBTQ community to frame itself at a potentially contributing subconstituency to the Democratic Party. This is the subject of the next section.

The Development of Lesbian and Gay Interest Groups

Little support for lesbian and gay rights was coming from parts of the country outside of the urban LGBTQ enclaves in the 1970s and 1980s. As chapter 3 explained, the gay liberation movement of the New Left had withered at a mass level and been replaced by more insular lesbian and gay–themed organizations during the mid-to-late 1970s. Urban members of Congress, susceptible to lobbying by LGBT rights activists in the urban enclaves, were already co-sponsors of the gay rights bill by the 1980s. Thus, the nexus of lobbying for support of the gay rights bill needed to extend beyond urban activist groups.

As progress in growing support for the gay rights bill stagnated after its initial introduction, lesbian and gay activists founded a different type of organization to replace the coalitions of local organizations that had attempted to broaden support for gay rights outside of the urban enclaves. These were formal Washington, DC–based interest groups devoted to increasing gay rights support, but at the expense of being isolated from the LGBTQ community in the urban enclaves. Interest group organizations do not need a broad membership base to function; nor do they require more than a small base of donors and activists to operate. Thus, in time periods like the late 1970s and early 1980s, when the majority of the lesbian and gay–identified community shunned direct political involvement, they could be staffed by a few political activists.

The first of these organizations was the National Gay Task Force, founded in 1974 and eventually renamed the National LGBTQ Taskforce (or NGLTF).[23] This New York–based organization became more of a think tank as time went on. The organization that replaced it in Washington is currently the largest pro–lesbian and gay lobbying operation: the Human Rights Campaign (HRC).

The Human Rights Campaign Fund, the original name of the HRC, was founded in 1980.[24] By 1982, it had given $140,000 to candidates for federal office.[25] Of the 118 candidates given money in that cycle, the overwhelming majority were Democrats. This trend in giving almost exclusively to Democrats continued. For example, by 2008 $1,215,425 of the $1,268,464 given out by HRC to candidates went to Democrats. This represented money given to 187 Democrats and only six Republicans. Indeed, from 1990 to 2008 the level of organizational giving of the HRC to Democrats never dropped below 84 percent.[26]

Whether the HRC's decisions to give were based explicitly on party or some other factor is difficult to tell, although evidence exists that these donations were effective at swinging votes.[27] A few criteria may lead to an illusion of partisan-based giving, when in reality the HRC may have been giving only to members of Congress who they thought were "movable" on gay rights. In terms of ideology, most of the supporters who co-sponsored the gay rights bill were solidly liberal in the early years. Because a liberal ideology is strongly related to a tolerant predisposition toward out-groups, that may have resulted in more giving to Democrats. Furthermore, giving donations to individuals who were moderately liberal, potentially on the verge of supporting lesbian and gay rights, and in need of a nudge would have involved giving donations to Democrats. Since Democrats appeared to be in a "permanent" majority in the House in the 1980s, the lack of support from Republicans did not appear to endanger the eventual passage of legislation.

Another factor leading to the HRC's decision to give to Democrats may involve the election of President Reagan in 1980, which brought a large number of socially conservative activists into the Republican Party base. Mobilized into politics for the first time in the 1970s in response to the policy successes of the women's rights movement and the LGBT movement, evangelical and born-again Christians were initially up for grabs in the 1976 presidential contest between Republican Gerald Ford, who endorsed the Equal Rights Amendment, and Democrat Jimmy Carter, himself a southern evangelical Christian. Once elected president, however, Carter alienated evangelicals by supporting the rights of women and other minorities. Thus, by 1980, evangelicals were firmly in the Republican camp under Ronald Reagan, and in the ensuing decades, they remained a core constituency for the Republican Party.

Naturally, new Republican candidates for office would want to appeal to this new group of potential supporters. Thus, they had an incentive to fight policies advocated by the leadership of the women's movement and LGBT movement and opposed by evangelicals. As the relationship between social conservatives and the Republicans strengthened, it likely resulted in a tactical decision by organizations like the NGLTF and HRC to focus nearly exclusively on the Democratic Party. The AIDS crisis and the Reagan Administration's slow response to the crisis intensified the perceptions among lesbians and gays that their rights would not get a hearing among the Republicans and that many of those in positions of power in the Reagan White House were out-and-out homophobes placed there to reward the Religious Right. In terms of the perceptions of LGBT activists, what had started as an urban issue in the 1970s was increasingly becoming a partisan issue by the 1980s.

Lesbian and gay rights activists did have some limited success at the presidential level in garnering endorsements of gay rights. President Ford's administration took indirect actions to counter discrimination when it occurred.[28] By and large, though, much of this early success was solely on account of liberal Democratic candidates. Ted Kennedy had supported nondiscrimination in 1971.[29] McGovern supported lesbian and gay rights "in principle" in 1972.[30] Walter Mondale, Gary Hart, and Jesse Jackson all supported nondiscrimination in 1984 and 1988.[31] One important thing to note, however, is that liberal candidates (with the notable exception of Jackson) would often preface their support as being motivated by a commitment to the *principle* of nondiscrimination. Often, they would explicitly state that their support did not constitute an endorsement of homosexuality.[32]

There is also considerable evidence that out lesbian and gay activists were becoming increasingly common within Democratic Party circles in the 1970s and 1980s, which in turn also predisposed lesbian and gay interest groups to give to Democrats. Jean O'Leary reports two out delegates to the Democratic national convention in 1972.[33] These numbers increased steadily over the next two decades. By the 1992 Democratic Convention, there were 110, though no formal quota mechanisms for lesbian and gay delegates were put in place until 2000. Among Democratic and liberal activists, contact with lesbian and gay activists was becoming increasingly common, much more so than among the larger public, and grew even more so after the ranks of these activists swelled during the peak of AIDS activism from 1987 to 1992.

Still, support for gay and lesbian rights was hit and miss, even among liberal officials, until the 1990s. In 1988, the LGBT movement attempted to donate money to the campaign of Michael Dukakis, the Democratic nominee for president. He returned the donation rather than allowing himself to be linked to an extremely unpopular minority.[34] When pressured by lesbian and gay activists to support gay rights in a closed-door meeting, Dukakis refused to budge. In justifying his lack of support, Dukakis eventually slammed his fist down on table saying, "Because it's wrong!"

From Congressional Support to Presidential: Bill Clinton's 1992 Campaign

By 1992, however, something had changed. In his quest to win the Democratic nomination, Bill Clinton had a problem. He was a southern governor from a poor, rural state running for the nomination of a party dominated by large liberal and urban blocs. Just how important those blocs were was underscored by the amount of support that Jesse Jackson had garnered in 1988, when he won twelve nomination contests and well over a thousand delegates.

At the same time, southern conservatives had been slowly moving over to the Republicans for the past 20 years. This had left the activist ranks of the Democratic Party with a decidedly liberal bent. The same could easily be said of the party's political donors and primary voters. After all, Jackson had won all the Democratic primaries in the Deep South in 1988, a bastion of white supremacy only thirty years prior. A white, southern governor was at distinct disadvantage in appealing to a party increasingly dominated by northern liberals.

What Clinton needed was a way to symbolically connect with liberal primary voters, donors, and activists in order to win the Democratic nomination in 1992. Little in his record as Arkansas's governor would allow him to do so. AIDS and lesbian and gay rights gave Clinton that symbolic issue. Tolerance for a neglected and disliked group would allow him to stress a commonality with urban liberals. AIDS and gay rights would also reinforce Clinton's campaign theme that George H.

W. Bush was out of touch with the rest of country. Not only was Bush unaware of a middle class in financial trouble as the economy declined, but his flippant attitude toward the AIDS plague, which had killed tens of thousands of Americans, reinforced Clinton's campaign theme that Bush was a patrician disconnected from the people he governed.

Unmistakably, many southern Democrats in the 1980s and 1990s were still closed off to taking pro-gay positions due to their own personal animus toward lesbians and gays (as Dukakis had similarly been). Clinton did not appear to harbor this animus, which freed him to draw on new avenues of political support that were closed to Dukakis and other potential presidential candidates. There is much in Clinton's background that likely predisposed him toward embracing lesbian and gay rights when the shifting circumstances of the early 1990s made it viable for a presidential candidate.

The most important of these was his friendship with political activist David Mixner in the late 1960s and 1970s. Mixner had come out to the Clintons in 1977, when he had written them a letter asking for support to oppose California's Prop 6, a potential ban on gay and lesbian teachers.[35] Bill had replied with a phone call: "We will always be your friends and you can count on us."[36]

Members of Clinton's presidential campaign were also fully aware of the rising levels of political participation among lesbians, gays, and AIDS activists, who were seeking support for fighting the epidemic from the government. According to Rahm Emmanuel, who played key roles in the 1992 campaign, "The gay community is the new Jewish community. It's highly politicized, with fundamental health and civil rights concerns. And it contributes money. All that makes for a potent political force, indeed."[37] The small shifts in public opinion at this time in favor of specific gay rights, such as employment nondiscrimination (in principle, and in the armed services, specifically), and civil liberties may have also convinced the campaign that a public backlash against those who supported gay rights was unlikely. The economy, after all, was the issue of the day. Apart from opposition from the already solidly Republican Religious Right, a position on lesbian and gay rights had never been significant to the majority of the public.

Clinton had contacted Mixner in September of 1991 to help him build a support base for his campaign in the lesbian and gay community.

Mixner advised him that, as of that moment, the majority of the lesbian and gay community would go with liberal Massachusetts Senator Paul Tsongas. Mixner advised Clinton to come out in favor of nondiscrimination in the armed forces and "to fight like hell to find a cure for AIDS."[38] When Clinton met with lesbian and gay activists in California at Mixner's request, he impressed them much more than Tsongas, who "was resentful that he had to explain his distinguished record [on gay rights]."[39] Subsequently, Clinton began to attract significant lesbian and gay support, particularly on the West Coast where Mixner was based.

By March of 1992, Tsongas had run out of money and dropped out of the campaign. This left Clinton the frontrunner. However, Clinton could still lose if the other remaining candidate, California Governor Jerry Brown, could dominate primaries in states like Connecticut, New York, and Wisconsin. Like Tsongas, Brown was a liberal with a strong record in support of lesbian and gay rights. However, like Tsongas in California, Brown was largely unknown in the East Coast lesbian and gay community. This left Clinton with an opening, and he began targeting New York City liberals including lesbians and gays. A strong win in the New York primary would knock Brown out of contention.

ACT-UP New York saw their chance. On April 2, 1992, Bob Rafsky of ACT-UP's media committee confronted Clinton during a campaign event:

> This is the center of the AIDS epidemic, what are you going to do? Are you going to start a war on AIDS? Are you going to just go on and ignore it? Are you going to declare war on AIDS? Are you going to put somebody in charge? Are you going to do more than you did as the Governor of Arkansas? We're dying in this state. What are you going to do about AIDS?[40]

Clinton was ready:

> That's why I'm running for President, to do something about it. I'll tell you what I'll do, I'll tell you what I'd do. First of all I would not just talk about it in campaign speeches; it would become a part of my obsession as President. There are two AIDS Commission reports gathering dust somewhere in the White House, presented by commissions appointed by a Republican President. There's some good recommendations in there.

> I would implement the recommendations of the AIDS Commission. I would broaden the H.I.V. definition to include women and I.V. drug users, for more research and development and treatment purposes. . . . I know you're dying of AIDS.[41]

Rafsky then cuts Clinton off—"You're dying of ambition." At that point Clinton started to get somewhat angry. Eventually he replied,

> I feel your pain, I feel your pain, but if you want to attack me personally you're no better than Jerry Brown and all the rest of these people who say whatever sounds good at the moment. If you want something to be done, you ask me a question and you listen. If you don't agree with me, go support somebody else for President but quit talking to me like that. This is not a matter of personal attack; it's a matter of human wrong.[42]

Clinton then met with activists from ACT-UP two days later. Rafsky's confrontation with Clinton drew attention to AIDS in the press. Furthermore, that month the *New York Times* printed an op-ed piece by Rafsky on AIDS activism. The confrontation clearly benefited ACT-UP in its goals of drawing national attention to the crisis and challenging Clinton on his lack of a record on AIDS.

Meanwhile, Clinton clearly benefited from the confrontation too. It gave him a clear and dramatic platform to show primary voters in New York that he had thought about how to fight the crisis and, indeed, did support several specific anti-AIDS policies. Furthermore, it demonstrated Clinton's ability to empathize with the pain of others to the New York electorate. Clinton won the New York primary with 40.9 percent of the vote to Brown's 28.6 percent, clinching the nomination.

In 1992 Clinton raised $100,000 at a fundraiser in Los Angeles hosted by the lesbian and gay community. The bigger impact of the event for the lesbian and gay community was Clinton's speech:

> Tonight I want to talk to you about how we can be one people again without regard to race or gender or sexual orientation or age or religion or income. Those of you who are here tonight represent a community of our nation's gifted people whom we have been willing to squander. We cannot afford to waste the capacity, the contributions, the heart, the soul, and the

> mind of the gay and lesbian Americans. . . . My fellow Americans . . . if I could—if I could wave my arm for those of you who are HIV-positive and make it go away tomorrow, I would do it, so help me God I would, if I gave up my race for the White House and everything else, I would do that. Let us never forget, there are things we can and cannot do, but the beginning of wisdom is pulling together and learning from one another, and being determined to do better. What I came here today to tell you in simple terms is, I have a vision, and you're a part of it.[43]

Now, not only did Clinton have the support of the mainstream lesbian and gay community, including political activists on both coasts; the community's enthusiasm for Clinton also rose to a fever pitch. Over the course of the summer, the tape of the speech was replayed again and again for lesbian and gay audiences. On Mixner's suggestion, lesbians and gays were mentioned in his acceptance speech at the Democratic National Convention, as well. By the end of the campaign, Clinton had raised over $3 million from the lesbian and gay community, and countless lesbians and gays had volunteered for his campaign.[44]

At the same time, the Republicans went firmly in the opposite direction. By 1992, the Republican right wing was strongly infused with religious conservatism. Although a moderate, George H. W. Bush won the 1992 primary, but then former Reagan White House Communications Director Patrick Buchanan, the man he defeated, was allowed to speak at the Republican National Convention as part of an attempt at bringing the conservative and moderate wings of the party back together. In what is regarded as one of the opening salvos of the culture war, he said the following to the convention:

> Yes, we disagreed with President [George H. W.] Bush, but we stand with him for freedom to choose religious schools, and we stand with him against the amoral idea that gay and lesbian couples should have the same standing in law as married men and women. . . . There is a religious war going on in our country for the soul of America. It is a cultural war, as critical to the kind of nation we will one day be as was the Cold War itself. And in that struggle for the soul of America, [Bill] Clinton and [Hillary] Clinton are on the other side, and George Bush is on our side. And so, we have to come home, and stand beside him.[45]

AIDS and the 1992 election had permanently linked the lesbian and gay community with the Democratic Party. Likewise, social conservatives had a clear home with the Republican Party after 1992. From this point on, there was no going back. LGBT activists and interest groups would be increasingly drawn to the Democratic Party as the path of least resistance. However, it is important to note that integration of lesbians and gays into the Democratic Party lagged behind the integration of the Religious Right into the Republican Party. This affected the timing of increases in support for lesbian and gay issues in Congress in the decade after.

The Era of Party Polarization: 1992–2004

Although the Democratic Party began to support gay rights more uniformly starting in 1991 and 1992, there was still considerable heterogeneity in the party as older and more conservative members continued to resist the party's nascent position.[46] All this is important to consider when and if an 'issue evolution' could have taken place on lesbian and gay rights issues in the 1990s.

With Clinton in the White House and Democrats in control of both the House and Senate, the passage of lesbian and gay rights became a real possibility for the first time since AIDS had galvanized the LGBTQ community. The omnibus gay rights bill was subdivided into various other bills, the most important of which was renamed the Employment Non-Discrimination Act (ENDA). This being the case, determining a common measure of support for lesbian and gay rights over time on the part of members of Congress is difficult, but not impossible. To accurately estimate support, I use not only roll-call votes on lesbian and gay related issues, but also information on co-sponsorship of pro-gay and anti-gay legislation. Different bills become the focus of differing lobbying efforts and legislative activity in various years, and only sporadically attract roll-call votes. After passage, there was no longer an incentive for members to announce their support for such legislation. Due to this congressional agenda change on lesbian and gay rights, even direct measures of lesbian and gay rights support provided by interest groups are, unfortunately, not directly comparable from year to year.

The rise of ideal point estimation techniques has revolutionized the study of roll-call voting by allowing for more accurate measurement of policy support on various issues in Congress. Ideal point estimates are based on the spatial model of voting, and are often used by scholars as proxy measures for legislator support on any particular issue.[47] For various reasons, I use just such an analysis to analyze change in congressional support for gay rights. If any other sharp shifts in support for LGBTQ rights in Congress occur in conjunction with events, they may provide insight into change. Ideal point estimation techniques provide the best possible solution when it comes to examining change from period to period on how uniform Democrats were in their support for gay rights and Republicans were in their opposition.

The trick to accurately estimating gay rights support in Congress involves gathering as much data on the revealed preferences of members of Congress as possible. Here, I use an ideal point model that determines support for pro-gay positions in Congress. I use not only roll-call votes on lesbian and gay related issues, but also information on co-sponsorship of pro-gay and anti-gay legislation. The specific statistical details of the estimation of the model are provided in the data appendix. A list of roll-call votes involving lesbian and gay issues was gathered from research done by Haider-Markel,[48] the Human Rights Campaign scorecards for various years, and a search of THOMAS for keywords involving lesbian and gay issues. THOMAS is the Library of Congress's online legislative database. (The statistical details of the procedures used are provided in the data appendix.) Support for pro-lesbian and gay positions was estimated in four time periods from the co-sponsorship and voting records: 1987–1992 (the last two years of Reagan's second term and G. H. W. Bush's single term in office), 1993–1996 (Clinton's first term), 1997–2000 (Clinton's second term), and 2001–2004 (G.W. Bush's first term). The results of the analyses are displayed graphically in figure 4.3 for the 150 members who served in Congress during all four of these time periods. Thus, we get a sense of how support for lesbian and gay rights in Congress changed for the Democratic and Republican Parties (while naturally controlling for membership turnover).

The scores range from about 80 to 115. Lower values indicate increasingly anti-LGBT positions on legislation. Higher values indicate increasingly pro-LGBT positions on legislation. The rough positions of Democratic and Republican members are given by density estimates of

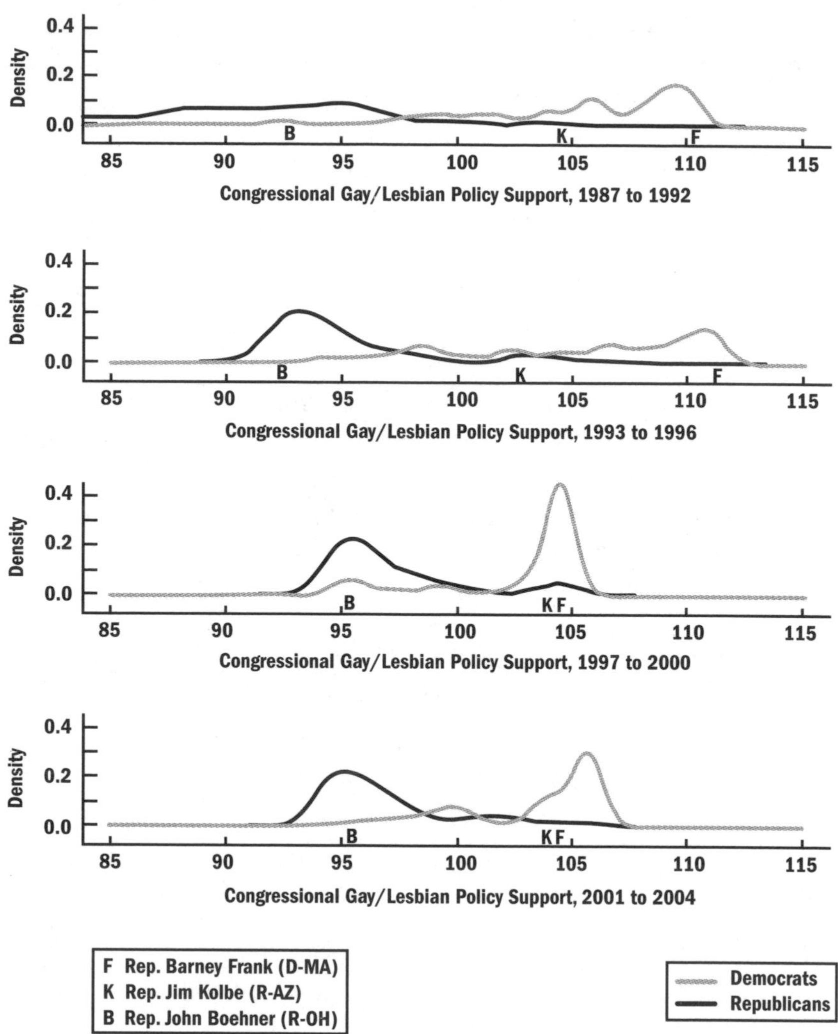

Figure 4.3. Latent Support for Pro-Gay and Lesbian Policies in Congress in Four Presidential Terms, 1987–2004.

Based on roll-call voting and co-sponsorship of legislation in Congress involving lesbian and gay-related issues, this figure displays latent support for pro-gay and lesbian policies among long-serving members of Congress. Greater values indicate higher support, while lower values indicate less support. Note that the relative positions of members can be accurately compared only cross-sectionally, not across time. The position of a few important members is also displayed for purposes of comparison.

each party's support in the four time periods. Also included in the figure are the estimated positions of three specific members for comparison: a typical Republican, future speaker John Boehner (R-OH), and two prominent gay members, Representative Jim Kolbe (R-AZ) and Representative Barney Frank (D-MA).

As I explain in the methodological appendix, caution should be taken when comparing these LGBT policy scores over time. The general distribution of support for the parties should be fairly accurate, however, in determining the spread of revealed support for gay rights in Congress.

Representative Barney Frank, an openly gay Democrat from Massachusetts (since 1987), is among the most liberal members on gay rights in each period. Furthermore, Representative Jim Kolbe, a Republican from Arizona who declared he was gay in the 104th Congress during the 1996 debate on the Defense of Marriage Act, showed increased liberalism on lesbian and gay rights after this event. In the earliest period, Kolbe was at the middle of the scale on lesbian and gay rights issues. This corresponds to being moderate on gay rights for a Republican, but still rather conservative when compared to a typical Democrat. However, by the later period, he had become markedly more liberal on lesbian and gay rights. His behavior on lesbian and gay rights was indistinguishable from that of a liberal Democrat in the latter two periods. In fact, it is not even statistically different from that of Barney Frank after 1996.

The more important changes over time involve the *relative positions* of the Democratic and Republican Parties on lesbian and gay rights. From the late 1980s to the end of the first Bush administration, votes involving LGBTQ issues were dominated by AIDS and HIV prevention policy. Moderate Republicans would often break off to support provisions that created programs to (modestly) curtail the epidemic. More conservative Republicans were perfectly happy to vote against such legislation, as were many conservative Democrats. In this time period, overlapping with the last few years the gay rights bill was introduced, more Democrats supported pro-lesbian and gay positions, yet both parties showed considerable heterogeneity in their support.

In Clinton's first term, after Pat Buchanan's surprisingly successful run for the White House in 1992, the heterogeneity in the Republican Party ended. When legislation like Clinton's 1993 Don't-Ask-Don't-Tell

(DADT) 'compromise' or the 1996 Defense of Marriage Act (DOMA) came up for a vote, the bulk of the party voted consistently for the anti-lesbian and gay position.

Two major factors are likely to have led to this consolidation. The first is the desire to appeal to the growing base of religious and social conservative activists who were flocking to the party after the 1992 campaign. Republican members running for Congress had incentives to move their individual support rightward on gay issues to appeal to socially conservative activists in a similar manner to the Democrats' leftward movement on gay rights in the early 1990s. The second factor was Republicans' winning control of Congress in the 1994 election.[49] At that point, they needed to appeal to religious activists not just as individual members of Congress but also as a party. Control of the congressional agenda gave them the ability to do that—and thus to keep moderate bills that divided the GOP on gay rights issues off the floor. This meant that moderate Republicans could not vote for moderately pro-gay bills, rendering them indistinguishable from conservative Republicans. As a result, the Republican Party came to look more conservative on lesbian and gay rights than it had been prior to the period of Democratic control, and this new party image—more consistently anti-gay—could be used to attract new socially conservative activists. The net result was a clearer party position against gay rights for the Republicans.

In sharp contrast, the Democrats remained heterogeneous in their support of lesbian and gay rights in Clinton's first term. For example, a significant number of Democrats (including Clinton) supported both DADT and DOMA, but significant numbers of Democrats also opposed both. It was not until Clinton's second term that the Democrats became much more unified in their support for such measures when they came up for a vote in Congress.

Why did the Democrats finally seem to converge in support of gay rights in 1997? As we have seen in chapter 1, this is the very time when mass liberalization with regard to gay and lesbian rights started to take place, especially among political liberals who overwhelmingly support Democrats. By this time, changes in constituents' attitudes, the focus of later chapters, were already working their effects on the remaining Democratic members of Congress. When constituency opinion demanded that representatives remain out-of-step with their urban colleagues on lesbian and gay nondiscrimination, it was in the political interests of rural and southern Democrats to oppose gay rights. But by 1997, all the forces that affected their support—pro-gay interest groups with resources, colleagues in Congress, and constituents' views—were now consistently aligning to push them in a pro-gay direction. Barring any deep-seated personal animus against lesbians and gays, there was no longer any political reason for Democrats to oppose ENDA or other gay rights issues, as such measures now had high levels of constituent support. Even still, on issues where a majority of the public was opposed to specific LGBTQ rights, such as marriage equality, Democrats appear to have lagged significantly until a majority of the public became supportive.[50]

Conclusion

The 1980s and 1990s showed a rapid rise in the power of political party in predicting congressional support for lesbian and gay rights. The events that solidified this division in 1992 and 1993—the election of Bill Clinton, the 1992 Republican Convention, and DADT—may be of key importance to attitude change on lesbian and gay rights. Some Democrats appeared to be moving to the Left in response to anti-AIDS activism and increases in media coverage in the early 1990s. Still others remained opposed to gay rights until after constituency opinion begin to shift later in the decade. Now that the lesbian and gay movement had support among elites in Congress in 1992 and then from the president, those elites could now persuade members of the public to change their positions. The next chapter searches for these effects of elite persuasion, or issue evolution, on mass opinion.

PART III

Public Response and the Nature of Social Change

Tonight every one of you knows deep in your heart that we are too divided. . . . For too long politicians have told the most of us that are doing all right that what's really wrong with America is . . . them. Them, the minorities. Them, the liberals. Them, the poor. Them, the homeless. Them, the people with disabilities. Them, the gays. We've gotten to where we've nearly them'ed ourselves to death. Them, and them, and them. But this is America. There is no them. There is only us.
—Bill Clinton, accepting the Democratic nomination for president, July 16, 1992

We have tracked the reasons for the national emergence of lesbian and gay issues: the desire of the Democratic Party to appeal to a more politically active lesbian and gay community mobilized by AIDS and the rise in media attention to gay issues caused by anti-AIDS activism. This book now pivots to its key focus, explaining change in public opinion. Clinton's presidency coincided with a large and significant turning point with respect to public opinion about gay rights in the United States.

Clinton's political positions in favor of employment protections for lesbians and gays, spotlighted in the 1992 campaign and the 1993 Don't-Ask-Don't-Tell (DADT) debate, would begin to restructure support for lesbian and gay rights in the mass public. However, while there was some positive movement in public opinion in the years before 1994, it was only political liberals who appeared receptive to rethinking their positions. Most of these positive gains in opinion were also somewhat offset by negative movement among conservatives and Republicans. These events are discussed in chapter 5.

Buried, however, in these seemingly mundane political changes (by the standards of political scientists) were all the simmering ingredients for much more profound social change, which took place from 1994 to

1998. As extreme negative feelings toward lesbians and gays declined and concerns about contracting AIDS among the public ebbed, LGBTQ people across the country reacted to the national emergence of a dialogue on LGBTQ rights by emerging from the closet. A record number of individuals across all ideological groups started to report increased contact with lesbians and gays in the mid-1990s. Likewise, mediated contact, or contact with fictional lesbians and gays through literature, television, and movies, also increased. Whereas television shows, as well as movies had only minor gay or lesbian characters at first, in the mid- and late 1990s these characters grew ever more prominent. The net effect of these two forces—the coming out of lesbians and gays and the rise in their fictional portrayals—would dramatically change mass attitudes.

In chapters 6 and 7, I discuss these two forces and the profound alteration in public views they inspired. The effect of interpersonal contact and exposure to lesbians and gays through media cannot be understated. I present evidence showing that the well-known cohort effects on gay rights are, to a large extent, also due to increases in contact with LGBTs, both interpersonally and via the media. These contact effects were disproportionately strong not only among the young, who lacked the strong negative impressions of gays held by older people, but also among those on the political Left. The net result was a solidification of political divisions on gay rights, which, in turn, set the stage for conflicts on marriage equality in the 2000s.

5

Issue Evolution?

Gay Politics in the Early Clinton Years

While there is demonstrable support for the belief that more and more people support gay rights [in terms of employment protections], the vast majority of the population continues to view homosexuality as just plain wrong. . . . Perhaps what is most surprising—or depressing—is the revelation that, despite activists' massive public education efforts, the perception of gays and lesbians appears to have changed little over the years. In 1982 51% of Gallup Poll respondents said homosexuality was "not acceptable." Nineteen years ago, 73% of respondents to the NORC [National Opinion Research Counsel's] Survey characterized homosexuality as "always wrong," a difference from the 1991 figure [of 75 percent] that is statistically insignificant.

—John Gallagher, "What America Thinks of You: The More Things Change, the More They Stay the Same," writing in *The Advocate*, October 6, 1992

As the epigraph to this chapter makes clear, although support for employment protections for lesbians and gays had been increasing since the 1970s, little change in the public's fundamental disapproval of lesbians and gays had occurred by the start of the 1990s. Public support for the principle of nondiscrimination based on sexual orientation had increased. But when most members of the public thought of lesbians and gays, the base negative emotions that arose were much the same as in previous decades.

What changes had occurred were in the narrow issue area of employment nondiscrimination on the basis of sexual orientation. This was perhaps due to positions of AIDS activists that were starting to be conveyed by the news media, including reports of those with AIDS being fired from their jobs. Fading memories of the alleged links between homosexuals and communist subversives from the McCarthy era[1] and the changing positions of medical and mental health professions on homosexuality may have also had a minor effect.

Despite the apparent lack of progress on other forms of lesbian and gay rights support, even before Gallagher's article was published, political forces had already been unleashed and would start to transform these negative feelings. Lesbian and gay rights had entered into the national dialogue in the 1992 presidential campaign, and surveys in the field at the time of Gallagher's writing, including the 1992 American National Elections Study (ANES), addressed more in this chapter and the next, were already starting to detect a mild warming of feelings toward lesbians and gays among political liberals and Democrats. Clinton's new tolerant rhetoric involving lesbians and gays, illustrated by his 1992 DNC acceptance speech, was likely a factor, too.

But from a policy standpoint, the early Clinton years were deeply disappointing for lesbians and gays. Clinton would quickly earn ire by failing to effectively advocate for gay rights after assuming office. For instance, not only was the Employment Non-Discrimination Act (ENDA) never enacted, but Clinton signed the Defense of Marriage Act (DOMA) into law. The eventual enforcement of the Don't-Ask-Don't-Tell policy was little different from the explicit pre-1993 ban on gays in the military. Despite these setbacks, however, real, positive changes began stirring underneath this string of disappointments.

This chapter begins by first briefly describing the effects of the 1992 campaign on public attitudes. Differences between the 1988 and 1992 ANES surveys allow for an analysis of the effects of the 1992 campaign specifically, as the 1992 wave of the study was fielded *after* the conclusion of the 1992 Democratic convention and *before* Don't-Ask-Don't-Tell in 1993.

The DADT controversy itself looms large over any discussion of gays and lesbians in the 1990s. I give a brief description of the rightward shift that Clinton took on the issue in 1993, following an examination of attitude change that subsequently occurred during the controversy using the ANES's mid-1990s panel study of political and voting behavior. This panel study tracked the changing opinions of hundreds of individuals from 1992 to 1996. Because they resurveyed the same respondents in different years, this study allows for better tests of hypotheses involving attitudinal change. Three specific gay rights questions were repeatedly asked in the panel study: (1) support for employment protections for lesbians and gays; (2) support for gays in the military; and (3) support for lesbian and gay adoption rights. The ANES also included the feeling thermometer for lesbians and gays, which asked how much respondents felt warmly or coolly towards lesbians and gays as a group as expressed by giving a number from 0 (cold) to 100 (warm) with 50 being neutral. The last of these most accurately measures the general feelings of the public toward lesbians and gays as groups. This is what Gallagher alluded to when he mentioned "perceptions of gays and lesbians" in the epigraph to this chapter. The chapter then concludes by addressing a topic that has been a nagging concern of those who study public opinion involving lesbians and gays, yet never adequately addressed using cross-time survey data: the ebb of public fears over contracting AIDS on public opinion on lesbian and gay rights in the late 1990s. I show that some attitude change, consistent with the theories of issues evolution and elite-led polarization,[2] did occur during Clinton's 1992 campaign for president and the DADT controversy. However, I find that the magnitude of these changes were small, casting doubt on the notion that changes in LGBTQ rights support among American political leaders caused the bulk of attitudinal change that occurred in the 1990s.

Effects of the 1992 Presidential Campaign

As we have seen in chapter 4, President Clinton took clear positions in favor of a tolerant approach to lesbian and gay issues in 1992. At the same time, the GOP moved in the opposite direction. By highlighting their opposition to the rights of lesbians and gays and allowing Pat Buchanan to give his "culture war" speech during their convention, Republicans did their part to establish a sharp contrast between the two parties on gay rights for the first time. To date, no one has looked for change in public opinion solely from these 1992 events without also combining them with the effects of the DADT debate months later.

Still, there are several reasons for separating out the effects of the two. First, according to political science theories of issue evolution and elite-led polarization,[3] we would expect a clear polarization between Democrats and Republicans in the public at the same time as the 1992 campaign. This polarization should be most evident on public viewpoints of the two gay rights policy issues most discussed during this time: employment protections and gays in the military. More important, the analysis in the first chapter suggests that this is the time period in which attitude change first started to occur. This fact in and of itself merits a finer-grained examination of the early 1990s.

Two questions were asked on the ANES in 1992 that were also asked in 1984 or in 1988. Recall that the ANES is a nationally representative set of surveys taken in elections years, which asks the same questions to different sets of respondents in different years. Some questions on the ANES involve support for employment protections for lesbians and gays (first asked in 1988) and the feeling thermometer (asked in 1984, 1988, and 1992). The exact wording of the thermometer and its specifics were described in the first chapter. Table 5.1 displays the basic pattern of responses to these questions. On the employment protections question, respondents indicated whether they favored or opposed legal bans on discrimination and, if so, whether their support was strong or not strong. In 1988, respondents could also indicate that their support "depends"; this was a voluntary response in 1992. On the feeling thermometer, respondents rated their impression of lesbians and gays from 0 (negative) to 100 (positive).

There is some modest evidence of attitudinal change on the employment protections question from 1988 to 1992.[4] The percentage of people who "strongly favor" laws codifying these protections increased by 7 percent. There is also a 10 percent increase in overall support. However, many of these respondents appear to have migrated from the "depends" category, which was absent in 1992, so these results are suggestive at best.

A similar story emerges on feelings toward lesbians and gays after the 1992 campaign. In 1984, 30 percent of those who offered a rating of lesbians and gays gave 0, indicating the most negative response possible. Things got worse as the AIDS crisis took its toll. By 1988, 35 percent of respondents rated lesbians and gays at 0. The trend in the average response is similar. In 1984, the average rating among respondents was about 30 degrees. In 1988, it had dropped slightly to 28.5 degrees. From 1988 to 1992, positive feelings toward lesbians and gays rebounded. The

TABLE 5.1. Change in National Opinion on Gay Rights on the ANES, 1984, 1988, 1992

Employment Protections	1984	1988	1992
Oppose, Strongly		22.0%	21.2%
Oppose, Weakly		12.3%	12.8%
Depends		10.5%	2.1%
Favor, Weakly		20.7%	23.8%
Favor, Strongly		20.1%	27.9%
LG Feeling Thermometer	**1984**	**1988**	**1992**
0	30.5%	35.2%	22.7%
1–25	15.5%	12.1%	10.3%
26–49	15.5%	15.3%	16.7%
50	25.8%	26.5%	27.3%
51–74	7.8%	6.2%	15.3%
75–96	3.1%	3.5%	5.7%
97–100	1.8%	1.3%	2.0%
Average Response	29.9	28.5	37.7

percentage of respondents giving 0 dropped by one-third to 22.7 percent. While still relatively low, the average response rose nine points to 37.7.

Did any specific political or social groups in the public shift *more* from 1988 to 1992? Specifically, were liberals or Democrats more likely to respond to Clinton's expressed tolerance at the top of the Democratic ticket in the heat of the campaign? We can test this in a rather straightforward fashion using the ANES data from these years. In order to answer this question, I combined the 1988 and 1992 cross-sections from the ANES in order to see what factors became more powerful using regression analyses. (The details of this analysis in terms of variable coding are in the data appendix at the end of the book.) In both years, questions about ideology, political party, church attendance, gender (female), race (African American), educational attainment, and year of birth were asked. Thus, I was able to look for a strengthening or weakening relationship between any demographic variable and gay rights support.

So how did the factors that predict support for gay rights change during the 1992 campaign? Put another way, what demographic "gaps"

TABLE 5.2. Change in Gay Rights Attitudes by Demographic Characteristics, 1988–1992

	Job Protections for LGs
	Coef. Est. *(S.E.)*
LG Feeling Thermometer	0.040*** *(0.002)*
Ideology	0.993*** *(0.187)*
Party ID	0.112 *(0.166)*
Gender	0.418*** *(0.075)*
African American	–0.049 *(0.099)*
Year of Birth	0.236 *(0.307)*
Religiosity	–0.412*** *(0.099)*
Education	0.463*** *(0.128)*
1992 Dummy	–0.507*** *(0.131)*
1992 * Party ID	0.871*** *(0.213)*
Cut 1	0.857 *(0.267)*
Cut 2	1.694 *(0.268)*
Cut 3	1.997 *(0.269)*
Cut 4	3.495 *(0.275)*
Akaike Information Criteria (AIC)	6903.65
Deviance	6875.65
N	2704

*** ~ p < .001, ** ~ p < .01, * ~ p < .05, @ ~ p < .1 (two-tailed tests)

on gay rights support expanded or contracted? Table 5.2, which examines change in support for employment protections, indicates that the only relationship that changed was that of party identification, which strengthened considerably. While political party appears to have had no discernible relationship to employment protections support in 1988, there was a modest effect (or gap in support for employment protections by party) in 1992, exactly as theories of elite-led attitude change would predict.

Table 5.3 models strong Democrats' and strong Republicans' views for the years 1988 and 1992, with all other demographic factors held at their mean values. In 1988, controlling for demographics, ideology, and feelings toward lesbians and gays, there was no difference between Democrats and Republicans in their support for employment protections. However, by 1992, things had changed considerably. Strong Democrats were now 16 percent more likely to strongly favor such laws, while strong Republicans were 16 percent more likely to strongly oppose them. The change in the "depends" response had little effect on the results. As would be expected, in both 1988 and 1992, feelings toward lesbians

TABLE 5.3. Change in Probability of Support of Employment Protections from 1988 to 1992, Based on Table 5.2

In 1988			
	Strong Republican	Strong Democrat	Difference
Oppose, Strongly	0.204	0.204	0.000
Oppose, Weakly	0.168	0.168	0.000
Depends	0.072	0.072	0.000
Favor, Weakly	0.337	0.338	0.001
Favor, Strongly	0.219	0.219	0.000
In 1992			
	Strong Republican	Strong Democrat	Difference
Oppose, Strongly	0.298	0.138	0.160
Oppose, Weakly	0.197	0.132	0.055
Depends	0.073	0.062	0.011
Favor, Weakly	0.286	0.358	−0.072
Favor, Strongly	0.144	0.310	−0.166

and gays, ideology, gender (female), and education all predicted higher support for employment protections about equally. Church attendance predicted weaker support in both years.

Turning to the feeling thermometer results in table 5.4, we see that liberalism and education are both strongly related to more positive feelings in both 1988 and 1992. Gender and political party seem weakly

TABLE 5.4. Change in Gay Rights Attitudes, by Demographic Characteristics, 1988–1992

	LG Feeling Thermometer
	Coef. Est. *(S.E.)*
Intercept	1.333 *(3.594)*
Ideology	26.682*** *(2.256)*
Party ID	5.023* *(2.124)*
Gender	4.876*** *(1.409)*
African American	−2.451* *(1.214)*
Year of Birth	4.484 *(3.870)*
Religiosity	−8.847*** *(1.221)*
Education	25.407*** *(2.338)*
1992 Dummy	8.084** *(2.768)*
1992 * Party ID	5.848* *(2.678)*
1992 * Gender	3.179@ *(1.859)*
1992 * Education	−7.588* *(3.069)*
Adjusted R^2	0.216
σ	24.03
N	2757

*** ~ p < .001, ** ~ p <. 01, * ~ p <. 05, @ ~ p < .1 (two-tailed tests)

related to more positive feelings in both years. Race (African American) and church attendance are also weakly related to more negative feelings. There appears to be no statistically discernible relationship between year of birth or age in either 1988 or 1992.

Between 1988 and 1992 the effect of gender increased marginally. Women became more supportive by about 3 points, going from about 5 points to 8 points, perhaps out of greater sympathy over AIDS. More meaningfully, the effect of political party doubled from a 5 point difference in 1988 to a 10 point difference in 1992 between strong Republicans and strong Democrats. Unexpectedly, the effect of education decreased. The gap separating the most highly educated from the least educated decreased from 25 points to 17 points. What appears to have happened is that educated individuals mostly stayed in place in terms of their support during the 1992 campaign, while uneducated individuals caught up. Moreover, those without an education became warmer toward lesbians and gays, especially if they were Democrats or women. Across demographics, feelings toward lesbians and gays improved about 8 points.

What we are starting to see, in the broadest sense, is the start of a reconstruction of attitudes toward lesbian and gay caused by the political conflict on gay rights between the two national political parties. From the 1970s to the peak of the AIDS crisis, the determinants of positive (or non-negative) feelings toward lesbians and gays had less to do with lesbians and gays as a group and more to do with the various things that indicate a general predisposition of tolerance held by some toward out-groups and their rights in general. It seems unlikely to be a coincidence that characteristics such as education and ideology, which featured prominently in studies predicting tolerance toward out-groups, such as communists and atheists, also dominate these early predictors of attitudes involving lesbians and gays in 1988.[5] Other studies of support for gay rights based on pre-1990s opinion data (where education was a prominent predictor of tolerance) substantiate this argument.[6] Moreover, the marquis predictor of political attitudes in general, party identification, had little effect on attitudes in 1988. What occurred with the 1992 presidential campaign was a shift in the central axis of support and non-support of lesbian and gay rights from one that divided the tolerant from the intolerant to one that cleaved the political Left from the political Right.

The Don't-Ask-Don't-Tell Controversy

Clinton's victory in 1992 was met with immense elation among gay and lesbian activists. A seemingly supportive president and Congress now appeared on the horizon. Clinton had promised to pass ENDA and to end the ban on gays in the military. However, support for gays rights among members of Congress—and Clinton—would prove to be much weaker than it appeared to be on Election Day in 1992.

Hints of what would come began days after the election. Senator Sam Nunn (D-GA) publicly voiced his opposition to lifting the ban on gays in the military.[7] This opposition to allowing openly lesbian and gay people to serve had until that point remained silent. As long as a Clinton presidency was theoretical, there was no need for those opposed to lifting the ban to voice their disapproval. This lack of a pushback from social conservatives gave both Clinton and the lesbian and gay movement the impression that there would be little resistance to a change in policy. Now that a Clinton presidency was a certainty, the forces opposed to allowing gays in the military needed to act.

As both chairman of the Senate Armed Forces Committee and a moderate in Clinton's own party, Senator Sam Nunn was in a position to easily assemble a majority in Congress to undo any executive order allowing gays in the military. The Georgia senator was generally unsupportive of lesbians and gays and had other political incentives to confront the new president.[8] Nunn firmly held the power to veto any policy changes implemented by Clinton.

Clinton, always the compromiser, refused to strongly support his previous position in the face of growing congressional opposition. Clinton wished to resolve the issue with a minimal expenditure of political capital, which he wanted to save for use on issues of greater importance to the public, including healthcare reform and economic growth. As the Clinton administration tried to find middle ground with Nunn, a compromise proposal advanced by Charlie Markos emerged.[9] This proposal would legalize status as gay or lesbian among those who served, but any homosexual "behavior" would still be banned. What constituted homosexual "behavior" was not clearly defined.[10] In practice, although new recruits would no longer be asked about their sexual orientation when they entered the military, this policy differed little from the past policy in its effect on the lives of lesbians and gays in the military.

As time passed, Nunn continued to use his chairmanship and strategic position in Congress to spotlight both his opposition to removing the ban and his own power to block the president's will on the issue. He began to hold hearings on gays in the military in Congress and highlighted concepts such as "unit cohesion" in order to undermine the positions of the ban's opponents.[11]

As the controversy dragged on into summer of 1993, Nunn never lost the institutional upper hand. The president remained unwilling to expend actual political capital on the issue by actively lobbying members of Congress to support a policy change. A series of compromise proposals floated about, each more limited in changing policy than the last, including one by Barney Frank that would allow members of the military to be open about their orientation off-base but not on-base. Earlier, Clinton himself had even entertained the possibility of allowing segregated units on the basis of sexual orientation as part of compromise legislation. Here, the response from David Mixner, who was still a key link between the administration and the lesbian and gay movement, was categorical. Mixner denounced Clinton's willingness to consider segregation on *Nightline*. "There is one thing that is very unacceptable to talk about as a legitimate alternative and that is the segregation of the military once again. It is morally wrong. It is repugnant. It is something we cannot accept."[12] After his appearance on *Nightline*, Mixner found his connection with the administration effectively severed.

When the Don't-Ask-Don't-Tell measure came up for a vote in the Senate Armed Services committee, only Democrats opposed it. On the floor of the Senate, thirty mostly liberal Democrats voted against the compromise. In the House, the old conservative coalition of Republicans and southern Democrats reemerged, with 121 mostly northern Democrats and twelve moderate Republicans opposing the measure.[13]

Clinton should not take all of the blame for the resulting policy. The lesbian and gay movement, having been on the outside for so long, had little institutional experience navigating the complexities of Washington policymaking. Both Clinton and the movement overestimated their hands heading into 1993, conveying an advantage to those opposed to lifting the ban. Despite a national march on Washington in early 1993, the movement could not match the volume of letters and visits with members of Congress coming from social and religious conservatives.[14] That said, the White House, feeling it had greater influence with lawmakers than the lesbian and gay community, had wanted to take the lead on the lobbying Congress on the issue.[15]

The DADT Controversy and Public Attitudes

If the 1992 campaign started to forge a link between national politics and gay rights, the months of focus on the gays in the military issue solidified that link. At the same time, though, even as the 1992 campaign clarified party positions on gay rights, the prominent role played by Democratic Senator Sam Nunn undermined this clarification. With the southern Democrat taking the lead in watering down policy change, and a North-South split reemerging within the Democratic party on DADT, it seems reasonable to suspect that the "proper" positions for liberals and conservatives in the public to take on lesbian and gay rights were being clarified for those following the issue. This contrasts with the way polarization and issue evolution typically takes place on most issues—between Democrats or Republicans. Although Clinton himself ended up on the conservative side of the issue, he was framed as being a liberal trying to upset the status quo throughout most of the controversy. Despite the opposition to DADT by gay and lesbian organizations and congressional liberals, Clinton rhetorically maintained that DADT was a pro-gay policy shift.

In 1992, the ANES started a panel study in which the same set of nationally representative respondents would be asked their attitudes at multiple points in time. In addition to being surveyed before the 1992 election, these respondents would be resurveyed in 1994 and 1996. Half of them would be resurveyed in 1993 with special batteries of questions. The second half would be resurveyed with a different special battery in 1995. In addition, the prominence of DADT in the summer of 1993 led to the inclusion of a special battery of questions designed to probe the effects of attention to DADT and gay rights on support for Clinton. The feeling thermometer was asked in all four years (1992, 1993, 1994, and

1996), attitudes toward employment protections and gays in the military were asked in 1992, 1993, and 1996, and attitudes toward gay adoption were asked in 1992 and 1993. Attitudes on employment protections and gays in the military were asked using the same 4-point scales as 1988, while the question on allowing gay adoption only asked if respondents were in favor or opposed.

Table 5.5 shows response frequencies for each of these questions over the course of the study. General feelings involving lesbians and gays, support for employment protections, and views involving gay adoption changed little among the panel respondents. Feelings involving lesbians and gays appear to have dropped slightly in 1994, but rebound immediately after. In contrast, support for gays in the military improved overall, although it should be noted that the people who tend to stay in a panel study over a period of years are generally more interested in politics and thus already tend to have more stable positions on issues. However, the trend on the feeling thermometer among the panel shows little change from 1992 to 1996.

Thus, it appears on the whole that there was little change in gay-related attitudes during the DADT controversy, with the natural exception being attitudes toward gays in the military. Could there be any significant movement between political groups on gay rights from 1992 to 1993, despite the seeming stability across all respondents?

Using the panel, we can track actual change in attitudes from 1992 to 1993 among the *same* individuals, unlike in the prior analysis of change from 1988 to 1992, which used different samples of respondents. Starting with the three issue-based attitudes, I modeled change in each individual policy (employment nondiscrimination, gays in the military, and gay adoption) from 1992 to 1993 as a function of the same demographics as in the previous 1988–1992 analysis: gender, education, ideology, party, year of birth, and religiosity.[16] This resulted in three different analyses: one for change in attitudes on employment protections, one for change in attitudes on gays in the military, and one for change in attitudes involving gay adoption. I also include the value of the 1992 feeling thermometer and change in feelings from 1992 to 1993 in these models in case change in feelings is driving any liberalization. In keeping with other studies of this period, I also include a scale of support for egalitarian values. This scale measures individual support for equal treatment

TABLE 5.5. Change in National Opinion on Gay Rights, ANES Panel Study for 1992, 1993, 1994, and 1996

	1992	1993	1994	1996
Employment Protections				
Oppose, Strongly	22.9%	23.1%		23.1%
Oppose, Weakly	12.9%	13.7%		13.7%
Favor, Weakly	28.1%	24.2%		24.2%
Favor, Strongly	36.0%	38.9%		38.9%
Don't Know	0.1%	0.1%		0.1%
	1992	1993	1994	1996
Gays in the Military				
Oppose, Strongly	31.3%	30.2%		24.4%
Oppose, Weakly	7.6%	8.0%		6.7%
Favor, Weakly	27.8%	17.3%		24.8%
Favor, Strongly	33.2%	44.4%		43.9%
Don't Know	0.1%	0.1%		0.1%
	1992	1993	1994	1996
Gay Adoption				
Oppose, Strongly	59.4%	61.7%		
Oppose, Weakly	12.0%	9.2%		
Favor, Weakly	15.2%	13.7%		
Favor, Strongly	13.4%	15.1%		
Don't Know	0.0%	0.1%		
	1992	1993	1994	1996
Gay Feeling Thermometer				
0	21.9%	16.5%	28.3%	20.0%
1–25	9.1%	17.3%	11.3%	9.1%
26–49	16.0%	12.8%	12.4%	16.2%
50	27.4%	35.8%	25.3%	31.0%
51–74	17.2%	7.2%	14.2%	15.8%
75–99	6.0%	8.6%	4.2%	5.4%
100	2.3%	2.2%	3.5%	2.6%
Average Response	39.4	38.9	35.9	39.9

of social groups by the government.[17] Because those who already have strong support for gay rights in 1992 cannot express greater support in 1993, I include the 1992 measure of support for each question in order to control for these "ceiling" effects.[18] Table 5.6 shows these three models. In all three models, feelings toward lesbians and gays emerge as a key predictor of shifts in favor of gay rights. This is particularly the case for gays in the military, but in general feelings toward lesbians and gays were becoming a stronger predictor on all gay rights issues, even on those like gay adoption that received little press attention.

After feelings are taken into account, little similarity between changing support across gay rights issues is found. Those high in egalitarianism and those who identify as Democrats shifted in favor of employment protections. Surprisingly, those who were younger became *less* supportive of these protections as compared to those who were older. Democrats and women become more supportive of gays in the military. Women and the more highly educated become more supportive of gay adoption, while those who attend religious services become less supportive.

Democrats in general appeared to be moving in a more supportive direction of gays in the military regardless of Nunn's opposition. What about those who were paying closer attention to the controversy and were more aware of the role of Nunn and other southern conservative Democrats in blocking reform? Here ideology becomes more important. In table 5.7, I allow the effect of ideology to vary with a respondent's ability to answer general questions about national politics. The ability to answer knowledge-based questions about politics is generally regarded as a better measure of television news watching than self-reports of viewing. Political scientists have shown that people feel more social pressure to say they follow politics when they generally do not. However, basic knowledge about politics, learned by watching the news, cannot be as easily faked. The models show that, among those likely paying closer attention to politics, ideological polarization generally took place rather than partisan polarization. Nunn's leadership did influence conservative Democrats and liberal Republicans if they were paying closer attention to the controversy. Thus it was *not* egalitarian values that caused the shift on gay rights among Democrats, as value-framing theory would predict. Despite the fact that the DADT issue was extensively covered by the news media in 1993, elite-signaling appears to have been more significant than value-framing.

TABLE 5.6. Change in Gay Rights Support during the DADT Controversy

	DV: Δ in Employment Protections (1992–94)	DV: Δ in Gays in the Military (1992–94)	DV: Δ in Gay Adoption (1992–94)
	Coef. Est. *(S.E.)*	Coef. Est. *(S.E.)*	Coef. Est. *(S.E.)*
Intercept	0.154* *(0.070)*	0.119@ *(0.068)*	−0.065 *(0.057)*
Party ID	0.127* *(0.051)*	0.116* *(0.050)*	0.048 *(0.042)*
Ideology	0.074 *(0.078)*	0.049 *(0.075)*	0.055 *(0.064)*
Education	0.021 *(0.053)*	−0.048 *(0.052)*	0.120** *(0.043)*
Gender	0.044 *(0.030)*	0.056@ *(0.029)*	0.042@ *(0.024)*
Religiosity	−0.063 *(0.038)*	−0.036 *(0.037)*	−0.071* *(0.031)*
Year of Birth	−0.218*** *(0.065)*	−0.038 *(0.063)*	0.009 *(0.052)*
'92 Employment Protections	−0.636*** *(0.047)*		
'92 Gays in the Military		−0.518*** *(0.047)*	
'92 Gay Adoption			−0.403*** *(0.041)*
LG Feelings in 92	0.002** *(0.001)*	0.005*** *(0.001)*	0.003*** *(0.001)*
Δ in LG Feelings (92 to 94)	0.002@ *(0.001)*	0.003*** *(0.001)*	0.002** *(0.001)*
Egalitarianism	0.296*** *(0.081)*	−0.038 *(0.081)*	−0.060 *(0.066)*
Adj. R^2	0.307	0.224	0.184
F-statistic	21.28	14.3	11.35
σ	0.304	0.298	0.249
N	460	463	459

TABLE 5.7. Political Awareness and Change in Attitude to DADT

	DV: Δ in Gays in the Military (92 to 94)
	Coef. Est. *(S.E.)*
Intercept	0.303* *(0.140)*
Party ID	0.251* *(0.121)*
Ideology	–0.364* *(0.160)*
Religiosity	–0.004 *(0.037)*
Year of Birth	–0.015 *(0.065)*
Education	–0.080 *(0.056)*
Gender	0.063* *(0.030)*
'92 Gays in the Military	–0.532*** (0.047)
LG Feelings in 92	0.005*** *(0.001)*
Δ in LG Feelings (92 to 94)	0.003*** *(0.001)*
Egalitarianism	–0.172 *(0.215)*
Political Awareness (PA)	–0.305 *(0.199)*
Party ID * PA	–0.300 *(0.209)*
Ideology * PA	0.799** *(0.274)*
Egalitarianism * PA	0.020 *(0.337)*
Adj. R^2	0.246
F-statistic	11.69
σ	0.294
N	460

Disgust and the Ideological Basis of Changing Feelings

The results discussed above show that the link between feelings toward lesbians and gays and gay rights was strong and that changes in feelings translated directly into increased or decreased support for gay rights. But how were these feelings changing? While the average of the feeling thermometer may have changed little between 1992 and 1996, this may mask substantive polarization between groups. In table 5–8, I model the change in the feeling thermometer as a function of the same demographics used earlier. The results are nearly identical when change from 1992 to 1993, 1992 to 1994, or 1992 to 1996 is modeled.

The findings of this analysis are surprising and ultimately serve as a prelude to the next chapter. Based on the findings in table 5.6, we would expect that party, and not ideology, would serve as a basis for polarization on gay rights for the larger public. After all, partisan polarization on gay rights was seen among most respondents on gays in the military and employment protections from 1992 to 1994, with the exception of those high in political awareness on gays in the military, who understood that the conflict was actually between liberals and conservatives in both parties. Table 5.8, however, reveals that the big political variable on which the gulf on lesbian and gay feelings increases was *ideology* not party. Conservatives stayed about the same, while liberals grew about 8 points warmer in their feelings toward lesbians and gays. Those who were more educated and women also tended to grow more positive toward lesbians and gays.

But why ideology and not party? This analysis was conducted with all respondents, not just those that followed politics closer and may have been responding to the DADT controversy. Why would an ideological divide strengthen here, while a partisan divide had emerged on the specific gay rights issues that the media were discussing at the time? A full answer to this question will emerge in chapters 6 and 7, but the 1993 pilot study of the ANES allows for a preliminary exploration. In addition to ideology and party, the 1993 panel study asked specific questions involving common stereotypes of lesbians and gays and the emotional reactions that people have toward them. This was specifically to study the effects of the DADT debate on public opinion. These include attitudes on the immutability of homosexuality, feelings of disgust toward homosexuality, anxieties that gay coworkers can transmit AIDS in the workplace, feelings

TABLE 5.8. Change in LG Feelings during DADT

	DV: Δ in LG Feelings (1992–93)	DV: Δ in LG Feelings (1992–93)
	Coef. Est. *(S.E.)*	Coef Est. *(S.E.)*
Intercept	−1.902 *(3.843)*	16.515** (5.119)
Party ID	4.707 *(2.861)*	2.705 *(2.957)*
Ideology	8.765* *(4.292)*	2.594 *(4.489)*
Year of Birth	3.514 *(3.608)*	7.440@ *(3.988)*
Gender	3.270* *(1.642)*	0.762 *(1.726)*
Religiosity	−1.389 *(2.113)*	3.292 *(2.230)*
LG Feelings in 92	−0.370*** *(0.035)*	−0.508*** *(0.042)*
Egalitarianism	3.668 *(4.534)*	0.962 *(4.792)*
Education	8.506** *(2.930)*	4.032 *(3.105)*
"Homosexuality Is Not a Choice"		2.847 *(2.679)*
"Gays and Lesbians Are Disgusting"		−13.217*** *(2.568)*
"Worried about Catching AIDS"		−1.194 *(3.236)*
"Homosexuality Is Unnatural"		−5.297@ *(2.782)*
"Gays Will Seduce Heterosexuals"		−4.188 *(2.973)*
Adj. R^2	0.182	0.276
F-statistic	14.74	12.85
σ	17.66	16.5
N	493	405

that homosexuality is unnatural, and a fear that gays and lesbians will try to seduce heterosexuals. Including these measures in a model of lesbian and gay feelings allows us to determine exactly what it may be that is causing this polarization to be ideological in nature rather than partisan.

Model 2 in table 5.8 displays just such an analysis. Ideology, gender, and education all lose statistical significance, meaning that gaps on these variables are so small that they could have occurred due to random chance in terms of the sample of ANES respondents. This suggests that these variables were just proxies for the gay-specific stereotypes and emotions that were added to the model and were not actually responsible for any direct effect. Those who feel that homosexuality is unnatural appear to have grown slightly colder toward gays and lesbians, but the gap changes only by about 5 points on the feeling thermometer. The only other variable that appears to explain shifts in lesbian and gay feelings is if a respondent reported *feeling disgust toward homosexuality*. Generally, most respondents grew 16 points more positive toward homosexuality. However, if respondents reported feeling various levels of disgust at or discomfort from homosexuality, their attitudes remained unchanged from 1992 to 1993. Because liberals and educated people are less likely to report feeling disgust, this explains why ideological polarization took place. Also, older Americans appear to have shifted marginally toward more positive feelings.

Few surveys directly ask respondents about their level of disgust toward homosexuality in general. This means that a cross-time analysis of the impact of disgust on gay rights is not possible. However, political psychology research is beginning to establish that there is a very strong relationship between biological predispositions to feel disgust and political ideology.[19] This connection is important for understanding why ideology may be so much more important than party in terms of its effect on affectively laden feelings toward lesbians and gays in general.

Just what caused this ideological polarization of feelings toward lesbians and gays, based on feelings of disgust, cannot at this point be fully determined. That said, improvement in attitudes clearly occurred among those who did not report feeling disgust and regardless of news consumption. The value for the intercept in the model shows a 16-point increase in feelings for all respondents. The effect is canceled by the 13-point decrease in feelings among those who report disgust. These numbers drop to about 8 and 7 points if we track change from 1992 to 1994 or from 1992 to 1996. This is a small effect, but still substantive. Biological attributions for homosexuality also likely played a role in ideological polarization, as liberals in this time period were overwhelmingly coming to believe that gays are "born that way."[20] This, in turn, increased support for gay rights.[21] However, the rising frequency of the belief that gays and lesbians are "born that way" was actually a very minor part of the story in terms of aggregate change.[22]

The Declining Impact of AIDS in the 1990s

One question never adequately answered but often asked by those studying mass attitudes toward lesbians and gays is how fear of catching AIDS played a role. Presumably, this fear lowered support for gay rights in the early and mid-1980s, but the effect likely declined as the public became more educated about AIDS and as new medical breakthroughs transformed an HIV infection into a manageable condition (for those with access to treatment). The ANES battery of more specific gay-related questions in 1993 allows for an analysis of the role of AIDS in changing feelings toward lesbians and gays.

Since one question specifically asked respondents about their worry over catching AIDS from an HIV-positive coworker, just how strongly responses to this question are related to the feeling thermometer can be assessed. Those asked about their worry of AIDS in 1993 faced the same self-assesment on the feeling thermometer in 1992, 1994, and 1996. In table 5.9, I model these feeling thermometer measures separately as a function of party, ideology, and the five more specific questions asked about gay rights. The demographic categories are dropped here, with the exception of ideology and party, as this analysis seeks to uncover the attitudinal basis of feelings, regardless of any underlying demographic factors that may ultimately influence the answers to the attitudinal questions asked about gay rights. Adding egalitarianism to the mix decreases the effect of ideology by about 2 points, but leaves the other effects mostly unchanged. The effects of egalitarianism is generally about 13 points over time, representing the difference in the thermometer between those at the highest and lowest levels of support for egalitarian values.

Ideology was a fairly consistent and large predictor. Strong liberals and strong conservatives were, on average, roughly 20 points apart,

TABLE 5.9. Change in Feelings toward Lesbian and Gays, 1992–1996

	Model 1 LG Feelings (1992)	Model 2 LG Feelings (1993)	Model 3 LG Feelings (1994)	Model 4 LG Feelings (1996)
	Coef. Est. *(S.E.)*	Coef. Est. *(S.E.)*	Coef. Est. *(S.E.)*	Coef. Est. *(S.E.)*
Intercept	**39.557*** (3.776)**	**44.764*** (3.678)**	**35.040*** (4.238)**	**34.393*** (4.311)**
Party ID	1.782 *(3.272)*	2.411 *(3.211)*	**7.983* (3.630)**	**8.850 * (3.974)**
Ideology	**23.043*** (4.882)**	**13.968** (4.847)**	**18.471*** (5.431)**	**20.759*** (5.844)**
"Homosexuality Is Not a Choice"	**8.306** (3.052)**	**8.059** (2.997)**	**12.114*** (3.459)**	**9.889** (3.510)**
"Gays and Lesbians Are Disgusting"	**−12.868*** (2.880)**	**−18.355*** (2.810)**	**−14.161*** (3.171)**	**−15.010*** (3.287)**
"Worried about Catching AIDS"	**−15.225*** (3.637)**	**−10.191** (3.597)**	**−14.507*** (3.994)**	−3.334 *(4.225)*
"Homosexuality Is Unnatural"	**−10.834*** (3.132)**	**−9.822** (3.084)**	**−8.923* (3.552)**	**−8.712* (3.613)**
"Gays Will Seduce Heterosexuals"	−3.820 *(3.414)*	**−7.675* (3.380)**	−5.459 *(3.810)*	−0.850 *(3.982)*
Adj. R^2	0.462	0.483	0.479	0.438
F-statistic	54.3	58.2	51.9	34.5
σ	19.8	19.32	20.59	19.43
N	435	430	387	302

although at 13 points, the gap was slightly smaller in 1993. The partisan gap also grew over time. While there was no relationship between party and feelings in 1992 and 1993, modest gaps of around 8 points appeared in 1994 and 1996. Those who believed that gays do not choose their orientation and those who believed that being gay is a choice were consistently separated by about 8–12 points over time. Again, disgust is a major explainer of differences in the thermometer scores in this analysis. Those who felt disgust toward homosexuality rated lesbians and gays roughly 15 points lower over time, and somewhat more so in 1993. The belief that homosexuality is unnatural dropped evaluations by roughly 10 points across time. The belief that gays and lesbians will seduce heterosexuals appeared to be predictive only in 1993 at the height of DADT, but only slightly so.

The biggest shift seen in the analysis was the decline in 1996 of fear of contracting AIDS. From 1992 to 1994, this fear was associated with lower ratings of lesbians and gays between 10 and 15 points. By 1996, four years into the Clinton administration and after the discovery of the first generally effective treatment for HIV, the triple cocktail, the effect of reported worry about contracting AIDS on feelings toward lesbians and gays had evaporated. None of the other predictors saw quite as large a decline, which further suggests that the relationship between AIDS and views of lesbians and gays had, at the very least, weakened considerable by the middle of the 1990s.

In terms of change in the aggregate attitudes of the entire sample, however, the effect of this shift was quite small. Only about 13 percent of respondents said that they were worried about catching AIDS from a co-worker in 1993. This means that the net result of the declining relationship between worry over AIDS and feelings resulted in an increase of less than two-thirds of a point on the thermometer in aggregate because of the small proportion of people who expressed fear over AIDS in 1993.

Conclusion

While attitudes toward lesbians and gays started to shift in the early 1990s, these shifts were generally small and occurred mainly among Democrats (on policy issues) or liberals (on general feelings toward lesbians and gays). Conservatives, for the most part, stayed in place or grew less supportive of gay rights. Thus, there is little indication that we are starting to see a broad liberalization of attitudes beyond some modest increases in political polarization on gay rights. These shifts appear to be consistent with the effects that we would expect from elite-signaling on any issue in which the parties take a clear and divergent position: a few percentage point shifts among partisans but no exceptional changes.

It was later in the 1990s that greater changes developed. The decline of worry about AIDS and the increase in support for gay rights among liberals and Democrats may have pushed gay rights support just enough to move it past a tipping point, but the drivers of social change would not come from the political arena. Rather, they would come from a cultural and social revolution that took place in the mid- and late 1990s.

6

Coming Out, Entertainment Television, and the Youth Revolt

Unless you have dialogue, unless you open the walls of dialogue, you can never reach to change people's opinion.
—Harvey Milk, 1978

Decreasing mass anxiety over AIDS and rising tolerance among liberals and Democrats coincided with changes in both the entertainment industry and the behavior of individual lesbians and gays. This chapter tracks these changes and analyses their effects on public opinion. In doing so, two key puzzles raised in the introduction will be addressed in the context of testing the theory of *affective liberalization*: What has caused the magnitude of observed attitude change on lesbian and gay rights to be so large when compared to other changes in mass opinion? Why has this change been concentrated among the young?

In the 1970s and 1980s, what divided members of the public that supported gay rights from those that did not were factors that predisposed some people to be tolerant of all out-groups generally: educational attainment and being exposed to more out groups by living in a densely populated urban area. The early 1990s saw the start of a trend of political polarization on gay rights, as the Left's views grew more liberal as compared to the Right's. This new partisan division became superimposed on the old division that had existed in the 1970s and 1980s. Democrats were growing slightly more supportive of gay rights regardless of where they lived or how much time they had spent attending university. Either way, the attitudinal change on gay rights among political liberals and Democrats in the early 1990s was not out of the ordinary, given the polarization at the elite level on the issue.[1]

As we move into the mid- and late 1990s, the major drivers of change in attitudes, according to the theory of affective liberalization are unleashed: increases in interpersonal exposure to lesbian and gay people and increases in depictions of the lives of lesbians and gays in entertainment media. As more people encountered gays and lesbians in workplaces, public spaces, and in their own homes, and as images and narratives of the lives of lesbians and gays proliferated in literature, film, and television, change in attitudes occurred among nearly all political and social groups. In addition, subtle differences in the ways that younger people and older people process new information about social groups caused a third major fault line to emerge: a separation in support for gay rights between the young and the old.

This chapter discusses the direct causal forces that changed American attitudes on LGBTQ rights. As this chapter shows, this is the time when we see the origin of a rare intergenerational schism in public opinion. First, increases in reported interpersonal contact with lesbians and gays that began in the early 1990s are discussed. Second, the slow proliferation of LGBT characters on American television across the course of 1990s is described in some detail. The timing of these two phenomena suggests that media attention to LGBTQ and AIDS issues in the early 1990s was a precondition for the emergence of both. The chapter then examines the effects of direct and mediated interpersonal contact on attitudinal change using a wide variety of data sources and shows how these forms of contact paved the path to mass support for LGBTQ rights.

Politics at the Personal Level

Although substantial media attention was drawn to lesbian and gay issues in 1992 and 1993, it is likely that many Americans did not pay much attention. Survey research into who watches the evening news or regularly reads newspapers has concluded that a large segment of the public is generally inattentive to, or ignorant of, political developments. This is especially true of younger individuals and those without higher levels of formal education.[2] Thus, it seems unlikely that the developments described in the previous chapters hold the key to the immediate causes of mass liberalism on gay rights. Politics and media may have been able to slightly warm the public's attitudes toward lesbians and gays in the early 1990s, but what brought on the heat wave?

Having cast aside the major political science explanations for change, what was the proximate cause of the social revolution? Figure 6.1 displays

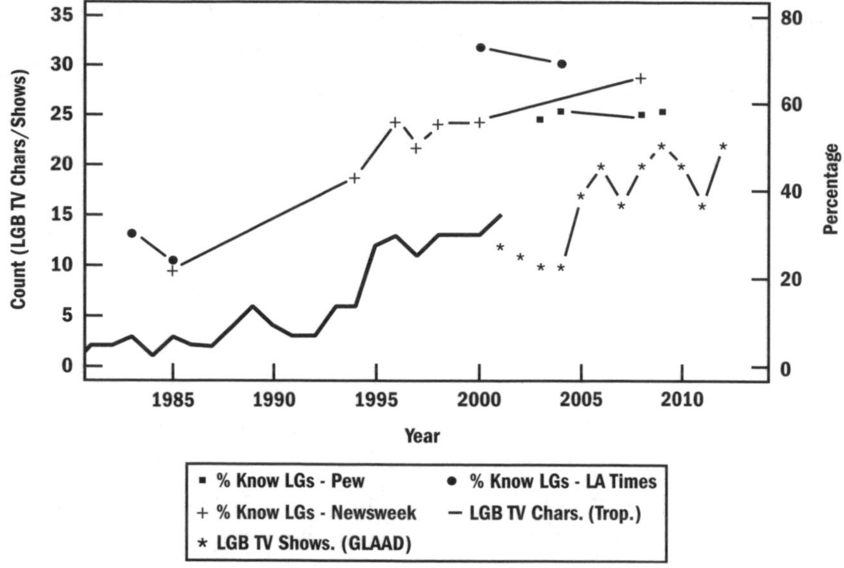

Figure 6.1. Trends in Interpersonal Contact with Lesbians and Gays in Popular Culture.

This figure displays change in the percentage of people that report interpersonal contact with lesbians and gays and counts of prominent lesbian and gay characters on the Big 3 networks (ABC, NBC, CBS). The number of prominent lesbian and gay characters increased dramatically in 1995. The roles of these characters increased in prominence until *Ellen*'s puppy episode in early 1997 and the premier of *Will and Grace* in 1998.

Source: Bowman and Fostor, "Attitudes about Homosexuality and Gay Marriage"; Tropiano, *The Prime Time Closet*; compilation by author from various GLAAD Where We Are on TV documents.

trends from several polling firms that have asked respondents whether they have close friends, acquaintances, family members, or co-workers who are lesbian or gay. The results are unmistakable. Until the late 1980s or early 1990s, few respondents reported knowing lesbians or gays personally. In the 1990s, this proportion ballooned. In the mid-1980s, both the *LA Times* and *Newsweek* reported that between approximately 20 percent and 30 percent of the public knew lesbian or gay people. By the end of the 2000s, both firms were reporting that roughly 70 percent of the public had direct interpersonal contact with lesbians and gays—an increase of between roughly 40 percent and 50 percent. A shift of this magnitude is almost unheard of in terms of survey research and raises serious questions as to its specific causes. The rise of anti-AIDS activism is the first likely cause of these increases in interpersonal contact. The timing of these increases seems to indicate that they occurred contemporaneously with the development of ACT-UP, discussed at the end of chapter 3. Unfortunately, few polling firms asked about interpersonal contact with lesbians and gays from the late 1980s to the start of the 1992 presidential election. This makes it difficult to analytically separate out exactly why lesbian and gay people felt increasingly more comfortable living openly as the 1990s unfolded.

There is strong cause to believe that the wave of LGBT activism in the late 1980s and early 1990s was stronger than prior waves in the 1950s and early 1970s.[3] The devastation that AIDS wrought on the gay community in the early and mid-1980s, in terms of death and despair, eclipsed anything that had happened before. For instance, while the death of Harvey Milk was a horrific event for the lesbian and gay movement, Milk could be mourned and those remaining could move on. AIDS in the early 1980s gave no such respite. We need only to read the accounts of the period to remember this. From Gould, quoting an article by Arnie Kantrowitz in the *Advocate*:

> For centuries we have heard from the heterosexual majority, "You may not live among us as homosexuals." . . . We are now hearing, "You may not live among us" in the form of the threatened compulsory HIV testing and quarantine that several states are actively considering as law. Does it take much imagination to hear in the wind, "You may not live"?[4]

Larry Kramer was more succinct: "I repeat: Our continued existence as gay men upon the face of this earth is at stake. Unless we fight for our lives, we shall die."[5] While prior negative developments in lesbian and gay rights in the 1970s threatened the loss of employment or movement leadership (in the case of Milk's assassination), inaction in the face of AIDS was portrayed by some as aiding in genocide. For many LGBTQ people, their lives and the lives of everyone they knew were in the balance.

There is one problem with this narrative, however. Very few LGBTQ people outside of the urban enclaves likely had direct contact with anti-AIDS activists and anti-AIDS activism in general. Despite this increase in activism, it was still mostly situated in communities in urban areas that already had visible LGBTQ communities of some size.

The major mechanism for the increase in coming out was almost certainly the increase in mass media coverage of AIDS and LGBTQ issues. In the 1970s, the primary mechanism for strengthening the lesbian and gay identity was lesbian and gay-themed organizations in the urban enclaves. However, when resistance to covering lesbian and gay issues in the media finally broke down in the early 1990s, this may have shifted the locus for where those with same-sex attraction learned that they shared their sexual orientation with others and that they were potential members of a larger gay and lesbian community. From 1990 to 1993, the AIDS crisis, the 1992 campaign, and the gays-in-the-military debate were all covered in the national press. This represented the first time that LGBTQ issues were covered in any depth. Recall from chapter 3 that the national media, inadvertently perhaps, may have taken over the role of spreading the lesbian and gay identity outside of the LGBTQ enclaves in major cities, as witnessed by the drop in the average age of people's coming out from their twenties to their high school years in the 1990s. This coverage may have inadvertently caused a strengthening of gay and lesbian identity across the country. Same-sex attracted people in suburban and rural areas, where there were no gay-themed organizations or active lesbian and gay communities, were most affected. As the gay and lesbian identities of people in these areas strengthened and they came out to others, reported contact naturally increased.

While it is likely that few gay or lesbian individuals nationally had direct contact with AIDS activists, especially those outside of the nation's major cities, lesbian and gay individuals across the country had to have been feeling the same mix of negative emotions in reaction to the AIDS crisis that Gould documented among activists in response to coverage of AIDS.[6] As AIDS activists finally began to see their struggle covered by the national media in the early 1990s, lesbians and gays outside of the nation's urban centers may have been inspired to take action based on their identity and the spread of LGBTQ movement framing of AIDS via the mass media[7] and to discuss their lives with friends and family. This would result in increased contact. Not doing so may have also resulted in increased negative emotions. Since the late 1960s, the lesbian and gay movement had encouraged individuals to come out as key to inspiring social change nationally and improving the quality of life for all lesbian and gay people, and now the media began to communicate this encouragement via coverage of AIDS and LGBTQ issues.

As the AIDS crisis deepened and the emotions it raised created a psychological need to engage in actions to both aid the lesbian and gay community and fight the crisis, coming out likely emerged as a relatively straightforward response in the minds of many lesbians and gays, especially those not living in urban areas and not having the opportunity to join activist groups. However, it was at this very time that public fear of AIDS further stigmatized lesbians and gays. These opposing impulses, an increased desire to come out countered by an increased fear of stigma, may have canceled each other out during the peak of the crisis. As the association between AIDS and feelings toward lesbians and gays decoupled during the 1990s, this fear of stigmatization may have decreased and resulted in a delayed boom in coming out in the later 1990s.

Were gays and lesbians coming out only to those whom they perceived as being already supportive of gay rights? Prior research has found that gays and lesbians do assess how supportive individuals are of lesbians and gays generally before choosing to come out to them.[8] Concern that research findings showing a correlation between contact and more tolerant attitudes are due only to these "selection effects" is common in gay rights research.[9] Furthermore, contact with members of social groups tends to be more effective in improving social attitudes when an authority figure (such as Clinton) is approving of the contact.[10] On an intuitive level, lesbians and gays may have anticipated that by coming out to likely supporters of Clinton—political liberals and Democrats—they would be met in a more positive fashion than in the past.

If this is the case, then the gains in contact depicted in figure 6.1 should have been more highly concentrated among political liberals. In figure 6.2, I show the results of several polls that asked respondents about both their interpersonal contact with lesbians and gays and their ideological self-placement. Although lesbians and gays are consistently more likely to come out to political liberals across time, the increases in self-reported contact across the 1990s are roughly the same for liberals, moderates, and conservatives.[11] Lesbians and gays *did not* become more likely to come out to liberals during the 1990s. In fact, figure 6.2

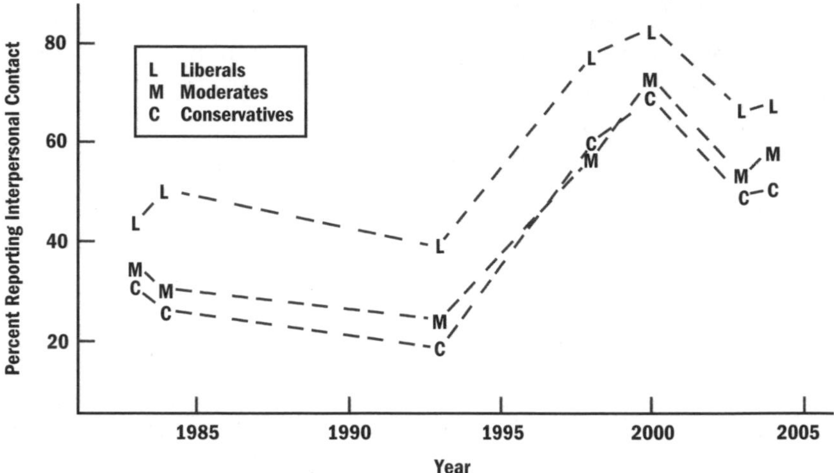

Figure 6.2. The Coming-Out Explosion in the Late 1990s.
Changes in reported contact with lesbians and gays by ideological group from the early 1980s to the early 2000s based on television news polling. Notice that change in interpersonal exposure to lesbians and gays lags the political events of the early 1990s and increases uniformly across political lines of difference. The dip in 1992 may be a question-wording effect.
Source: Calculation by author from various Pew, Gallup, *Newsweek*, *Los Angeles Times*, and *CBS News* polls.

shows that they actually became less politically discriminating in who they come out to. This strongly suggests that "selection effects" regarding those who reported knowing lesbians and gays were on the decline.

The Televised Revolution

In terms of people's exposure to lesbians and gays, nothing has increased more dramatically—other than the likelihood of meeting a lesbian or gay person—than the representation of gays and lesbians on television. In the early 1980s, there were few televised portrayals of lesbians and gays or major lesbian- or gay-related plots on television. What few there were would often reinforce the negative stereotypes of lesbians and gays as being depressed or leading lonely existences.[12] Over the course of the 1990s, representation of homosexuality on television was still the "love that not dare speak its name." In the middle of the decade, homosexuality on television was a controversial issue triggering mass boycotts and generating large amounts of media attention. Finally, by the end of the 1990s, homosexuality became a virtual non-issue among most television viewers. *Modern Family*, a television show featuring a same-sex couple raising an adopted child, was revealed to be one of the most popular shows on television *among Republicans*.[13] The most dramatic shifts in portrayals of homosexuality and the public's reception of these portrayals occurred in the years from 1993 to 1999.

LGBTQ characters on television are important because as discussed in prior chapters, this "mediated" contact may be just as effective in improving attitudes toward outgroups as interpersonal contact. Theoretically, these characters should play on the same mental processes that lead to attitude change as more direct contact. Moreover, fictional characters that are recurring and positive are more likely to result in successful contact, as these factors foster an emotional attachment to the character in the viewer. Thus, a rise in LGBTQ characters in fiction, and especially fictional television, could have a similar effect on mass opinion as a rise in interpersonal contact with LGBTQs.

Such a rise is displayed quantitatively in figure 6.1, which tracks the number of major recurring lesbian and gay characters from 1980 to 2000 on ABC, NBC, and CBS. These data were aggregated from Stephen Tropiano's meticulous list of characters featured in his book *The Prime Time Closet: A History of Gays and Lesbians on TV*.[14] For years after the publication of Tropiano's book, press releases from the Gay and Lesbian Alliance Against Defamation (GLAAD) gave counts of the number of shows with recurring and regular LGBTQ characters on these three networks. In the early 1980s, the series shown on each of the networks had on average less than a single LGBTQ character. Although this number rose to six characters by 1988, it declined back to the early 1980s levels in 1991 and 1993. Real movement did not begin to occur until 1993–1995, when portrayals doubled. Subsequently, they remained high until the end of the decade.

Many studies have tracked and described this shift,[15] but the exact reasons for the rise in lesbian and gay portrayals in the mid-1990s remain elusive. What is likely is that a confluence of mutually reinforcing factors was behind this cultural transformation, all of which unfolded sequentially and reinforced one another across time. They include, in chronological order: (1) the personal experiences of those who worked in the entertainment industry and knew gays affected by the AIDS crisis and who may have felt pressure from AIDS activists to tell the stories of those with AIDS; (2) the gains in tolerance among those on the political Left documented in the previous chapter (a group from which those who work in the entertainment industry may be disproportionately drawn); (3) the subtle effect of having a president (rhetorically) committed to support for lesbian and gay rights; (4) the lack of a drop in ratings when already successful shows (such as *Roseanne* and *Seinfeld*) dealt with homosexuality in the early 1990s; and (5) the success of the film *Philadelphia* in early 1994, which proved that the national market could turn a profit on a film that dealt with homosexuality in a (somewhat) more explicit fashion than in the past.

The rise in lesbians and gays on television may have also been a response to increases in interpersonal contact with lesbians and gays. Conversely, increased portrayals of lesbians and gays on television may have also served a role-modeling function in the 1990s. By providing examples of lesbians and gays openly living their lives, television may have encouraged additional individuals to come out.

I do not wish to suggest that all of these new characters were universally depicted in positive ways. However, I focus on recurring characters in this study and elsewhere, as these characters are more difficult to negatively stereotype, given that interest groups can engage in protests of such depictions more easily than they can sporadic or one-shot characters. Elsewhere, I have discussed how negatively depicted characters can and do reduce tolerance among the public and how recurring positive depictions maybe necessary to increase tolerance among the public.[16]

Regardless of the actual causes of the change in portrayals of lesbians and gays, television introduced homosexuality and homosexual issues to a large proportion of the country for the first time. Changes on the order of magnitude of those seen in figure 6.1 should result in massive changes in public attitudes, according to the research discussed in chapter 2. Also, there is reason to believe that these changes may have given rise to one distinctive development: namely, the recent relative liberalism on gay rights among young people. In the next section, I give a short recap of why this might be the case according to the theory of affective liberalization.

Increases in Exposure and the Rise of Generation Gaps in Gay Rights Support

The political psychology literature has shown that as individuals are exposed to more information about a group or person, the automatic emotional reaction that people have when that group or person is mentioned tends to solidify.[17] Once this happens, new information that contradicts the affectively laden reaction, whether positive or negative, has less of an impact on updating evaluations of a person or group.[18] For instance, the more people read or learn about Hillary Clinton or undocumented immigrants, the more their immediate reactions to that individual or group, either positive or negative, becomes consistent over time.

Because of this, information gained earlier has a primacy effect and is likely to color the interpretation of any new information. Affectively laden feelings formed when the earlier information is encountered will reappear the next time information on the topic is encountered and bias the processing of that new information. Gay rights issues are no different. Someone who has learned only negative information and stereotypes about lesbians and gays will be more likely to have negative emotions spring immediately to mind when seeing a gay or lesbian person appear on his or her television screen. This initial negative impression may then act as barrier to accepting any positive or counter-stereotypical information that follows, including information gained from an encounter with a person known to be lesbian or gay.

Until AIDS activists broke down the media's resistance to reporting on lesbians and gays in the early 1990s, very little positive information about lesbian and gay people was being presented to the public by the media. People also reported little interpersonal contact with lesbians and gays, as figure 6.1 illustrates. This all suggests that individuals who grew up in the 1980s and prior were likely to have developed negative initial emotional reactions to lesbians and gays. These initial reactions could therefore make it more difficult for positive attitudinal change to take place when an older individual met a lesbian or gay person or saw one on television.

A parallel line of research in the public opinion literature suggests that individuals go through a period when their political identities and attitudes toward various political and social groups solidify. The years in which these predispositions are formed, before age thirty or forty, are termed the "impressionable years."[19]

If individuals learn information about lesbians and gays from interacting with them at a personal level or from viewing positive depictions of them on television (particularly counter-stereotypical depictions), it stands to reason that this exposure will be more effective in changing attitudes of younger individuals as compared to older individuals. Meta-analytic findings in social psychology have confirmed that interpersonal contact is more effective in improving attitudes toward outgroups among college students, adolescents, and children as compared to adults.[20] Therefore, there is a strong theoretical and empirical basis for the hypothesis that increases in exposure to lesbians and gays across the 1990s, documented in figure 6.1, may have led to the pronounced gap in gay rights support between younger and older individuals. It is to a direct test of this theory that I now turn.

A Natural Experiment: Emmet's Coming Out on *Grace under Fire* in 1995

Does exposure to LGBTQ characters on television increase support for LGBTQ rights in ways consistent with affective liberalization? Although previous studies have demonstrated that mediated contact with lesbians and gays has an effect on attitudes involving gay rights,[21] these findings were either contingent on using measures of *recalled* television viewing, which may be reported by survey respondents in error or based on experimental designs that may have lacked adequate control conditions.[22]

The early and mid-1990s American National Election Study (ANES) panel study allows for a direct test of these findings in the form of a "natural experiment" that sidesteps such concerns. A natural experiment is a research design that matches as closely as possible a traditional experiment in that exposure to the cause of change is nearly or very nearly random. Recall that the ANES panel study resurveyed the same nationally representative group of respondents in 1992, 1994, and 1996. Half of those respondents were asked a battery of gay rights questions in 1993, the results of which were discussed in the previous chapter. The other half received a battery of questions about their television viewing habits in 1995, including some factual questions about fictional television shows.

Among these factual questions were ones asking the number of children that Grace had on *Grace under Fire* (3–4), the first name of Kramer on *Seinfeld* (Cosmo), and the name of the show on which one would see Dan Connor (*Roseanne*). If a person can answer a question about a program correctly, it stands to reason that she has probably watched that show somewhat regularly. As mentioned before, these knowledge-based questions are often better at determining who is paying attention to (or interested in) something than actual self-reports of attention or interest. Knowledge-based questions can thus be used as a safe measure of who watched certain programs in 1995. The 1994 and 1996 waves of the panel study also asked the standard feeling thermometer questions involving social groups.

The question mentioned above about the fictional program *Grace under Fire* is important. Quite unexpectedly, the writers and creators of the show decided to radically change a traditional, married, heterosexual recurring character: Grace's father-in-law Emmet (played by Bryan Clark). On the December 15th, 1995, episode of the show Grace was shocked to find her father-in-law in a gay sports bar when stopping to ask directions. Emmet then confesses to have been in a hidden gay relationship for fifteen years. Then, in an episode that premiered on December 18, 1995, Emmet passed away suddenly. At his funeral, his lover, Dan, arrived and expressed anguish to Grace over the fact that the relationship was hidden.[23]

This was all after the ANES question involving *Grace* was asked, but before the 1996 wave of the study asked questions on gay rights and the lesbian and gay feeling thermometer. The two episodes provided a powerful and emotionally engaging treatment of a gay relationship, which, if the theory of affective liberalization is correct, should improve affective feelings toward lesbians and gays. Everyone inevitably experiences death, most anticipating it with dread, and this provides an experience that any person can potentially empathize with any other person over. In other words, watching the show should manifest in a positive shift in the feeling thermometer score between the 1994 and 1996 waves. The show had few references to homosexuality prior to the Emmet episodes. This means that individuals were likely not watching *Grace* because of pro-gay messages prior to the Emmet episodes in late 1995. Even if more pro-gay individuals did watch the show, we can control for that using respondents' feelings involving lesbians and gays in 1994. Other shows on the 1995 ANES television battery did have lesbian and gay characters and plotlines (*Roseanne*, for instance), but these were prominent *prior* to the 1995 wave and thus may have been attracting more pro-gay viewers rather than changing the attitudes of regular viewers. It is the sudden shift in *Grace*'s content that makes it the basis for a natural experiment, as this plot shift was unlikely and almost random given the prior content on *Grace*.

I present a regression analysis of the change in the difference in the feeling thermometer scores of lesbians and gays for the respondents of the survey from the 1994 to the 1996 wave in column 1 of table 6.1. The details of this and subsequent regression analyses in this chapter are in the data appendix at the end of the book. The key variable of interest is whether or not individuals can answer the question about *Grace under Fire* correctly. This is a proxy for likely exposure to Emmet.

I also use the number of total correct responses about television programs in general on the ANES battery, not including *Grace*, as a control variable. This is included in case any positive effect on answering the Grace question is just due to higher general television viewing. The feeling thermometer value in 1994 is also included to control for both prior pro-gay attitudes and "ceiling effects" in terms of thermometer value change. Those at higher values in 1994 cannot shift their expressed feelings more positive as compared to those with less warm feelings, and including past values as a control helps deal with this problem. I recommend any readers who are still uncomfortable with such an analysis to return to the description of regression analysis and its interpretation at the end of chapter 2.

In column 2 of table 6.1, I include an interaction of *Grace* with respondent age. This allows for a direct test of whether or not the effect of *Grace* is dependent on year of birth. For this interaction to be significantly sized in terms of the results of the regression analysis, it would indicate that both variables (year of birth and watching Grace) would have to take on large or positive values, rather than just one of the two, for Grace to affect the thermometer score for lesbians and gays. Because younger viewers were less likely to have lived through or to remember

TABLE 6.1. OLS Regressions Predicting Change in Feeling Thermometer Score of Lesbians and Gays from 1994 to 1996

	Model 1		Model 2		Model 3	
	Est.	*S.E*	Est.	*S.E*	Est.	*S.E*
Constant	7.277	*5.428*	9.278	*5.522*@	−1.960	*8.114*
Total TV	−0.237	*0.708*	−0.129	*0.710*	0.086	*0.710*
Grace under Fire	6.155	*2.253**	−7.346	*7.919*	67.934	*19.505**
Party ID (Republican)	−5.870	*3.388*@	−5.544	*3.380*	−5.259	*3.361*
Ideology (Conservative)	6.226	*6.171*	6.058	*6.150*	6.052	*6.109*
Bible = Word of God	3.397	*3.928*	3.587	*3.894*	4.954	*3.919*
Church Attendance	−0.062	*2.917*	−0.159	*2.907*	0.405	*3.919*
Age (Younger)	5.198	*5.020*	0.354	*5.681*	47.347	*25.887*@
Age^2					−43.644	*23.212*@
Education (Years)	5.459	*4.136*	5.847	*4.127*	4.381	*4.156*
Female	0.320	*2.243*	0.630	*2.242*	0.703	*2.237*
African American	−5.115	*4.083*	−5.165	*4.069*	−5.660	*4.051*
Lesbian and Gay Therm. in 94	−0.367	*0.043****	−0.363	*0.043****	−0.359	*0.043****
Grace under Fire *Age			20.276	*11.273*@	−109.003	*57.192*@
Grace under Fire *Age^2					112.711	*48.144**
Adj. R^2	0.240		0.245		0.255	
σ^2	325		323		318	
N	322		322		322	

*** ~ $p < .001$, ** ~ $p < .01$, * ~ $p < .05$, @ ~ $p < .1$ (two-tailed tests)

time periods of heightened anti-gay prejudice, they should not have negative emotions spring to mind when learning Emmet is gay. Young viewers should therefore be more open to changing their views based on Emmet's story. This is a quick test of the hypothesis that cohort effects on attitudes toward lesbians and gays may be partially due to fictional media effects or "parasocial" contact.

Are effects of watching the Emmet episodes in *Grace under Fire* stronger among younger people, as predicted by the theory of affective liberalization? The results in table 6,1 are strong and unequivocal. Not only does the ability to correctly answer a question about *Grace under Fire* predict positive attitude change from 1994 to 1996, but it is also the *only* statistically significant predictor of positive change on the feeling thermometer with the exception of the prior value of the thermometer. Answering the knowledge question on *Grace* correctly corresponds to a shift of 6.2 points in the positive direction on the feeling thermometer from 1994 to 1996. Keep in mind that this is well after the DADT controversy. Although attention to lesbian and gay issues in the news had dropped considerably, the mass public's attitude toward gay rights was still liberalizing at this time. As column 2 of table 6.1 reveals, when an interaction between age and *Grace* is included, it detects a much stronger effect for younger viewers.

What exactly do these results in table 6.1 mean substantively? It turns out that all of the control variables in the regression model earlier are unrelated to the *Grace* effect.

To more clearly illustrate what was actually going on, figure 6.3 plots the change in respondents' feelings toward lesbians and gays from 1994 to 1996 by both age and their ability to answer the *Grace* question correctly. The figure shows that knowledge of *Grace under Fire* has a clear causal effect on feelings toward lesbians and gays and that this effect is heavily dependent on age. Unlike those who were ignorant of *Grace*, few younger respondents who knew about *Grace* developed negative feelings. The feelings of several respondents under age thirty-five warmed by *40 points or more*, a fifth of the possible range of change in feelings of 200 points (corresponding to the difference between a possible drop of 100 points and increase of 100 points). Average shifts among the youngest respondents were 30 points according to the figure. The magnitude of these shifts is astronomical by public opinion standards. They occur

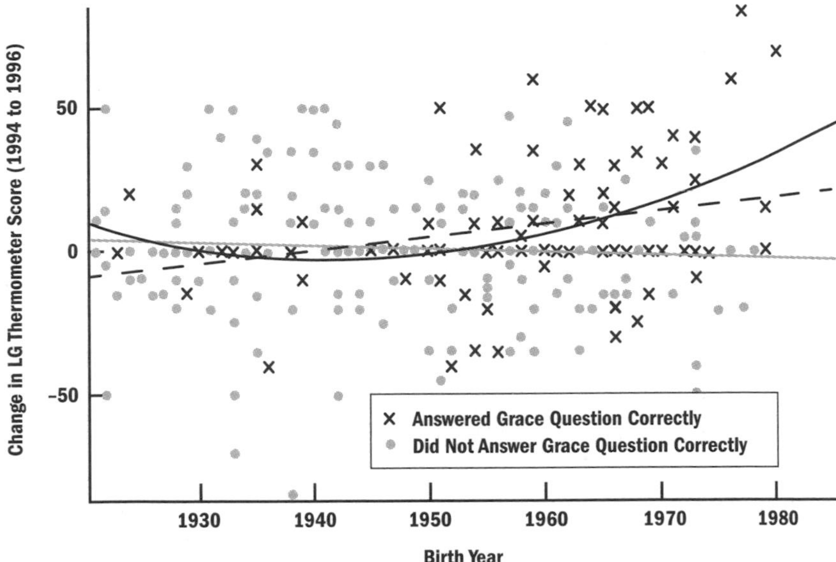

Figure 6.3. Change in LG Feeling Thermometer Score from 1994 to 1996 by Age and Knowledge of *Grace under Fire*.
A character came out on the television show *Grace under Fire* between the 1995 and 1996 waves of the American National Election Study Panel. Knowledge of the show was also assessed with a factual question about the show in 1995. The grey line is a linear regression fit by year of birth for those who either did not answer the *Grace* question or failed to answer it correctly. The dashed black line is the same fit for those who answered it correctly indicating that they likely watched *Grace*. Finally, the black curve represents a quadratic (or birth year^2) fit for those who answered the question correctly. A curve appears to be a much better fit for the relationship.

almost exclusively among younger individuals who knew about *Grace under Fire* and confirm theoretical expectations that younger respondents would be more likely to change their attitudes.

The image also reveals that the effects are not quite linear. That is, they do not diminish uniformly as we move from younger to older individuals. They drop off more quickly from age eighteen to thirty-five. For those over age forty, the effect of knowledge of *Grace* appears to be uniformly zero. Thus, those over age forty appear to be largely immune to the effects of media contact. Because the effect of *Grace* drops off with age, a more appropriate statistical model is a curve, as illustrated in figure 6.3. For the mathematically inclined, I model this relationship as a *quadratic* (or *age-squared*) curve. If the effect is indeed related to age-squared rather than age, then when both age and age-squared are entered into the model as variables, age squared should become statistically significant. The final model in table 6.1 allows for just such a fit.

The Birth of Cohort Effects in the Late 1990s

Although this discussion of a "curved" relationship for the effect of contact on gay rights support based on year of birth, rather than a "linear" relationship may seem a bit technical, this curved relationship of increasing contact effects with younger people occurs with such frequency across datasets that it appears to provide a marker of intergroup contact, even when such contact cannot be directly measured. What does this mean? If we see this curved effect of year of birth appear, it may provide evidence that contact is occurring. In doing so, we gain a way to detect such effects and to gauge their impact on mass attitude change, even on surveys that do not ask about viewing television shows with lesbians and gays or about interacting with lesbians and gays in person. Thus, the presence of these curved effects is actually a big deal for the purposes of testing the theory of affective liberalization, even if they add a little complication to an analysis. If contact effects are much greater among younger individuals, and contact increased in the second half of the 1990s, does this distinctive age-squared effect show up in other public opinion data?

To answer this question, I first turn to the cumulative ANES, rather than just the panel. Recall that in chapters 1, 2, and 5, we discussed this large cross-time survey, which surveys a different nationally representative group of respondents in each year. Using the combined dataset from 1984 to 2008, I modeled feelings toward lesbians and gays as a function of the key known predictors of gay rights regularly asked by the ANES across time in chapter 2. Specifically, I modeled feelings toward lesbians and gays as a function of year, liberalism, party identification, church attendance, gender (female), race (black), and education (all coded the same ways as in the prior statistical analysis at the end of chapter 2). Using this modeling strategy allows us to model the gaps in gay rights support, controlling for or holding constant the other factors or demographics included in the analysis. However, I wanted to allow the effects of most of these variables to change with time. To do that, I interacted all of these variables with dummy variables for the various years of the survey, similar to the analysis in chapter 2. Recall that these interaction terms represented how different in magnitude each of the effects (or gaps) of the demographic variables is as compared to the first year of the survey used (1984).

I also include the *square* of year of birth, as I did in the prior analysis, and interact this with each year. As in chapter 2, the effect of each variable can change dynamically, thereby allowing for an assessment of change in effects over time. This type of analysis leads to a very large table of regression coefficients, which I display in the data appendix at the end of the book for that reason. Coding of these variables are the same as in the analysis at the end of chapter 2.

This model was estimated to test a very specific hypothesis: Does the effect of year of birth change in a fashion consistent with an age-squared effect (or year of birth–squared effect) immediately after the shift in interpersonal and mediated contact in the mid-1990s? If so, then the interaction of year of birth and year of birth–squared in the late 1990s should be significantly larger than the effect in 1984 and the years immediately after. Figures 6.1, 6.2, and the earlier discussion suggest the peak years of this increased exposure should be 1996–2000.

In 1984, there was no evidence of year of birth effects, or differences between the young and the old, on affective feelings toward lesbians and gays according to the results in the data appendix. The full model suggests that the year of birth–squared effect was zero as late as 1992. However, after 1992, the year of birth effect rose slightly in a statistically insignificant fashion until 1996. In 1998, a curved effect of year of birth skyrocketed in size and became statistically significant. This curved effect receded in magnitude in 2000, before becoming a typical linear effect.

Figure 6.4 displays the shift in year of birth effects in the year 1998 graphically from the baseline of no discernable effect in 1984. It matches the shape of the year of birth effects among the *Grace* viewers almost exactly. Changes in the feeling thermometer score for most individuals are less than ten points in 1998 and only marginally statistically significant for older respondents versus the 1984 baseline. But among the younger respondents in 1998, the effects are twice that size—20 points—and

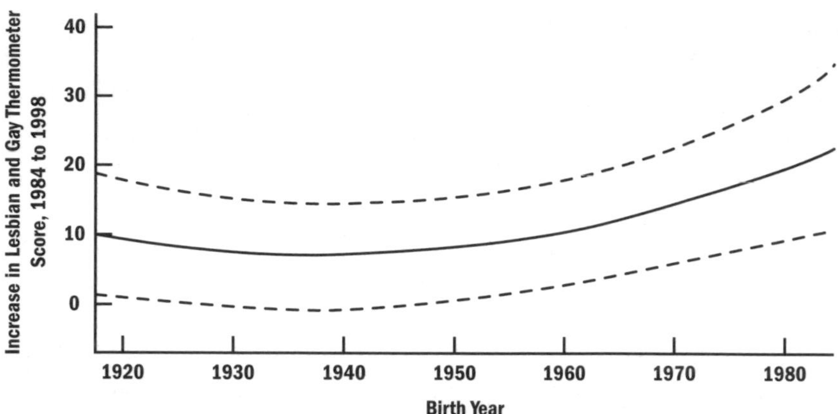

Figure 6.4. Change in Feelings toward Lesbians and Gays by Year of Birth (cumulative ANES) in 1998.

Using the larger cumulative ANES, this figure illustrates the emergence of the same distinctive cohort effect as found in the separate *Grace under Fire* analysis.

clearly large enough that statistical significance is no longer an issue. Similar figures for other years find no large effects concentrated among the youngest respondents in this quadratic fashion with the exception of a more modest quadratic effect in 2000.

The results show that the age-squared effect appeared in survey data in the late 1990s, and not just among the viewers of *Grace under Fire*. A similar "ordered probit" analysis of the GSS's same-sex relations question also reveals the same age-square effects, although they peak just prior to those in the ANES in 1996 rather than 1998.

Interpersonal and Mediated Contact: Two Sides of the Same Coin?

In the *Grace under Fire* natural experiment, I isolated effects of mediated contact with a television character and showed that the effects of this mediated contact were strongest among young people. In the previous section, I showed that younger people's distinctive liberalism in affective feelings toward lesbians and gays appears to have emerged in the late 1990s, at the same time that interpersonal and mediated contact boomed.[24]

The *Grace under Fire* analysis showed that mediated contact resulted in cohort effects in terms of attitudes toward gay rights. Does interpersonal contact with lesbians and gays do the same? Is it both mediated contact *and* interpersonal contact that pushed young people to become disproportionately more liberal on gay rights in the late 1990s, or just mediated contact?

Unfortunately, the ANES did not asked respondents if they know any lesbian or gay people. However, television news polls since the mid-1980s have asked individuals if they know any lesbians or gays somewhat frequently, so they can be used to examine whether knowing lesbians and gays has an effect similar to that of mediated contact. This motivated the collection of a unique set of cross-time television news polls that asked respondents if they had direct contact with any lesbians or gays. This dataset was also put together to control for a second hypothesis—that increases over time in the belief that individuals are born lesbian or gay has influenced mass attitude liberalization, which is often put forth as another potential cause of change on attitudes toward gay rights. Thus, I collected any surveys that asked about these beliefs, contact with lesbians and gays, and viewpoints on employment protections for gays. A total of six surveys (taken in 1983, 1985, 1993, 1998, and twice in 2000) from the *LA Times*, *CBS News*, the *Washington Post*, and *Newsweek* asked these questions. All of these surveys measured other key predictors of gay rights support: ideological identification, party identification, education, race (black), gender (female), and year of birth. Collecting this dataset allows for both a much more nuanced examination of the effects of both interpersonal contact and mediated contact over time and for a check that my results do not disappear when controlling for changing views on the origins of homosexuality. Interpersonal contact is measured as 1 if someone states on the survey that he or she knows lesbians, gays, or bisexuals and 0 otherwise. Also included as a variable is the number of lesbian, gay, and bisexual television characters active in each year (as demonstrated in figure 6.1). Most research and theories on attitude change in political communication and on change in lesbian and gay rights tend to focus specifically on hard and soft news. Because television news is also important, I also include my measure of television evening news attention to lesbian and gay issues (see figure 3.1).

I am specifically interested in whether interpersonal and cultural experiences with lesbians and gays are felt more powerfully for the very young. Thus, I include year of birth and its square in the model and interact both of these with reported interpersonal contact and the number of lesbian and gay characters in a given year. I also interact the year of birth variables with the number of television news stories on lesbian and gay issues, although I do not expect to find a quadratic or curved age effect due to television news stories, as these do not represent recurring exposure to lesbians and gays in most instances.

If interpersonal and cultural contact are both cognitively processed in a similar fashion, with affective feelings playing a mediating role on change in gay rights, then their effects on support for gay and lesbian employment protections should *both* be curved in age as they were in the previous models. The model fits are displayed in table 6.2. Figure 6.5 graphically shows the joint differences in support for employment protections by cohort, levels of lesbian and gay fictional television representation, and knowing gays and lesbians, keeping all other variables constant, and is generally easier to interpret than the regression table.

The results in figure 6.5 illustrate that as exposure to lesbians and gays increases, either interpersonally or through television, the probability of supporting job protections for lesbians and gays goes up by birth year and the effects of increased contact—either interpersonally or through the cultural representation of lesbians and gays—are disproportionately large among the youngest respondents. Specifically, the change in the probability of support for gay rights is 10 to 20 percent larger for younger individuals versus older individuals in the pressence of either form of contact—a very large effect for social science data. In contrast, when cultural representation of lesbians and gays is low, the effect of year of birth on support for gay rights is actually *reversed* among those who also do not know any lesbians or gays. Younger individuals are about 5 percent *less* likely to support gay employment protections than older people in this scenario. This fits with older research based on data from the early 1990s, which found that support for employment protections was *higher* among older individuals.[25] In the context of the 1980s—with its low levels of reported contact with lesbians and gays and low cultural representation—these earlier findings make perfect sense based on the theory of affective liberalization.

TABLE 6.2. Year of Birth and Contact Effects on Gay Rights Support (Media Polls)

	Coef. Est. *(S.E.)*
Intercept	−2.219*** *(0.489)*
Reported Contact with LGs	1.197** *(0.486)*
"Born Gay" Belief	0.895*** *(0.068)*
Year of Birth	3.316@ *(2.162)*
Year of Birth^2	−3.206 *(2.255)*
Education	0.535*** *(0.084)*
Gender (Female)	0.179** *(0.053)*
Race (African American)	0.010 *(0.083)*
Democrat	0.307*** *(0.072)*
Independent	0.149* *(0.061)*
Liberal	0.880*** *(0.078)*
Moderate	0.449*** *(0.061)*
LGB TV Characters	0.202*** *(0.057)*
LGB TV News Stories	0.014 *(0.019)*
Year of Birth * LGB Chars.	−0.465* *(0.226)*
Year of Birth * LGB News	−0.001 *(0.079)*
Year of Birth * Contact	−3.499@ *(1.896)*
Year of Birth^2 * LGB Chars.	0.451* *(0.213)*
Year of Birth^2 * LGB News	0.018 *(0.078)*
Year of Birth^2 * Contact	3.957* *(1.779)*

(*continued*)

Table 6.2. Year of Birth and Contact Effects on Gay Rights Support (Media Polls) (*continued*)	
	Coef. Est. *(S.E.)*
σ | Intercept	0.142
σ | Year of Birth	0.451
σ | Year of Birth²	0.038
AIC	8681.1
Deviance	8639.1
N	8214

*** ~ p < .001, ** ~ p <. 01, * ~ p < .05, @ ~ p < .1 (two-tailed tests)

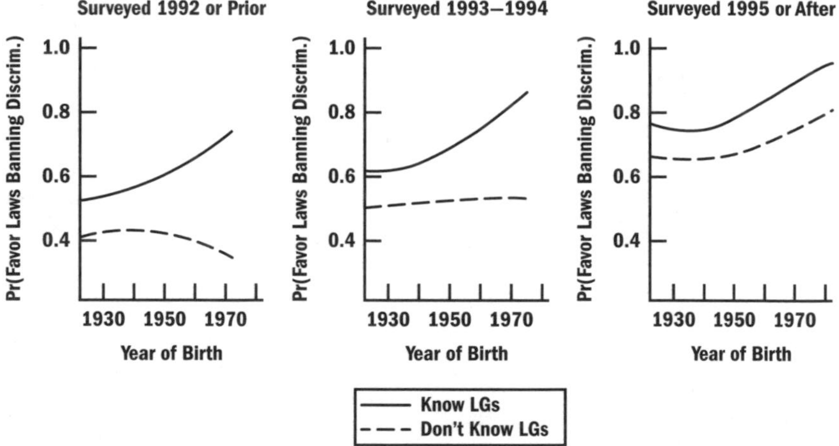

Figure 6.5. Change in the Probability of Supporting Employment Protections for Lesbians and Gays by Year of Birth, Reported Contact with Gays, and the Number of Television Portrayals of Lesbians and Gays, early 1980s to 2001.

This image depicts the change in the year of birth effects among both those who did and those who did not report contact with lesbians and gays as cultural representation of gays increased. The first panel analyzes survey data from 1992 and prior, when there were few televised portrayals of lesbians or gays in those years. The second examines data from 1993 and 1994, when there was an intermediate number of portrayals. The final panel examines data from 1995 to 2001, when those portrayals were common. The horizontal axis in each figure is the respondents' year of birth. Notice that only younger individuals who report contact or who live in time periods with higher levels of televised contact are generally more liberal on gay rights than older individuals. Also, the age effects are inverted for those who report no contact when television representation of lesbians and gays was low. These inverted cohort effects on support for employment protections match prior findings from before 1993.

Turning to the model in table 6.2, we see that liberalism, education, and the view that lesbians and gays are born gay also have considerable effect on gay rights support, depending on if respondents are high or low on these factors. These effects are generally smaller, however, than the joint effects of birth cohort with interpersonal and mediated exposure to lesbians and gays. Other control variables have even smaller effects. Race and television news are the only variables to have to no statistically discernable impact.

Mediated Exposure and Television Usage

We have just analyzed exposure to lesbian and gay characters in terms of an annual count of LGBTQ television characters, but there is a possibility that some omitted variable that resembles this increase may be responsible for the positive findings. Although the last model includes controls for the most prominent of these—namely, views that individuals are born gay and actual interpersonal contact with lesbians and gays—there may be doubt in the minds of some that television is responsible for these effects, although the results of the natural experiment are not so easy to explain away.

In this section, I test to see if these effects of the annual number of lesbian and gay characters are related to reported television usage. If the effect is greater for those who report watching television, then this finding will constitute strong evidence that the contextual effects found earlier are due to television programming.

The General Social Survey frequently asks individuals to estimate the number of hours they watch television, and, like the ANES, asks a different nationally representative sample of Americans the same questions every year or so. The major difference between this survey and the ANES is that the former is run mostly by sociologists rather than political scientists. Recall that this survey also asks a question on approval of same-sex relations, as discussed in chapter 1. This allows for a test to see if the contextual effects of the number of lesbian and gay characters on the major channels are stronger for those who watch television versus those who do not.

Reported use of television, particularly in the context of television news, is generally viewed with suspicion by media researchers (as opposed to knowledge-based measures such as the measure used in the natural experiment). The validity of reports of general television exposure have not been studied as extensively, however. It turns out that self-reported television consumption is directly related to both reported viewing of *individual* fictional television programs and the preferred knowledge-based measures of fictional television programming used in the natural experiment discussed earlier.[26] This suggests that self-reported television viewing indeed measures actual television watching.

Turning to the analysis, I use the cross-time responses to the General Social Survey's same-sex relations question as discussed in chapter 1. I created a statistical model based on the work of Loftus.[27] My dependent variable is if the respondent said that same-sex relations are "not wrong at all" (= 1; 0 otherwise), the most liberal response on the GSS.

As with the news polling dataset, I entered the number of television news stories relating to lesbian and gay issues and the number of lesbian and gay characters as aggregate annual variables. These are interacted with self-reported television usage to examine if the relationship between the number of characters on these channels and support for same-sex relationships are greater for those that report more television viewing. I split the sample in two groups: those born prior to the start of 1956 and those born after. The evidence presented earlier suggests strongly that there is no effect of mediated contact for those born in the earlier time period. It makes little sense to find an effect among older individuals given the earlier results. Table 6.3 displays the fitted model for those born before and after 1955.

For younger respondents, the effect of the annual number of lesbian and gay characters is positive and increases strongly as respondents report more television usage. The relative change in the effect size of this variable is contingent on television usage as displayed in figure 6.6. The effect of each additional television character on support for same-sex relationships increases with reported hours of viewing. Moving from zero hours upward, the effect of each additional LGBTQ character on gay rights becomes statistically larger at five hours of viewing (as compared to the effect at zero hours of viewing) where it has nearly doubled in size. The effect at zero hours is due to the strong cross-time correlation in increases in interpersonal contact and media contact that cannot be modeled separately in the dataset displayed in figure 6.1 (as interpersonal contact has not been commonly asked on the General Social Survey). If

TABLE 6.3. GSS Same-Sex Relations Approval, Television Viewing, and LGBTQ Television Representation

	Model 1 (Born 1956 or After)	Model 2 (Born 1955 or Before)
	Coef. Est. *(S.E.)*	Coef. Est. *(S.E.)*
Intercept	−4.209*** *(0.602)*	−3.623*** *(0.455)*
Ideology (Conservatism)	−0.255*** *(0.041)*	−0.244*** *(0.031)*
Party (Republican)	−0.108*** *(0.029)*	−0.059 *(0.022)*
African American	−0.728*** *(0.175)*	−0.460*** *(0.148)*
Other (Non-White) Race	−0.592** *(0.211)*	−0.318 *(0.255)*
Gender (Female)	0.522*** *(0.100)*	0.397*** *(0.079)*
Education	0.106*** *(0.022)*	0.096*** *(0.014)*
South Atlantic	−0.152 *(0.233)*	−0.468** *(0.175)*
North Central	−0.255 *(0.219)*	−0.445** *(0.161)*
South Central	−0.836*** *(0.248)*	−0.774*** *(0.198)*
Mountain	−0.222 *(0.268)*	−0.118 *(0.204)*
Pacific	−0.155 *(0.232)*	−0.105 *(0.167)*
Mid-Atlantic	−0.184 *(0.229)*	−0.304@ *(0.167)*
Rural Childhood	0.376*** *(0.100)*	0.264*** *(0.080)*
Lib./Mod. Protestant	−0.248 *(0.221)*	0.067 *(0.238)*
Fund. Protestant	−0.458@ *(0.241)*	−0.119 *(0.253)*
Catholic	0.152 *(0.120)*	0.122 *(0.098)*
Jewish	0.761* *(0.352)*	0.666 *(0.19)*
Religious Attendance	−0.133*** *(0.024)*	−0.172*** *(0.017)*

(*continued*)

TABLE 6.3. GSS Same-Sex Relations Approval, Television Viewing, and LGBTQ Television Representation (*continued*)

	Model 1 (Born 1956 or After)	Model 2 (Born 1955 or Before)
	Coef. Est. *(S.E.)*	Coef. Est. *(S.E.)*
Biblical Interpretation	−0.594*** *(0.145)*	−0.869*** *(0.143)*
Interracial Marriage	1.258*** *(0.258)*	1.441*** *(0.150)*
Premarital Sex	0.462*** *(0.049)*	0.237*** *(0.027)*
Extra-Marital Sex	0.134* *(0.049)*	0.162*** *(0.032)*
TV Consumption	−2.235 *(1.443)*	−1.053 *(1.420)*
LGB News Stories	0.010 *(0.008)*	−0.007 *(0.009)*
LGB TV Characters	0.055** *(0.018)*	0.061** *(0.020)*
LGB News * TV Cons.	0.000 *(0.050)*	0.050 *(0.048)*
LGB Char. * TV Cons.	0.273** *(0.103)*	−0.016 *(0.118)*
σ | Intercept	0.000	0.174
σ | TV Consumption	0.586	1.201
AIC	2724.1	4582.5
Deviance	2662.1	4520.5
N | Individuals	3093	6969
N | Years	12	12

*** ~ p < .001, ** ~ p <. 01, * ~ p <. 05, @ ~ p < .1 (two-tailed tests)

these results were due only to interpersonal contact, however, we would not see them strengthen along with television consumption. In fact, we would suspect that they would decrease with greater viewing, as more time spent watching television generally corresponds with less time to interact with other people interpersonally, including lesbians or gays, especially at extremely high levels of television usage.

No such differences in support by television viewing and annual number of characters were found among the older respondents. The

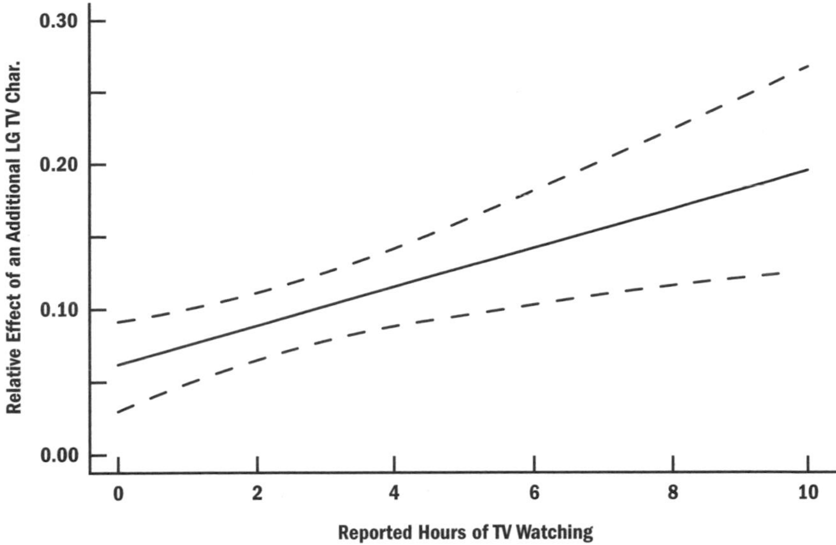

Figure 6.6. The Marginal Effect of an Additional Lesbian or Gay Television Character on Support for Same-Sex Relations.

direct effect of increases in television characters, unmediated by television usage, is similarly sized when compared to younger individuals who do not watch television. Television news, as in the earlier analysis, has no effect for either group. This is strong evidence that, at least for younger people, fictional television can be a source of positive exposure to the lives of lesbians and gays and matters significantly more than television news in terms of support for gay rights.

Conclusion

The 1990s saw a dramatic increase in interpersonal and mediated contact with lesbians and gays. At the start of the decade, when only about one-third of individuals knew lesbians or gays and few lesbian and gay characters were on television, the bulk of liberalization on gay rights had not yet begun (as demonstrated in the first chapter). Likewise, younger people were as likely to be as intolerant of lesbians and gays as older people. By the end of the decade, exposure dramatically changed the magnitude of support for lesbian and gay rights. As individuals encountered newly out lesbians and gays interpersonally, their likelihood of supporting gay rights increased. Depending on the person's age and the time period of the encounter, the result was a 10–35 percent increase in support for gay rights among the third of the public that reported knowing lesbians and gays in the late 1990s, but not in the 1980s.

The results are more impressive when we factor in mediated exposure. For those who did not meet any lesbian or gay people by end of the 1990s, increasing depictions of lesbians and gays on television and other forms of popular culture also had a liberalizing effect on the same order of magnitude as that of interpersonal contact: 10–35 percent, depending on age, and controlling for other prominent explanations of changed views on lesbian and gay rights, such as the increasing belief that lesbian and gays are born gay and increases in televised news attention to lesbian and gay issues. These findings are consistent with those discussed in chapter 1 concerning the 15 percent rise in public support for employment protections in this time period. As figure 6.1 indicates, roughly 70 percent of the public met lesbians or gays or likely saw them substantively portrayed on television for the first time in the 1990s.With 70 percent of the public gaining exposure, and that exposure causing a 10 to 35 percent increase in support among those members of the public, increased contact easily explains the 15 percent increases in gay rights support across issues described in chapter 1 without the need for any additional explanations such as value-framing or elite signaling. Additionally, young people's greater sensitivity to contact meant that younger Americans liberalized much faster than older Americans. The net effect of this was that an entire generation (the youngest members of Generation X and the Millennials) has significantly more positive affect toward lesbians and gays, and because of that, higher levels of support for gay rights.

Despite this new public tolerance and overwhelming majorities in favor of allowing gays in the military and laws banning employment discrimination, by the end of the 1990s, gay rights did not disappear as a political issue. We saw evidence of this in chapter 4, as Republican members of Congress remained largely opposed to lesbian and gay rights. In fact, with the start of same-sex marriages in the early 2000s, political conflict on lesbian and gay rights intensified, and same-sex marriage went on to play a prominent role in the 2004 presidential election. Just as Democrats and political liberals diverged from mass opinion on gay rights in the early and mid-1990s, strong conservatives resisted this liberalizing trend and found their attitudes to be out-of-step in the 2000s. In the next chapter, I complete my story of attitude change in the United States by explaining just why political conflict regarding gay rights has persisted in the United States despite the effects of increased exposure to lesbians and gays.

7

The Persistence of Political Conflict over Gay Rights

> The National Gay and Lesbian Task Force frequently receives calls from same-sex couples asking for a list of states in which they can legally marry. These individuals see shows like "Will and Grace" or "Dawson's Creek." They worship in churches or synagogues that welcome them. They are out in the workplace or at school. They just assume, like many heterosexual Americans, that the barriers of discrimination have been eradicated. . . . The reality, of course, is quite different.
>
> —Elizabeth Toledo, Executive Director of the NGLTF, April 5, 2000

Increased interpersonal and mediated exposure to lesbians and gays appears to provide a compelling explanation for the bulk of attitude liberalization on homosexuality. This increased exposure, which began in the mid-1990s, has continued to rise to this day. For instance, in 2014, Pew reported that 87 percent of the public knew at least one lesbian or gay person—an astoundingly high number.[1]

Furthermore, for reasons of self-interest, corporate America came to see the gay and lesbian community as an acceptable niche market. This likely encouraged the normalization of portrayals of lesbians and gays in entertainment programming. Insofar as the viewers of these programs were likely to be disproportionally gay or pro-gay, advertisers had an easy way to reach this new market. In addition to near universal interpersonal exposure to lesbians and gays reported on surveys, 2012 and 2013 produced record numbers of lesbian and gay characters on the "Big 3" networks (ABC, NBC, and CBS).

A tipping point thus occurred in the late 1990s or early 2000s, and increases in coming out and support for gay rights began to be mutually reinforcing. As negative affect dissipated, public disapproval of homosexuality could no longer provide an effective cudgel to force lesbians and gays to keep their lives hidden. Consequently, one would expect that as ever larger majorities of the public began to support lesbian and gay rights, first on employment protections and more recently on same-sex marriage, opposition on the part of elected officials would wane.

There is ample evidence, however, that this has not occurred.[2] As of 2017, it was still legal to discriminate based on sexual orientation in employment in twenty-six states. The national version of the Employment Non-Discrimination Act (ENDA), considered by many lesbian and gay activists to be the most important piece of gay rights legislation, has not been passed into law. This is odd. Not only does the majority of constituents in all fifty states support nondiscrimination laws, but every single congressional district also has a majority of constituents in support of such laws.[3] It certainly appears as if unelected federal judges and justices, rather than elected officials, are more often than not the ones advancing gay rights. Either way, a disjunction has opened up between the preferences of the public and the actions taken by elected officials in support of gay rights once in office.

Of course, as previous chapters have made clear, not all elected officials have been unresponsive to changing attitudes. Same-sex marriage and ENDA have now been co-sponsored by nearly every Democrat in Congress. However, only a handful of Republican members of Congress have endorsed or co-sponsored pieces of legislation that represent either of these positions. Before the Supreme Court legalized same-sex marriage nationally in 2015, the order in which states legalized same-sex marriage followed an interesting pattern. Of the states (and the District of Colombia) that voted for either John Kerry or Al Gore, the two Democratic nominees for President in the early 2000s, all but Michigan and Wisconsin allowed same-sex couples to marry by the summer of 2014.[4] None of the states that voted twice for George W. Bush allowed such unions at that time. Most of the states that allowed same-sex marriage were legislatively controlled by Democrats, while the majority of the states without same-sex marriage had at least one branch of government controlled by Republicans.

Despite mass attitude change, as we move up the ladder of political activity from liberals and conservatives in the public to liberal and conservative activists to members of Congress, we find more and more political polarization on the issue of gay rights. This elite polarization has not declined as the mass public has liberalized. On the contrary, it has intensified. It is as if the more politically active people are, the more likely they are to adopt their ideological group's position on gay rights, regardless of any national trends.

This chapter examines why, despite increased exposure to lesbians and gays and the liberalizing effects of that exposure, the old political divisions on lesbian and gay rights have not only endured, but have continued to thrive. I suggest that liberals and conservatives who are highly knowledgeable about politics have engaged in what is known as *motivated reasoning*. When individuals engage in motivated reasoning, they become increasingly likely to seek out and process information in ways that confirm predispositions, thereby reinforcing existing attitudes.[5] A growing literature has found that new information on an issue on which the stances of the political parties are clear and divergent is especially likely to trigger this politically motivated reasoning.[6] The net impact of this process on gay rights attitudes is that liberals are more likely to adopt pro-gay positions when exposed to lesbians and gays,[7] while conservatives are increasingly likely to engage in mental gymnastics to resist the effect of pro-gay intergroup contact and maintain consistency in holding uniformly "conservative" beliefs.

This increased incentive for liberals to change may have contributed to the rapidity of public opinion changes in the 1990s and 2000s. Conversely, motivated reasoning may have led conservatives, and especially politically astute conservatives, to discount any exposure to lesbians and gays that displaced negative stereotypes. Many conservative activists and elected officials personally know lesbians and gays, but have either ignored any positive information gleaned from that contact or relied on older political rationales for not supporting gay rights when anti-gay views are threatened by any such positive exposure. In fact, anti-gay attitudes can sometimes be reinforced for conservatives when this intergroup contact occurs, as I demonstrate later in this chapter.

No doubt, subconstituency politics is in play among elected officials. Recall from chapter 4 that the theory of subconstituency politics predicts that elected officials will deviate from the majority preferences of their constituents on a public policy issue if a minority group incentivizes that deviation by providing political and campaign resources. In this case, socially conservative constituents may be providing resources in such a manner to Republican elected officials.

At the same time, as demonstrated in this chapter, strong conservatives in the public and conservative activists without ties to any given constituency appear to be as resistant to change. Given that by the early 2000s, roughly 60–70 percent of the public reported contact with lesbians and gays, how have anti-gay subconstituencies managed to maintain their views in the face of such change? Motivated reasoning explains why these subconstituencies (strong conservatives and the Religious Right), as well as elected conservatives, have been largely immune to the liberalizing effect of increased exposure to lesbians and gays. It also explains why a small, but politically influential group of citizens remains anti-gay and why gay rights rarely advance in political arenas dominated by Republicans, even when supermajorities of the population generally favor gay and lesbian rights.

This chapter addresses how the political system has reacted to change in mass support for LGBTQ issues, focusing mainly on the Republican Party. After first describing the existing political divide on LGBTQ rights support, I consider the psychological process of motivated reasoning in greater detail. This process suggests that those committed to a political or religious ideology will actively resist attitude change when it contradicts some component of that ideology. I then demonstrate that the effects of exposure to LGBTQ people or LGBTQ characters are remarkably different for strong liberals and strong conservatives. Lastly, using an original psychology experiment, I demonstrate that providing a political frame that activates people's political ideologies results in polarization on LGBTQ rights across the lines of ideological difference rather than causing increases in tolerance as seen in the last chapter. This explains why conservative and religious right activists continue to resist support for LGBTQ rights despite exposure to lesbian and gay people and why public policy on lesbian and gay rights has lagged public opinion so drastically.

The Ideological Gulf on Gay and Lesbian Rights

Before outlining just how motivated reasoning works, it is worth pointing out that as we shift our focus from mass opinion to elite opinion, attitudes on lesbian and gay issues become increasingly polarized. Furthermore, this polarization tends to persist on the most prominent gay rights issues of the day—employment protections and same-sex marriage.

While figure 1.5 displayed the trend from the 1970s onward in the responses to the General Social Survey (GSS) questions regarding support for same-sex relations, figure 7.1 breaks down this trend by ideological group. The familiar findings of the previous chapters immediately become clear. Liberals began to change their attitudes during the 1992 campaign and the 1993 gays-in-the-military debate, while conservatives changed little in those years. In the middle of the 1990s, as exposure began to increase, attitude liberalization continued modestly among moderates and liberals and, to a very small degree, among conservatives. The largest increases among conservatives have taken place in the last few years, but even these are tiny compared to the changes seen among liberals and moderates. This makes sense, given that conservatives had less interpersonal contact with lesbians and gays than liberals or moderates, as the previous chapter showed. Only after rates

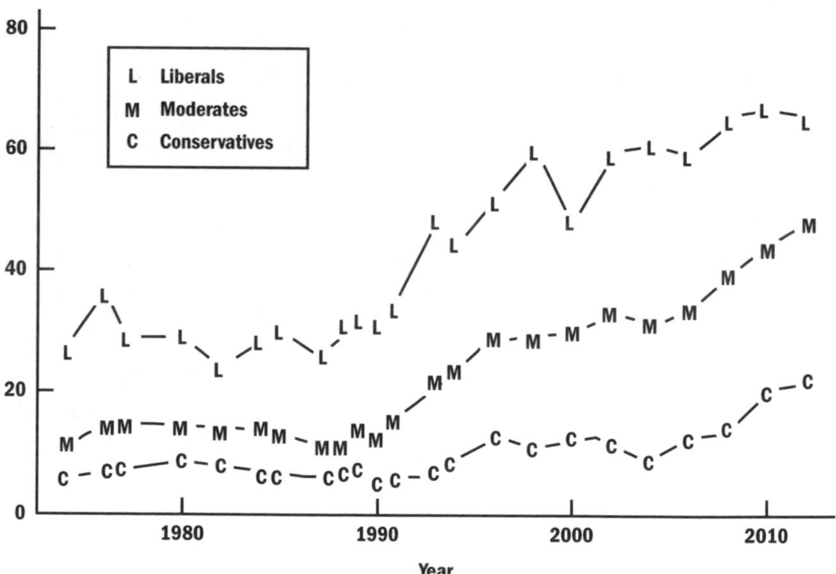

Figure 7.1. Percentage of Respondents Reporting Same-Sex Relations Are "Not Wrong at All," 1974–2012.
Source: Calculation by author from Smith et al., *General Social Surveys, 1972–2016*.

of mediated contact started to rise in the mid-1990s did they begin to liberalize to the extent that they did; they did not do so in response to Clinton's endorsement of gay rights before that.

The general trend seen in attitudes on the same-sex relations question on the GSS matches recent trends in support for same-sex marriage on other surveys. Same-sex marriage has been regularly polled by the Pew organization since Massachusetts legalized it in 2003. Pew's breakdown in support by ideological group is displayed in figure 7.2,[8] which shows that as the public has rapidly liberalized, the gap between liberals and conservatives on same-sex marriage has remained remarkably consistent at 35–50 percent. Liberals and moderates have increased their support by about 25 to 30 percent. Conservatives have increased it by a more modest 15 percent.

That is not to say that conservatives (in the mass public) have been completely unchanged by the events of the last twenty-five years. When we move to other prominent gay rights policies, such as support for employment protections and gays in the military, public opinion among conservative Americans has changed radically. In the 2012 round of the ANES, 54 percent of conservatives supported employment protections

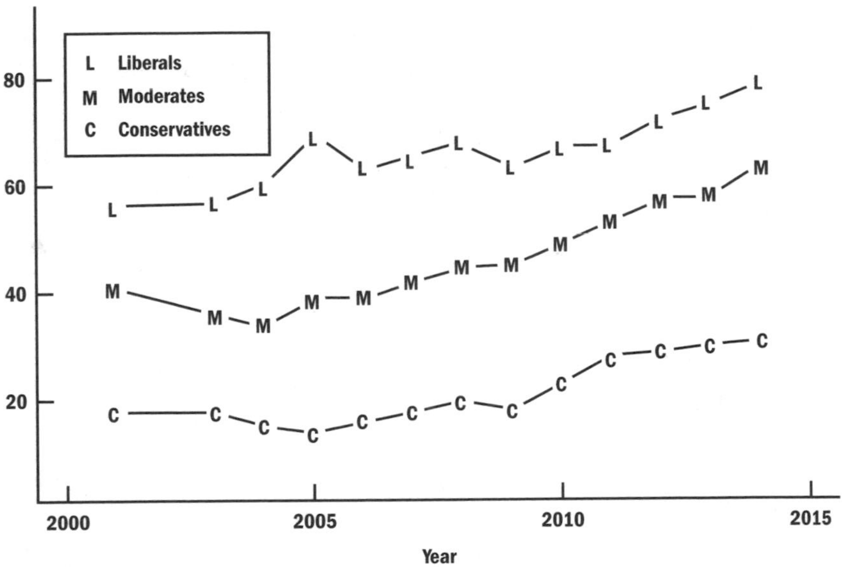

Figure 7.2. Percentage of Respondents in Favor of Same-Sex Marriage, Early 2000s. *Source*: Various Pew Polls, www.people-press.org.

for lesbians and gays and 70 percent supported allowing gays and lesbians to serve openly in the military. The feeling thermometer on the cross-time ANES also revealed a warming of affective reactions toward lesbians and gays among conservatives in the 1990s as mediated exposure increased (see also figure 1.5).

Change among conservatives on gay rights, however, has not taken place among those who are in a position to actually implement gay rights policy or to influence those who are. That is to say, change among conservatives has been largely among those who are the least politically active or influential. The best way to gauge change among political activists, whose support is generally necessary to win elections and who represent the face of their respective parties in their communities, is to examine surveys of the convention delegates who attend the Democratic and Republican National Conventions every four years. In 2004 and 2008 these surveys asked a three-point question involving support for either same-sex marriage or civil unions for same-sex couples. Support among the Democratic delegates for marriage equality increased from 44 percent to 55 percent from 2004 to 2008, foreshadowing the party's endorsement of same-sex marriage in 2012. Support for civil unions, however, dropped from 43 percent to 35 percent. Five percent in both years supported no recognition for same-sex couples. As a means of comparison, in 2008, 49 percent of Democratic Party identifiers in the public supported same-sex marriage, 19 percent civil unions, and 29 percent no recognition.[9]

From 2004 to 2008, the Republican delegates hardly budged according to the delegate surveys. Three percent supported same-sex marriage in 2004, 41 percent supported civil unions, and 49 percent supported no recognition. In 2008, the numbers were 6 percent, 43 percent, and 46 percent, respectively. While mass support among Republicans was generally lower (in the form of lower support for civil unions), it should be noted that Republican convention delegates were fairly wealthy and highly educated, characteristics that are usually associated with high support for gay rights.[10]

Turning to members of Congress, 183 out of 201 Democrats endorsed same-sex marriage in the House of Representatives as of 2014,[11] compared to only 4 out of 234 Republicans. Support for employment nondiscrimination at the congressional level was little different. While 196 out of 201 Democrats in the House of Representatives co-sponsored ENDA in 2014, only 7 out of 234 Republicans had endorsed the legislation. This actually represents a drop in Republican support from 2000, when 17 out of 223 Republicans co-sponsored that year's version of the bill. Most of this drop has been due to the defeat or retirement of moderate Republicans in the intervening years. In effect, little has changed in party polarization vis-à-vis gay rights since Clinton's second term, with the notable exception of support for same-sex marriage catching up to support for other gay rights policies among the Democrats.

Politically Motivated Reasoning

Why do Republicans in government remain recalcitrant on gay rights, when so much of the public has become more supportive in the last twenty-five years? To answer this question, I turn to the process of motivated reasoning, which is likely to occur once ideological or partisan lines are drawn by elites and cued to the public.[12] One aspect of motivated reasoning is especially important to this study: selective perception, whereby people tend to accept arguments congruent with their attitudinal predispositions more easily and to critique those that run counter to them more severely.[13]

Although some have suggested that party identification may moderate information on gay rights,[14] ideology is a better candidate for this predisposition. Unlike party, it has a much longer history of predicting gay rights preferences prior to the 1990s.[15] As I demonstrated in chapter 5, partisanship had no role in predicting public support for gay rights support as late as 1988. Even in the absence of elite signals on gay rights, liberals were naturally more supportive of gay rights because of their ideology in the 1970s and 1980s. Democrats were not. It would have probably taken more than just a suggestion from Clinton and other elites that gay rights should be supported to trigger motivated reasoning. Instead, Clinton's position may have suggested to liberals that their deep-seated tolerance of nonthreatening out-groups should be applied to lesbians and gays,[16] which in turn led to further motivated processing.

Another reason to suspect that ideology will form the basis of motivated reasoning involves the findings regarding feelings of "disgust" toward lesbians and gays discussed in chapter 5. Because conservatives have been found to be more likely to feel disgust in various contexts,[17] they are more likely than liberals to have this negative reaction to gays and lesbians. These negative feelings would, in turn, trigger an affective contagion as discussed in chapter 2.[18] . This means that negative information involving lesbians and gays, which is affectively congruent with visceral feelings of disgust at homosexuality, would be more likely to be recalled by conservatives when exposed to lesbians and gays. It also means that conservatives who feel this visceral disgust would be more likely to engage in motivated reasoning. Since partisanship is not associated with a predisposition to feel disgust, party identification is less likely to provide a basis for it.

Further evidence suggests that politically motivated reasoning is occurring on gay rights. Recent studies have found lesbian and gay contact effects moderated by both religious and political identity.[19] Quite unexpectedly, these studies showed that in some situations interpersonal contact can result in *lower* support for gay rights among social conservatives. Here, motivated reasoning may provide some insight. These studies had not predicted that outcome, as a drop in gay rights support when exposed to a pro-gay consideration such as positive exposure seems paradoxical at first. However, if those with a socially conservative predisposition encounter pro-gay information in the form of brief social or mediated contact, they may be motivated to search their memory for counterbalancing, anti-gay information, thereby contributing to a *drop* in gay rights support. Looked at from a liberal point of view, during the emergence of elite conflict in national politics on lesbian and gay issues in 1992 and 1993, liberals learned reasons to support lesbians and gays from the rhetoric of their elites, which in turn colored their responses to contact with lesbians and gays interpersonally and through popular culture. As these changes worked their way through the 1990s, they should, theoretically, have driven more liberal attitudes toward lesbians and gays via motivated reasoning on the political Left as political liberals were predisposed by the supportiveness of liberal leaders for gay rights to interpret new information on gay rights, included intergroup contact, in ways that would allow them to hold consistent views with other political liberals. In other words, due to the events of the 1990s, including Clinton's rhetoric, liberals were looking for reasons to support gay rights. On the Right, however, this clarification of elite positions should have had the opposite effect. It should have weakened (or even reversed among the most conservative) the effectiveness of increasing rates of interpersonal and mediated contact with lesbians and gays. When strong conservatives meet lesbians and gays, especially when politics is salient, negative information, often drawn from elite rhetoric, is brought up from memory. For instance, a strong conservative who meets a lesbian or gay person may remember George W. Bush's campaign rhetoric against gay marriage from his 2004 reelection campaign. In spite of this conservative's positive exposure to an LGBT individual, he or she may actually become *less* supportive of same-sex marriage as a result of memories of this campaign rhetoric being actively recalled.

In the remainder of this chapter, I empirically verify that when we examine ideologues who are more politically aware, the exposure effects documented in chapter 6 are distorted, likely by motivated reasoning, in a fashion that results in ideological polarization rather than liberalization. First, I revisit my set of time-series cross-sectional media polls in order to show that exposure effects are generally weaker among political conservatives. I also verify that the effect of exposure to *Grace under Fire* in the natural experiment from the previous chapter had differing effects for liberals and conservatives.

After narrowing my focus to strong ideologues, I use a dataset from 2006 to examine how different types of reported interpersonal contact had polarizing effects on strong liberals and strong conservatives. Lastly, I present the results of an experiment in which subjects saw a picture of talk-show host Ellen DeGeneres with various politically charged figures. The experimental results strongly suggest that for those who are highly politically active or knowledgeable about politics, exposure to lesbians and gays can polarize people on gay rights rather than liberalize them.

Exposure Effects for Liberals and Conservatives

The first step in showing that differences in exposure effects have led to increased polarization among the nation's political elite is to demonstrate that the exposure effects from chapter 6 are felt differently for liberals and conservatives in the public. To do that, I use two of the datasets from the previous chapter that established these contact effects, but now allow the effect of exposure to vary by respondent political ideology.

The first such analysis uses the time-series cross-sectional media polls introduced in chapter 6. Recall that this is a set of six polls that asked about employment protections for lesbians and gays, reported contact with lesbians and gays, and biological attributions for homosexuality. The easiest way to allow the effect of exposure to vary by ideology is merely to form new variables by multiplying the dummy variables that measured liberal and moderate identification times the various types of exposure used in the previous chapter. This is akin to allowing the effects of various variables to vary by year by multiplying them by variables representing the year a respondent was surveyed and entering them into the model as in previous analyses. The interaction variables now represent a potential effect that only occurs when both variables are high in value (or alternatively, low, if they can both take on negative values). Once these multiplicative interactions have been constructed, they can then be added to the model estimated in table 6.2. As a reminder, this previous model included variables for the number of regular lesbian and gay television characters on the 'Big 3' networks in the years the surveys were taken and the number of news stories relating to lesbian and gay issues on the evening news in each year.

These two variables, as well as interpersonal contact, were interacted with "liberal" and "moderate." When these interactions are included, the effect of the un-interacted exposure variables, LGBTQ characters or interpersonal contact with LGBs, becomes the effect of such exposure for conservatives (who get a value of 0 for both the "liberal" and "moderate" variables). The interactions terms then measure the difference in the exposure effect between liberals and conservatives (for the interactions with the "liberal" variables) and between moderates and conservatives (for the interactions with the "moderate" variables). The modified model appears in table 7.1.

The results in table 7.1 show that interpersonal and mediated exposure is still effective in improving attitudes for liberals, moderates, and conservatives. However, these effects are stronger for liberals and moderates, at least when it comes to lesbian and gay television characters and interpersonal contact. The effect of an increase in television news stories, however, seems to correspond only with more pro-gay attitudes for liberals.

TABLE 7.1. Ideological Differences and Gay Rights Support (Media Polls)

	Coef. Est. *(S.E.)*
Intercept	−1.958* *(0.652)*
Reported Contact with LG's	1.007* *(0.480)*
"Born Gay" Belief	0.863*** *(0.068)*
Year of Birth	3.441* *(2.073)*
Year of Birth^2	−3.147@ *(2.227)*
Education	0.528*** *(0.084)*
Gender (Female)	0.176*** *(0.054)*
Race (Afr. Amer.)	0.022 *(0.083)*
Democrat	0.295*** *(0.073)*
Independent	0.131** *(0.069)*
Liberal	0.082 *(0.188)*
Moderate	−0.014 *(0.147)*
LGB TV Characters	0.206** *(0.065)*
LGB TV News Stories	0.009 *(0.022)*
Year of Birth * LGB Chars.	−0.500* *(0.206)*
Year of Birth * LGB News	−0.002 *(0.079)*
Year of Birth * Contact	−3.375@ *(1.849)*
Year of Birth^2 * LGB Chars.	0.446* *(0.199)*
Year of Birth^2 * LGB News	0.019 *(0.078)*

(*continued*)

TABLE 7.1. Ideological Differences and Gay Rights Support (Media Polls) (*continued*)

	Coef. Est. (*S.E.*)
Year of Birth² * Contact	3.645* (*1.726*)
Liberal * LGB Chars	0.045** (*0.017*)
Liberal * LGB News	0.022*** (*0.008*)
Liberal * Contact	0.400** (*0.158*)
Moderate * LGB Chars	0.028* (*0.013*)
Moderate * LGB News	0.007 (*0.005*)
Moderate * Contact	0.377** (*0.127*)
σ | Intercept	0414
AIC	8661.4
Deviance	8607.4
N	8214

*** ~ p < .001, ** ~ p < .01, * ~ p < .05, @ ~ p <. 1 (two-tailed tests)

Table 7.2 shows how an increase in exposure affects the probability of an individual supporting laws protecting lesbians and gays from employment discrimination (holding all the other variables except ideology and exposure at their mean values) based on the results in table 7.1. Liberals are only about 9 percent more likely than conservatives to support employment protections based solely on their ideological stance. However, for those who report interpersonal contact, the ideological gap increases to about 16 percent. Liberals and moderates who report interpersonal contact are about 17 percent more likely to support employment protections than those without contact. Conservatives are a little less than 10 percent more likely to support employment protections when they personally know lesbians and gays. The effect of an increase in television characters of the order of magnitude of the one seen in figure 6.1 (the increase in characters from 1993 to 1996) is similarly sized and displayed in the third column. Liberals and moderates increased their support by

TABLE 7.2. Change in Probability of Support of Employment Protections Consistent with Exposure Increases by Ideological Group

	No Exposure	Contact Only	TV Characters Only	Contact and TV Characters	Difference from No Exposure	Percent of Possible Increase
Liberals	0.616	0.779	0.848	0.925	+0.309	80%
Moderates	0.553	0.727	0.784	0.886	+0.333	74%
Conservatives	0.524	0.619	0.710	0.783	+0.259	54%
Lib. Minus Con.	0.092	0.160	0.138	0.142	+0.050	26%

about 23 percent when more lesbian and gay characters were portrayed on television. Conservatives increased their support about 18 percent. For liberal and moderate respondents who reported contact with lesbians and gays and lived in time periods with a large number of lesbian and gay television characters, the probability of supporting such laws rose by over 30 percent. For conservatives, it was about 26 percent.

So exposure appears to have led to greater liberalism on gay rights, although it was somewhat less effective for conservatives. While the net effect of a large increase in exposure (as discussed in chapter 6), does lead to a small increase in polarization on gay rights, the roughly 5 percent increase in the difference in liberal and conservative support for employment protections seems like a small price to pay for a net increase in the probability of support for gay rights of over 25 percent across respondents. However, as we will see moving forward, this 5 percent increase in polarization really only begins to reflect the profound observable differences in how politically active liberals and conservatives react when encountering lesbians and gays.

Before moving to strong ideologies, it should be noted that the findings on the *Grace under Fire* quasi-experiment also appear to differ by ideological group. As described in chapter 6, this television show added a major gay character in late 1995, between two waves of the ANES panel, which asked a factual question about the show. Respondents who could answer the factual question about *Grace* likely watched the show and were found to have warmer feelings toward lesbians and gays in the later wave of the survey as compared to the earlier wave, while those who could not answer the question about the show had cooler feelings.

In the first model in table 7.3, I present a linear regression of this effect similar to the findings in chapter 6. Rather than test for differences by year of birth in the effect of *Grace*, as was the point of the analysis in chapter 6, in the second model of table 7.3, a multiplicative interaction between the 7 point scale, ranging from 'extremely liberal' to 'extremely conservative', used to measure respondent ideology with the variable that measured knowledge of *Grace under Fire* is included. When this interaction is added to the model, it allows the results to vary by ideological group in the same way as age in the last chapter.

According to the findings in table 7.3, the feelings of the most liberal respondents who could answer the *Grace* question correctly warmed

TABLE 7.3. OLS Regressions Predicting Change in Feeling Thermometer Score of Lesbians and Gays from 1994 to 1996

	Model 1		Model 2	
	Coef. Est.	*S.E*	Coef. Est.	*S.E*
Constant	22.547	*6.287*	17.261	*6.661***
Total TV	−0.342	*0.701*	−0.468	*0.699*
Grace under Fire	5.074	*2.778*@	24.040	*8.706***
Party ID (Republican)	−0.999	*3.388*	−0.333	*3.386*
Ideology (Conservative)	−8.894	*5.700*	−3.050	*6.264*
Bible = Word of God	−3.795	*3.913*	−3.941	*3.895*
Church Attendance	3.822	*2.968*	4.712	*2.980*
Age	−0.040	*0.069*	−0.040	*0.069*
Education (Years)	2.856	*4.142*	2.792	*4.120*
Female	0.626	*2.249*	0.745	*2.242*
African American	−7.314	*4.207*@	−8.309	*4.210**
Lesbian and Gay Therm. in 1994	−0.377	*0.043****	−0.337	*0.048****
*Grace under Fire** Ideology (Conservatism)	N/A		−24.464	*11.330**
*Grace under Fire** LG Therm. in 1994	N/A		−0.134	*0.088*
N	296		296	
Adj. R^2	0.250		0.258	
σ^2	301.7		296.9	

*** ~ p ≤ .001, ** ~ p ≤ .01, * ~ p ≤ .05, @ ~ p ≤ .1 (two-tailed tests)

by roughly 24 points on average. The feelings of the most conservative respondents who could answer the *Grace* question correctly saw no change. On average, the more individuals identified as conservative rather than liberal, the weaker the effect of *Grace*.

Strong Ideologues and Exposure Effects

Exposure seems to have widened the gap between liberals and conservatives, though the effects of exposure across liberals, moderates, and conservatives were always positive in previous analyses. However, as we move to individuals who feel their ideological identification strongly or who are experts on politics, this trend does not necessarily hold. Among strong conservatives, exposure can sometimes lead to *lower* levels of gay rights support due to motivated reasoning.

To demonstrate just how this works, I turn to the 2006 Cooperative Congressional Elections Study (CCES), initiated by a consortium of universities.[20] Several tens of thousands of individuals were surveyed across multiple states, though not every respondent was asked every question on the survey. Many were, however, asked their opinions on same-sex marriage as well as whether or not they had contact with any lesbians or gays. In a follow-up question, they were asked what type of relationship they had with the lesbian or gay person they indicated they knew—that is, whether that person was a co-worker, an acquaintance, a friend, or a family member. Same-sex marriage support was measured on a 4 point scale from "strongly support" to "strongly oppose." Respondents were also asked if they thought of themselves as very liberal, liberal, moderate, conservative, or very conservative. Using this data, I wanted to see whether different types of reported contact correspond to more opposition or support of same-sex marriage among strong liberals and strong conservatives. In order to do that, I interact dummy variables with each of the types of reported contact with the 5-point scale measuring conservatism and use these interactions to predict support for gay and lesbian rights as measured by responses to the same-sex marriage questions.

A previous study using the 2006 CCES had found that some forms of contact were generally weaker for strong Republicans.[21] In table 7.4, I reproduce that study and find the same results.

TABLE 7.4. Partisan vs. Ideological Moderation of Contact Effects from the 2006 CCES

	Model with Only Partisan Interactions of Contact		Model with Ideological Interactions	
	Coef. Est.	*S.E*	Coef. Est.	*S.E*
Intercept 1 (0|1)	20.36	*3.55****	19.92	*3.55****
Intercept 2 (1|2)	21.21	*3.55****	20.77	*3.55****
Intercept 3 (2|3)	22.17	*3.55****	21.73	*3.55****
Sex (Female)	−0.06	0.05	−0.06	0.05
Black	0.80	*0.11****	0.80	*0.11****
Latino	0.33	*0.10***	0.33	*0.10***
Other Race	0.19	*0.19*	0.19	*0.19*
Education	1.24	*0.10****	1.23	*0.10****
Age	0.74	*0.14****	0.74	*0.14****
Ideology (Cons.)	3.50	*0.16****	1.98	*0.47****
Born-Again	0.94	*0.05****	0.93	*0.05****
Income	−0.47	*0.11****	−0.47	*0.11****
Party ID (GOP)	0.05	*0.24*	0.64	*0.30**
Bush Approval	2.52	*0.10****	2.51	*0.10****
LGBT Acquaintance	−0.24	*0.16*	−0.95	*0.26****
LGBT Co-Worker	−0.25	*0.18*	−0.88	*0.30***
LGBT Friend	−0.94	*0.18****	−1.58	*0.28****
LGBT Family	−0.65	*0.17****	−1.24	*0.28****
LGBT Acquaint. * Party ID	0.60	*0.26**	−0.10	*0.33*
LGBT Co-Worker * Party ID	0.66	*0.29**	0.04	*0.37*
LGBT Friend * Party ID	1.32	*0.29****	0.68	*0.36*@
LGBT Family * Party ID	0.92	*0.28****	0.36	*0.36*
LGBT Acquaintance * Ideology			1.85	*0.54****
LGBT Coworker * Ideology			1.64	*0.62***
LGBT Friend * Ideology			1.68	*0.59***
LGBT Family * Ideology			1.53	*0.59***
Log-Likelihood	−7007.02		−7001.11	
N	9288		9288	

*** ~ p < .001, ** ~ p < .01, * ~ p < .05, @ ~ p < .1 (two-tailed tests)

Having a friend or family member who is lesbian or gay is associated with higher support for same-sex marriage, but the effects decrease to zero for those with greater Republican identification. Generally, the effects of contact do not reverse themselves for strong Republicans—that is, contact is not associated with *lower* support for gay rights.

When it comes to my hypothesis regarding ideological differences in exposure effects, the results are striking. The relationships between party and contact all but disappear, and in their place are much stronger and more significant differences based on ideology. All four forms of contact—with an acquaintance, a co-worker, a friend, and a family member—now appear to be effective for strong liberals, not just friends and family members as the previous study had found for strong Democrats. What is more shocking is that for strong conservatives, all of the positive effects of contact are canceled.[22] In fact, strong conservatives actually have statistically lower levels of support for same-sex marriage if they report contact with a lesbian or gay acquaintance or co-worker.

In table 7.5, I display the change in the predicted probabilities of different responses for strong liberals and strong conservatives who report different types of contact based on the second model in table 7.4. For strong liberals, all forms of contact result in over a 20 percent point increase in the probability of strongly supporting same-sex marriage. Having a gay or lesbian friend or family member is particularly effective. However, for strong conservatives, having a gay acquaintance or co-worker is associated with an 18 percent and 19 percent rise in strong *opposition* to same-sex marriage. It should be noted the differences between no contact and having a friend or family member who is lesbian and gay are not statistically significant in table 7.5 for strong conservatives just as they were not in table 7.4.

Thus, when we focus on strong ideologues, we find that, for strong liberals, contact with gays and lesbians is more effective at changing attitudes, whereas for strong conservatives, some forms of contact appear to result in lower support for lesbian and gay rights. It is probably not a coincidence that the two forms of contact least likely to be substantive and positive—contact with gay acquaintances and coworkers as opposed to contact with gay friends and family—were found to result

TABLE 7.5. Change in Probability of Support of Same-Sex Marriage for Strong Liberals and Conservatives Based on Type of Reported LGBT Contact

Strong Liberal	No Contact	Acquaintance	Co-Worker	Friend	Family Member
Strongly Oppose	0.149	0.060	0.069	0.048	0.056
Somewhat Oppose	0.164	0.081	0.092	0.068	0.078
Somewhat Support	0.204	0.139	0.150	0.120	0.133
Strongly Support	0.483	0.718	0.689	0.765	0.732
Strong Conservative	**No Contact**	**Acquaintance**	**Co-Worker**	**Friend**	**Family Member**
Strongly Oppose	0.558	0.747	0.734	0.661	0.667
Somewhat Oppose	0.209	0.138	0.144	0.174	0.172
Somewhat Support	0.119	0.063	0.066	0.087	0.085
Strongly Support	0.114	0.052	0.056	0.077	0.075

in less support for gay rights among strong conservatives. If strong liberals and conservatives generally dominate national politics, then the differing effects may provide part of the explanation of why political conflict on lesbian and gay rights has endured at the same time as mass liberalization.

Still only 6 percent of the respondents on the CCES said they were very liberal and 9.4 percent of the respondents said they were very conservative. These groups do not make up a large proportion of the mass public. But they are highly important for national politics insofar as they regularly vote in party primaries, give money to political candidates, and often choose to run for office themselves.

To separate those who are politically active (or could become politically active) from those who are generally apolitical, political scientists use a variable termed "political sophistication," "political awareness," or "political knowledge." This variable is generally measured by constructing a scale of how many factual questions about national politics individuals can get correct. For instance, on the 2006 CCES, individuals were asked what the party of their sitting governor, sitting senators, and sitting member of the House of Representatives was. They were also asked which party won the most seats in the two respective chambers of Congress in the 2006 elections (after the results were known). It turns out that people who can answer these questions correctly not only tend to know more about politics, but also tend to be more likely to watch news programming and opinion shows that focus on politics, to have well-formed and consistent opinions on issues, and to know how new information on the political issues of the day may advantage or disadvantage one party or the other.[23] This makes sense. If someone is a strong Democrat or Republican, or an activist affiliated with one of the parties, that person is likely to know basic information about politics—for instance, which elected officials belong to their party or control various branches of government or Congress.

To ascertain if high political awareness turns the liberalization effects of exposure into polarization based on ideology, I separated the CCES sample into two groups. One group missed only one or none of the factual questions about politics on the CCES. The other group missed two or more. The goal was to determine if exposure has a liberalizing effect for the low knowledge group and polarizing effect for the high knowledge group. I use a 3 point scale for ideology instead of the 5 point scale, collapsing strong and weak ideologues, because strength of ideology tends to be correlated with this political awareness. Also, for clarity, I combine the four categories of contact into a single measure equaling 1 if the respondent reports any contact.

In the first column in table 7.6, I model same-sex marriage support by ideology and contact in a model similar to the one in table 7.4 for the low knowledge group. Contact is only marginally significant (due to the smaller sample size in the low knowledge group). More important, for this low knowledge group, no statistically significant ideological differences in the contact effect were found. In the second column, which models the high knowledge group, the difference in the effect of contact between liberals and conservatives triples and easily reaches a high

TABLE 7.6. Ideological Moderation of Contact Effects and Political Knowledge on the 2006 CCES

	Against Same-Sex Marriage: Low Knowledge (2+ Questions Missed)		Against Same-Sex Marriage: High Knowledge (0–1 Questions Missed)	
	Coef. Est.	*S.E*	Coef. Est.	*S.E*
Intercept 1 (0|1)	1.24	*0.31****	1.49	*0.21****
Intercept 2 (1|2)	2.00	*0.32****	2.36	*0.21****
Intercept 3 (2|3)	2.78	*0.32****	3.36	*0.22****
Sex (Female)	−0.12	0.10	−0.04	0.06
Black	0.89	*0.19****	0.79	*0.12****
Latino	0.59	*0.17****	0.19	*0.12*
Other Race	−0.13	*0.36*	0.32	*0.20*
Education	0.90	*0.21****	1.27	*0.11****
Age	1.17	*0.26****	1.03	*0.16****
Ideology (Cons.)	1.99	*0.42****	1.36	*0.25****
Born-Again	1.02	*0.11****	0.92	*0.06****
Income	−0.58	*0.21***	−0.46	*0.12****
Party ID (GOP)	0.63	*0.22***	0.94	*0.12****
Bush Approval	2.05	*0.19****	2.61	*0.11****
LGBT Contact	−0.50	*0.28@*	−0.63	*0.18****
LGBT Contact * Ideology	0.27	*0.44*	0.90	*0.26****
Log-Likelihood	−1836.58		−5587.41	
N	2134		7066	

*** ~ p <. 001, ** ~ p < .01, * ~ p < .05, @ ~ p < .1 (two-tailed tests)

level of statistical significance. Table 7.7 shows the predicted probabilities for these two models given otherwise average respondents in these two groups. For both low knowledge liberals and conservatives, contact effects are generally weak, but they are in the expected positive direction. However, for the high knowledge conservatives, contact again appears to result in *less* support for gay rights. Coupled with the larger effect of contact for the high knowledge liberals, this signals that exposure to lesbians and gays is polarizing the high knowledge ideologues rather than liberalizing them.

TABLE 7.7. Change in Probability of Support of Same-Sex Marriage for Strong Liberals and Conservatives Based on Reported LGBT Contact and Political Knowledge

Strong Liberal	Low Knowledge			High Knowledge		
	No Contact	Contact	Δ	No Contact	Contact	Δ
Strongly Oppose	0.236	0.156	−0.080	0.154	0.089	−0.065
Somewhat Oppose	0.166	0.131	−0.035	0.177	0.120	−0.057
Somewhat Support	0.187	0.175	−0.012	0.210	0.178	−0.032
Strongly Support	0.412	0.538	+0.126	0.458	0.613	+0.155
Strong Conservative	**Low Knowledge**			**High Knowledge**		
	No Contact	Contact	Δ	No Contact	Contact	Δ
Strongly Oppose	0.694	0.640	−0.054	0.416	0.484	+0.068
Somewhat Oppose	0.138	0.154	+0.016	0.243	0.234	−0.009
Somewhat Support	0.081	0.097	+0.016	0.163	0.141	−0.015
Strongly Support	0.087	0.108	+0.021	0.178	0.141	−0.037

The DeGeneres Experiment: Polarization when Politics and Exposure Are Combined

There may still be some doubt that exposure can result in polarization for those high in political awareness. That is, it seems so counterintuitive that exposure to a lesbian or gay person can, for some people, result in less support for gay rights. The previous study found these effects only for self-reported exposure, and self-reports can always be in error. Here, I use an experimental method and find similar results. Exposure has a polarizing effect, likely due to selective perception, but only when politics are salient, as they are almost universally for highly involved political activists and national elected officials.

To examine the contingent effects of exposure on support for lesbian and gay rights, I used a traditional lab experiment modeled after interviews that took place on *The Ellen DeGeneres Show*. Ellen DeGeneres has been a national public figure since the mid-1990s, when she played a character on a sitcom with the same first name who came out as lesbian on television. This triggered a media firestorm, and it was widely reported that DeGeneres, the actress, was also a lesbian in real life. Although her sitcom was cancelled, DeGeneres currently hosts *The Ellen DeGeneres Show*, a daytime talk show.

Ellen DeGeneres is ideal as a treatment condition for testing the media contact hypothesis. Her status as a lesbian is well known by the public. Furthermore, Ellen, the actress, and Ellen, the sitcom character, are easy for the public to associate. Subjects may also have a long-term viewing relationship with Ellen DeGeneres as a celebrity figure, and repeated contact with the same person or character may be crucial to both the attitude liberalization process and mediated contact effects.[24]

The subjects in my experiment were 267 students at an elite southern university in early 2009, who were asked to take a computer survey. After answering several demographic questions and questions unrelated to lesbian and gay rights, the students were asked to read a paragraph stating that television can have a significant impact on politics. They were also told that on the next screen would be a picture and a written transcript of an interview that took place during the 2008 presidential election. The next screen then displayed one of several possibilities: a picture of Ellen interviewing Tom Brokaw (a nonpartisan journalist) with written dialogue beneath, another of Ellen interviewing Barack Obama, with the same Brokaw dialogue underneath (but with Brokaw's name replaced by "Obama"), and a third of her interviewing John McCain, again with the same dialogue. The latter two images combined exposure to Ellen with exposure to a political frame that should activate motivated reasoning. Obama is a clear liberal, while McCain was generally conservative at the time of the study, although he has at times had a reputation of being a moderate Republican. By comparing these conditions with the Brokaw condition, I can test for attitude change contingent on images of Obama or McCain raising the importance of political ideology in a subconscious fashion. The fourth and final image involved an interview with Brokaw, but the interviewer was changed to David Letterman, a heterosexual late night talk show host. The students saw only one of the three Ellen DeGeneres interviews or the control Letterman version. The transcript accompanying each was identical and always involved a discussion of one of the nation's most important problems. Comparison of the Ellen DeGeneres–Brokaw image with the Letterman-Brokaw image establishes the effect of mediated contact *without* a political stimuli activating selective perception. On the other hand, comparison of the effect of the Ellen DeGeneres–Brokaw image with the Ellen DeGeneres–Obama image and with the Ellen-McCain image establishes how the effect of mediated contact shifts when partisan figures create a political or ideological frame.

The post-test measure of lesbian and gay rights support involved a five-question battery assessing attitudes toward gay civil unions, gay marriage, gay adoption, employment protections for gays, and support for gays in the military. Each of these questions was then followed by a question asking individuals if they felt strongly or weakly about their position on that issue. These ten questions were combined into a scale of lesbian and gay rights support that ranges from 5 to 10, with 10 being the most supportive of gay rights. The items had a reasonable degree of reliability ($\alpha = .73$).

My key hypothesis was that knowledgeable liberals would become more pro-gay when they encountered Ellen and a political frame like Obama or McCain. Ellen, a positive nonthreatening lesbian, represents a positive consideration encouraging pro-gay attitudes. A political frame should activate motivated reasoning leading to easy acceptance of this positive consideration on the part of liberals. Conversely, knowledgeable conservatives may react *negatively* when exposed to Ellen in the context of a political frame. This is because motivated reasoning, when activated, will bring anti-gay considerations up from memory and cause them to mentally *argue against* support for gay rights.[25]

The potential of elite-led influence on attitudes also exists, but, in contrast, this should lead to *increased* pro-gay attitudes among knowledgeable conservatives. Meetings with Ellen on the part of either McCain or Obama can be interpreted as a tacit elite endorsement of Ellen and could strengthen the effect of the Ellen-Obama condition for liberals

Table 7.8. Experiment Study Results—Censored Linear Regression (Tobit)

(Dependent Variable = Lesbian/Gay Rights Support Scale)

	Liberals		Conservatives		Moderates	
	Coef. Est.	*S.E*	Coef. Est.	*S.E*	Coef. Est.	*S.E*
Intercept 1	10.7	*0.51****	11.3	*1.48****	9.56	*0.47****
Intercept 2	−0.19	*0.11*	0.02	*0.10*	−0.15	*0.07*
Party (Republican)	−2.47	*0.96**	−4.24	*1.45***	−1.13	*0.31****
Sex (Male)	−0.91	0.24***	−0.77	0.35*	−0.65	0.18***
Asian	−1.60	*0.60***	N/A		−0.81	*0.34**
Black	−0.89	*0.41**	N/A		−0.60	*0.28**
Latino	−0.07	*0.43*	N/A		0.65	*0.44*
Born-Again/ Evangelical	−0.34	*0.36*	−0.59	*0.39*	−0.62	*0.27**
Protestant	−0.32	*0.27*	−0.72	*0.52*	0.15	*0.23*
Catholic	−0.24	*0.33*	−0.57	*0.51*	−0.11	*0.23*
Muslim	0.95	*0.90*	N/A		N/A	
Political Knowledge	−0.04	*0.78*	2.26	*1.45*	0.84	*0.67*
Ellen-Obama Treatment	−2.08	*0.82**	2.08	*1.27*	1.30	*0.65**
Ellen-Obama * Knowledge	3.22	*1.33**	−3.27	*2.05*	−1.29	*1.03*
Ellen-McCain Treatment	−1.23	*0.70*	2.94	*1.17**	−0.07	*0.60*
Ellen-McCain* Knowledge	1.84	*1.04*	−4.65	*1.91**	−0.51	*0.91*
Ellen-Brokaw Treatment	0.36	*1.02*	1.00	*1.26*	0.51	*0.61*
Ellen-Brokaw* Knowledge	−0.36	*1.45*	−1.96	*1.97*	−0.79	*0.99*
Log-Likelihood	−83.6		−78.8		−141.7	
N	87		55		125	

*** ~ p ≤ .001, ** ~ p ≤ .01, * ~ p ≤ .05, @~ p ≤ .1 (two-tailed tests)

(and moderates, who were very pro-Obama in this sample) and cause a positive effect of the Ellen-McCain condition for unknowledgeable conservatives (who are less likely to engage in motivated reasoning). I also expected direct effects for moderates and the politically unknowledgeable based solely on the theory of mediated contact.

The results are in table 7.8, which shows that the Ellen-Obama and Ellen-Brokaw conditions resulted in slightly higher support for gay rights on average than the other two conditions across all subjects.

The effect of the Ellen-Obama condition was significantly greater than zero statistically for knowledgeable liberals ($b = 3.22 + -2.08 = 1.14$, $p < .05$) using the marginal effects interpretation for an interaction.[26] Conversely, the Ellen-McCain condition resulted in a statistically significant *negative* effect for knowledgeable Republicans ($b = -4.65 + 2.94 = -1.71$, $p < .05$). Furthermore, the effects of the Ellen-McCain condition for liberals and the Ellen-Obama condition for conservatives are in the correct direction and significant effects are also found for these

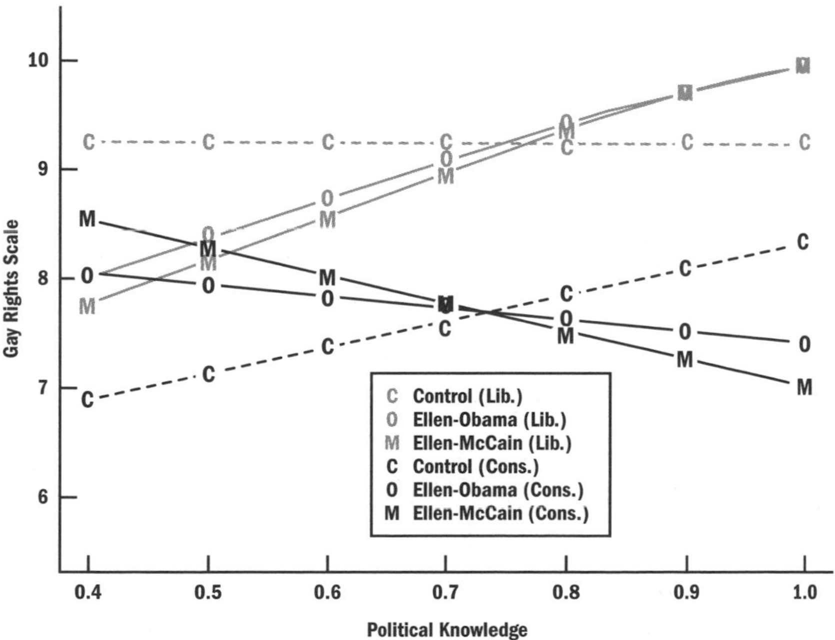

Figure 7.3. Exposure to Ellen DeGeneres in a Political Context and Polarization on Gay Rights by Political Sophistication.

conditions using a more complicated pooled analysis (see the data appendix), although they do not reach statistical significance in the subsamples in table 7.8.

Figure 7.3 displays the results for the Brokaw-Letterman control and the Ellen-Obama and Ellen-McCain conditions for liberals and conservatives. These models show the predicted fits for white protestant males (although these demographics do not matter in terms of the actual findings). Because there was a large amount of party polarization in the samples, the liberal model fit assumes a weak Democrat and the conservative model fit a weak Republican in order to more accurately portray the relationships. The results, again, are fairly clear. In the control Letterman-Brokaw condition, liberals are consistently highly supportive of gay rights. Conservatives with high levels of political knowledge also tend to support gay rights, which is not surprising in the context of past ANES results that found a robust relationship between gay rights and political knowledge.[27]

However, these relationships were rearranged when the subjects were exposed to Ellen DeGeneres in a political context. Ideologues low in knowledge appear to have surprisingly depolarized, while those high in knowledge appear to have polarized by several points on the gay rights scale. For the low knowledge conservatives, this makes sense, as exposure to Ellen should have a liberalizing effect. But for the low knowledge liberals this was surprising, as it constituted a drop in gay rights support from the control conditions. Thus, exposure in the presence of political frames appears to activate motivated reasoning and result in polarization on gay rights among those high in political knowledge. For those individuals, an elite endorsement effect explains little, given that the Ellen-McCain condition resulted in more *negative* attitudes rather than positive attitudes for conservatives. These results appear to match the lower support for gay rights among strong conservatives who reported more superficial relationships with lesbians and gays, as compared to those with no contact, on the 2006 CCES. This finding provides an independent confirmation that strong or knowledgeable conservatives are motivated reasoners on gay rights.

The experimental results also show some significant effects consistent with elite endorsements: politically unknowledgeable conservatives became more supportive of gay rights under the Ellen-McCain condition, and political moderates (who likely supported Obama in 2008 in this sample) became more supportive under the Ellen-Obama condition. Thus mediated contact in a political context appears to be more effective in improving gay rights attitudes than the neutral Ellen-Brokaw condition, which had no discernible effect across conditions.

Conclusion

Increased exposure to lesbians and gays has a liberalizing effect for most members of the mass public. However, among strong ideologues, motivated reasoning likely occurs and shifts this liberalizing effect into a polarizing effect. Although they make up a small segment of the population, ideologues dominate the ranks of primary voters, political activists, donors, political candidates, and elected officials. Because these are also the very people who have the power to pass laws that will advance gay rights, a gap has opened up between the mass public and elite support for gay rights. Republicans and conservatives have remained strongly against lesbian and gay rights, even those rights supported by a super majority of the public, because their most ardent supporters have been largely immune to the liberalizing effects of increased exposure with lesbians and gays.

PART IV

Looking toward the Future

8

The Global Shift in Attitudes toward Homosexuality

As the United States and other countries grapple with the issue of same-sex marriage, a new Pew Research Center survey finds huge variance by region on the broader question of whether homosexuality should be accepted or rejected by society. . . . The survey of publics in 39 countries finds broad acceptance of homosexuality in North America, the European Union, and much of Latin America, but equally widespread rejection in predominantly Muslim nations and in Africa, as well as in parts of Asia and in Russia.
—Pew Research, Global Attitude Projects, June 4, 2013

One can feel calm and at ease. Just leave kids alone, please.
—Russian President Vladimir Putin, to gays and lesbians attending the 2014 Sochi Olympic Games

As the epigraph from Vladimir Putin and the 2013 controversy surrounding laws to ban gay "propaganda" in Russia make clear, lesbian and gay issues have begun to emerge as a flash point between the more (classically) Liberal countries of the West and the more authoritarian parts of the world. This new schism in international politics, between nations with pro-gay and anti-gay majorities, appears only more likely to grow in importance, insofar as gay rights appears to fit into the United States' and the European Union's symbolic commitments to a global human rights agenda. In the past few years, the United Nations has, for the first time, debated and passed resolutions in favor of lesbian and gay rights.

Meanwhile, the fundamental rights of lesbians and gays have come under threat in nations such as Uganda and Nigeria, where penalties of life imprisonment and death have been attached to engaging in homosexual conduct (or merely advocating for more tolerant policies). Mass support for these measures has its roots in an anti-gay animus introduced by Western colonizers overly concerned with the morality of those in their overseas territories. Now this animus is further stoked by a new wave of fundamentalist religious missionaries from the West. Recent anti-gay laws are now being justified as necessary measures to defend local national cultures against "Western encroachment" in the form of a tolerance of sexual minorities.

In sharp contrast to these countries, liberalization in attitudes toward homosexuality has been not just an American phenomenon or even a Western phenomenon as some allege, but countries on nearly every continent have experienced a similar transformation in their understanding of lesbians and gays, even as others have grown more resistant. What can we learn from the experiences of those in other regions? Do the factors that have contributed to attitude change in the United States operative internationally? Or is this a case of so-called American exceptionalism?

Examining what has led to the global shift in attitudes requires us to think carefully about what specifically it is about the American context that has allowed the lesbian and gay movement to eventually find success. Generalizing from the American experience, two major factors appear to have aided the gay and lesbian movement. First, the adversarial nature of the American party system may have incentivized liberal politicians to endorse lesbian and gay rights in order to gain access to campaign resources including activist support in the early 1990s. The Democratic Party's repositioning on gay rights encouraged liberals and Democrats in the mass public to become more tolerant of sexual minorities when divisions between liberal and conservative elected officials on gay rights spilled over into the news. Still, while this factor may have encouraged mass attitude change among liberals, it may have more recently discouraged attitude change among political conservatives by triggering motivated reasoning as discussed in chapter 7.

A more important factor is the media itself, which provided lesbian, gay, and anti-AIDS activists with their first opportunity to garner public attention. If these activists could persuade reporters, journalists, and editors to cover AIDS and other gay issues, they could present their positions to the public and gain a much higher visibility for them. If images of lesbian and gay activism on the news in the late 1980s and early 1990s or the shift in entertainment programming that occurred later encouraged lesbians and gays to come out en masse in the 1990s, then a media system that allows for minority activists to potentially have the opportunity to express their views to the public would firmly undergird any attitudinal change.

In this chapter, I first survey global attitude change on homosexuality using the cumulative World Values Survey and European Values Survey (WVS/EVS).[1] Then, I examine how recent global attitudes involving homosexuality are similar or divergent across different national contexts. In testing whether countries that have government and media systems similar to those of the United States have also witnessed similar attitude change, I find strong evidence that suggests that the broader and freer a media system is, the more liberal public attitudes toward homosexuality are. This is especially the case among young people. These results are important for two reasons. First, they provide evidence supporting the assertion in the earlier chapters that it was the emergence of a national dialogue on lesbian and gay rights that was crucial to the attitude change process. Second, the results in this chapter explain why countries such as Russia have not experienced attitude change and why laws such as the anti-propaganda law in Russia are so detrimental. Without a free press, gays and lesbians simply cannot get their message out to the public. I also find suggestive evidence that the nature of a country's party system may encourage differences in how left-leaning and right-leaning voters may feel about homosexuality, but this evidence is weaker as there are only a small number of countries with competitive party systems from which we can generalize. Although broad-based comparisons of radically different national contexts can be problematic, this chapter serves as a preliminary test of whether the theory of affective liberalization holds in an international context. Any findings should be interpreted with caution, given how different cultures can interpret and perceive sexual and gender minorities in radically different ways.

An Outline of Global Change since the 1980s

Since the early 1980s, the World Values Survey and the European Values Survey (WVS/EVS) have sought to examine differences in public opinion in various nations of the world. Countries are resurveyed with the same questions about once every seven to ten years. While most of the original surveys focused principally on Western Europe, the number of countries studied has expanded greatly. Over one hundred nations have now been surveyed, many of them four or five times.

The WVS/EVS is very important when it comes to tracking change in global attitudes involving homosexuality since it has included a question about homosexuality on roughly three hundred of its surveys. This allows for an analysis of views involving homosexuality both over time and in different national contexts. The question asks respondents to rate how often they feel that homosexuality is justified. Respondents can express their opinion using a scale that ranges from 1 to 10. A value of 1 signifies that homosexuality is never justified. A value of 10 signifies that homosexuality is always justified. Thus, the way the question is worded is similar to the affective rating given by the feeling thermometer on the ANES described in previous chapters.

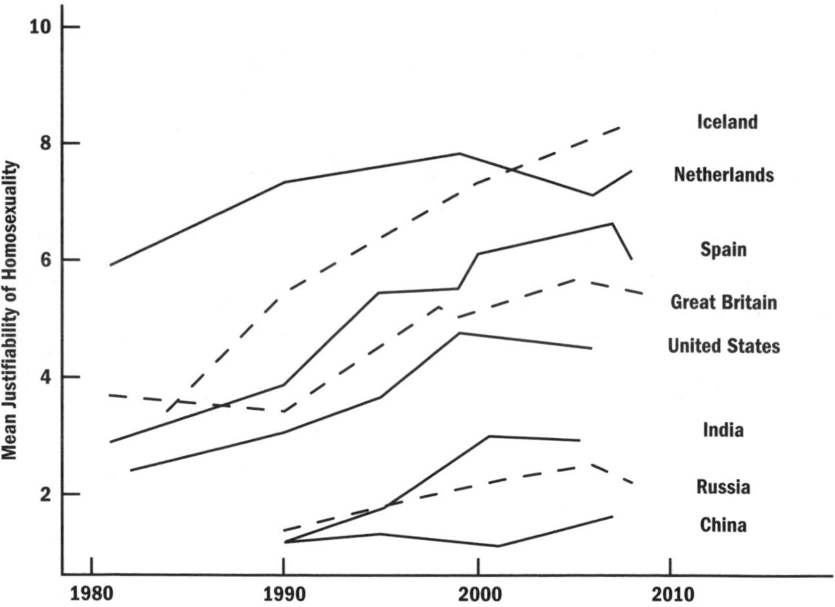

Figure 8.1. Average Response on the Justifiability of Homosexuality Question Asked by the WVS/EVS for Select Countries, 1980–2010.
Source: Calculation by author from the *World Values Survey* and *European Values Survey* cumulative files.

Figure 8.1 plots how the average rating changes over time for various countries, including the United States. The pattern of the American responses to the question are familiar, as they match both the feeling thermometer trend on the ANES and the trend on same-sex relations approval from the General Social Survey (GSS) discussed in chapter 1. Ratings of homosexuality on the WVS/EVS surveys in the United States are generally lower in the 1980s, show liberalization in the 1990s, and remain somewhat static in the 2000s.

But it is not just the United States that fits this pattern, as figure 8.1 makes clear. Most of the countries depicted (and most of those surveyed since the 1980s) also show a trend toward attitude liberalization. In Great Britain, India, and Spain this attitude change occurred in the 1990s, as it did in many countries that are not depicted including Sweden, Japan, Argentina, Chile, France, Mexico, Canada, the Philippines, and Germany. The Netherlands and Iceland are exceptions to this trend. The Netherlands has consistently rated homosexuality as more justified since the 1980s. Iceland, the first country to elect an out lesbian prime minister, has experienced rapidly changing attitudes in nearly every decade since the 1980s, not just in the 1990s.

Also depicted are Russia and China. While they are exceptions in that they have experienced little attitude change as compared to the other countries, their ratings of homosexuality are generally representative of many countries in Eastern Europe, Africa, and predominantly Muslim parts of South and Southeast Asia first surveyed by the WVS in the early 1990s.

To show change in world attitudes on homosexuality more broadly, figures 8.2 and 8.3 show maps of the average responses to the justifiability of homosexuality question in two different time periods, the 1980s and the 2000s. Lighter greys suggest that the mean rating for the justifiability of homosexuality is close to "Never Justified," while darker shades and black suggest the average rating is closer to "Always Justified." Countries in white were not surveyed, though it is apparent that many more countries were surveyed in the more recent rounds.

No countries except the Netherlands and Denmark had an average rating over 5 in the 1980s. Many of the countries with more liberal attitudes toward homosexuality had average ratings between 3 and 4 in that decade. However, nearly all of Western Europe, with the exception

Figure 8.2. Average Response on the Justifiability of Homosexuality by Country on the 1980s Rounds of the WVS/EVS.

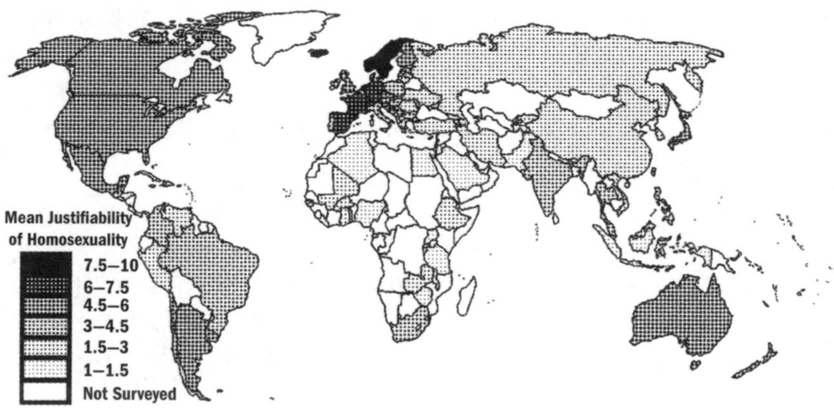

Figure 8.3. Average Response on the Justifiability of Homosexuality by Country on the 2000s Rounds of the WVS/EVS.

of socially conservative Italy, had average ratings over 5 by the end of the 2000s. So did Argentina, Australia, Canada, Chile, the Czech Republic, Slovenia, and Uruguay. Brazil, the United States, Greece, Israel, Japan, Mexico, New Zealand, Serbia, and Slovakia were close behind with average ratings over 4. Most of Eastern Europe and the former Soviet Union had average ratings between 2 and 3, while many parts of Latin America and Southeast Asia averaged between 2.5 and 3.5. South Africa averaged about 3, but all the other parts of Sub-Saharan Africa and the Islamic world showed ratings generally below 2. Egypt, Jordan, and Bangladesh had the lowest average ratings at 1.01, 1.02, and 1.05, respectively.

Changing Global Attitudes and Economics

While the Islamic world, China, and Africa generally have the lowest ratings when it comes to the justifiability of homosexuality and have experienced little attitude change on the issue in contrast to other countries, it would be a mistake to attribute this general pattern mainly to religious or cultural differences. The literature has found that the dominant predictor of liberalism toward homosexuality at a national level is the level of economic development of a country, generally measured by a country's gross domestic product per capita (GDP).

This relationship was first outlined by Robert Inglehart, who theorized that as a nation becomes more prosperous, the conflicts that are prioritized in its domestic politics change. Thus, as citizens increasingly have their material needs met, the nation's politics shifts from one characterized by conflicts about materialism, or redistribution between rich and poor, to a politics primarily concerned with symbolic or post-materialistic values. Generally, the latter involve allowing citizens to be self-expressive and self-actualizing. Naturally, under these circumstances, debates about sexuality and sexual freedom are common, and they may presage attitude change on homosexuality.

Anderson and Fetner, using the WVS/EVS, found that societies with greater economic development were more liberal on the justifiability of homosexuality question as would be predicted by Inglehart's post-materialistic thesis.[2] They controlled for a host of other individual-level demographic factors such as education, year of birth, gender, religion, and religiosity. In addition, Andersen and Fetner found that those who had their material needs met in developed countries (that is, non-manual workers, white-collar workers and managers) were more likely to give liberal responses when they lived in a country with a higher GDP.[3]

To get a sense of this pattern, I plot the average response on the justifiability of homosexuality by year of birth in figure 8.4. The results are quite striking. In countries with GDPs below $10,000, there is only a minor hint of a cohort effect. The average rating in such countries ranges

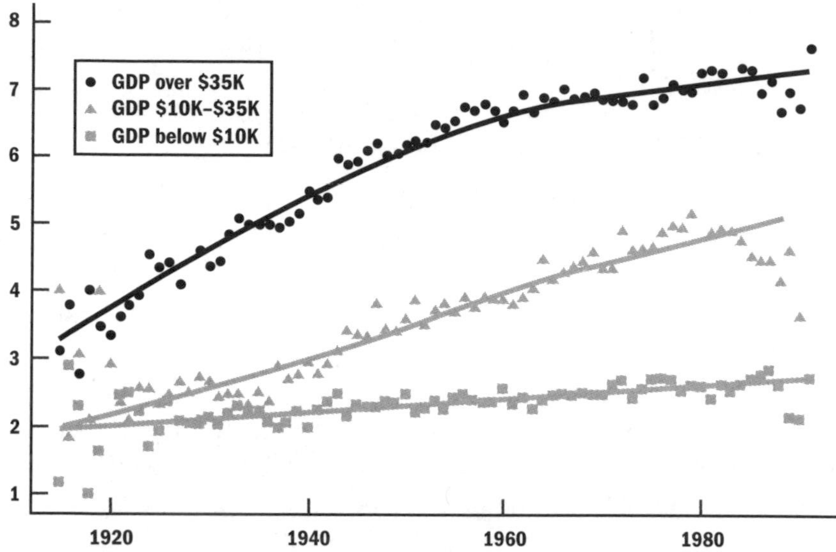

Figure 8.4. Justifiability of Homosexuality Respondents' by Year of Birth and Country GDP.

between 2 and 3 regardless of year of birth. In countries with moderate GDPs, a very sharp cohort effect emerges. Those born in the 1920s give an average rating of about 2.5 points on the scale and are not much different from those in the poorest countries. Those born around 1980 average a rating of 5.

For the richer countries (those with GDP per capita over $35,000) the average responses are much higher, especially for the youngest respondents. A cohort effect emerges in the richer countries, but the gap is much larger for those born between the 1920s and the 1950s. Those born after the 1950s in richer countries average a response of about 7.

Changing Global Attitudes and National Media

As previous studies like Anderson and Fetner's have shown, economic development does appear to explain part of the international variation in attitudes toward homosexuality. However, we would expect that countries that have a more developed and freer media system, one that could be taken advantage of by the lesbian and gay movement, would also have a higher GDP and more economic development. So, some of the variation in attitudes found by previous studies and based on GDP may actually be due to the fact that high GDP nations tend to have an extremely pervasive and free media. What would figure 8.4 look like if we used variables that measure a nation's media system to classify countries instead of GDP?

In figures 8.5 and 8.6, I reconstruct figure 8.4 using two very different variables: in figure 8.5, a measure of the number of televisions per capita in a country represents the pervasiveness of a nation's media. In Figure 8.6, I use a numerical measure produced by an organization called Freedom House that gauges how free a nation's press is. While these two variables measure very different aspects of a media system, we would expect that as both increase, it would be easier for gay and lesbian activists to get their point of view across to the rest of public. If few members of the public have televisions, then naturally, even if lesbians and gays could persuade decision-makers in politics and the media to support their rights, few would hear the message. Likewise, if the press is controlled by the state or open to intimidation by economic or political elites, this would discourage the press from conveying unpopular points

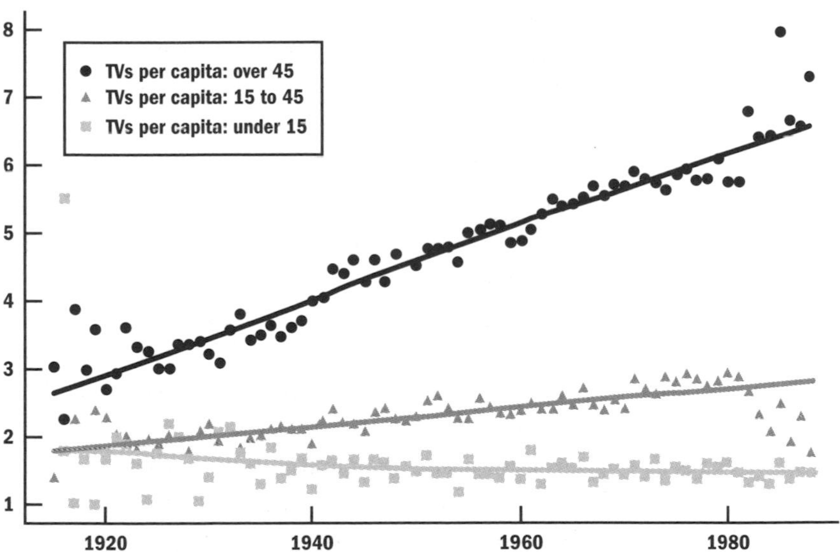

Figure 8.5. Justifiability of Homosexuality Respondents' by Year of Birth and Number of Televisions per Capita, 2002-2010.

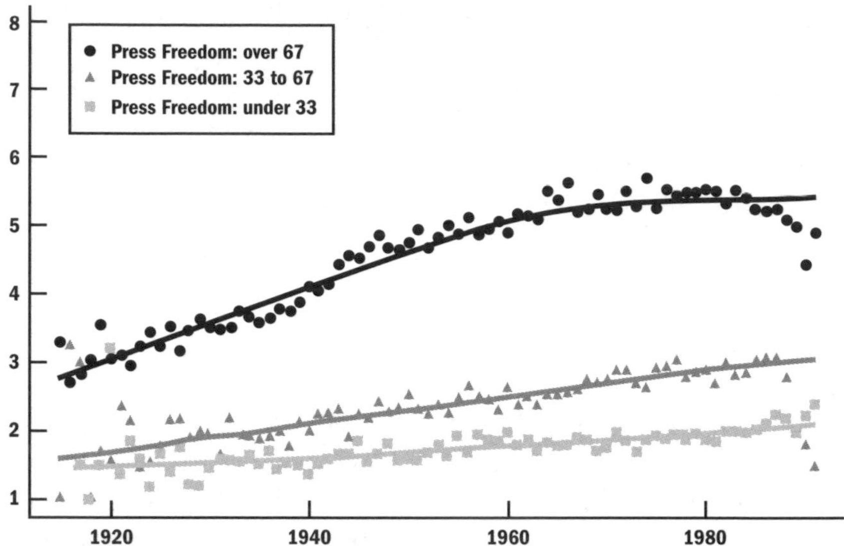

Figure 8.6. Justifiability of Homosexuality Respondents' by Year of Birth and Country Ratings of Press Freedom.

of view, especially those that could undermine the social or political power bases within a country. Where the role of the press does not extend to conveying opposing minority viewpoints in a given country, it would be next to impossible for lesbian and gay activists to persuade that nation's press to depict them in sympathetic ways.

Despite the fact that both of these variables measure very different aspects of the media, figures 8.5 and 8.6 are rather similar. Nations with low and medium levels of televisions per capita and low and medium press freedom generally have negative attitudes toward the justifiability of homosexuality, regardless of cohort or year of birth effects, although for nations with relatively few televisions, there is even a hint of a negative cohort effect. Those born *before* 1940 appear to be slightly more liberal than those born after. Additionally, those born prior to 1930 in countries with a relatively large number of televisions appear to be more liberal than those born in the same years in nations with fewer televisions. In both figures, prominent year of birth effects are present for nations with higher numbers of televisions and more press freedom. The cohort effects associated with the number of televisions in such nations appear to be completely linear. For those born in 1920, the average rating of homosexuality is about 3. For those born in 1980, the average rating is about 6. Thus the gap between the oldest and youngest in such countries is 3 points out of the 9 point scale. For nations high in press freedom, those born in 1920 average a rating of 3. The average rating increases for those born most recently, finally reaching about 5 for those born in 1960. The trend then flattens, and the average rating remains slightly over 5 for those born more recently than 1960.

It turns out that GDP, media density, and press freedom all emerge as very important predictors of more liberal attitudes about homosexuality in analyses of the WVS/EVS justifiability question. This is the case when all of these variables are included in a multivariate model.[4] When all three are included in such a model, along with a host of individual level demographic controls, differences in GDP correspond to a gap of about 4/5s of a scale point between the youngest and oldest respondents. Furthermore, differences in television density and press freedom both explain a little over an additional point each in terms of the gap between younger and older respondents. This means a total of 2 points is explained by media system differences, over twice the amount explained by GDP. Most of the gaps between younger and older respondents that have emerged in more developed and freer countries have been between 3½ to 4 points on this question, and there has consistently been little difference between the oldest respondents in less developed countries and the oldest respondents in more developed countries. This suggests that differences in national media correspond with about half the variation in more liberal responses that have emerged, with GDP differences explaining a remaining quarter of this change.

There is likely considerable validity to Inglehart's insight regarding the relationship of a nation's economic condition and its politics. This analysis may fill in some of the details. No doubt, lesbian and gay activists needed well-paying jobs to engage in their activism before the Stonewall Riots, and this may also be seen in terms of the remaining link between country GDP and attitudinal change on homosexuality. In very poor countries, where the most basic needs of the population are not being met, few lesbian and gay activists will emerge. But because a beneficial media context is also necessary for gay and lesbian activists to get their message out, it should not be a surprise that both a high GDP and a free media system are necessary for more liberal attitudes.

Changing Global Attitudes and Party System Dynamics

Before examining how a country's party system may affect support for lesbian and gay rights, a discussion of exactly what the terms "liberal" and "conservative" mean in an international context is in order. While they act as synonyms for "left-wing" and "right-wing" in the United States, internationally, their denotations are quite different. "Liberal" outside of North America (or "classically Liberal") tends to mean "supporting individual rights and greater liberty." Thus, internationally, the word "liberal" is closer to "libertarian" in its meaning. Internationally "liberal" parties tend to run the gamut from left-leaning to very far right economically. Many "center" parties in the European Union are, in reality, classically Liberal parties and are thus likely to be among the early supporters of gay rights in comparison to economically left-leaning parties. Here "Liberal" thus refers to the international meaning.

For the purposes of this analysis, "left-leaning" and "right-leaning" are thus more accurate labels than "liberal" or "conservative" when it comes to the ideological identification of voters in mass publics outside of the United States. The WVS/EVS measures ideological identification of voters by asking them to place themselves on a scale ranging from 0 to 9 where 0 is far left and 9 is far right. I consider a voter left-leaning if he or she picks 0, 1, or 2, and right-leaning if he or she selects 7, 8, or 9.

The role that various party systems may play in attitude change is complicated by two related issues. First, many nations do not have a competitive party system and must be excluded from any such analysis. Those that remain tend to be high GDP countries with free and pervasive media and tend to have more liberal attitudes on homosexuality, as we would expect from prior discussion. Second, competitive party systems are so varied that comparing one type with another type in a quantitative fashion is difficult. For instance, how can we compare change in a country with four parties that compete in a proportional representation system in which voters cast ballots as a single, national constituency with change in another country where each district elects one member of parliament? Thus, unlike the earlier analysis of media systems, factors specific to each country, like GDP or press freedom, may ultimately be more important than the role of party systems in support for gay rights. These issues mean we should move forward with caution.

To do so, I make a few basic assumptions. First, I assume that each country with a competitive system has a center-left and center-right party, that these parties are in competition for the median voter in a country, and that this median voter is generally up for grabs between these two parties. Second, I assume that the competition between these two parties generally defines the public's interpretation of the ideological continuum they are presented with on the WVS/EVS. When voters are left-leaning, I assume they are closer to the center-left party than the center-right party and vise-versa for right-leaning voters. They do not need to support that party; they are merely closer to it ideologically. I make these assumptions because if the center-left party is pressured into supporting gay rights by the context of a nation's party system, or by lesbian and gay activists, I would expect members of the public who are closer to them ideologically (and likely identify with that party more) to feel more favorable toward homosexuality and lesbians and gays. Similarly, if the center-right party is under added pressure from social conservatives on the right to keep anti-gay positions, it may remain locked in an anti-gay position, which in turn would discourage attitude change in members of the public who are right-leaning. This parallels the American experience from the previous chapters.

What situations may encourage the center-left and center-right parties to change on gay rights? One may be how powerful and credible more extreme third parties can be in competing for the votes of lesbians, gays, and their supporters on the Left and social or religious conservatives on the Right. Here it should be noted that multiparty systems provide greater incentives for third parties to form than two-party systems. In the latter, left-leaning voters (like lesbians and gays) would gain little by defecting to a third party, as these parties seldom win office or hold any real power. However, in a multiparty context, where third parties regularly win seats in a national congress or parliament and also regularly form coalition governments with center-left parties, the threat of lesbian and gay voters defecting to a pro-gay left-wing or Liberal party is quite real. Such a pro-gay third party would not be in competition for the median voter and would care little if taking a pro-gay position would alienate other voters. Thus, in a multiparty system, a center-left party should have an incentive to support gay rights in order to prevent lesbian and gay voters from defecting to a third, pro-gay party.

Center-left parties in two-party contexts should come around on gay rights, but perhaps much later. They are primarily concerned with attracting a country's median voter, not with pleasing or retaining left-wing supporters like lesbians and gays as these voters are unlikely to defect to the center-right party. Thus a center-left party in a two-party system will avoid supporting gay rights until party leaders come to believe that any resources gained from the lesbian and gay community will help more in attracting the support of the median voter than the shift to a pro-gay position will hurt in potentially alienating the median voter.

In contexts where third parties can easily form and are already common, I expect center-left parties to liberalize in order to prevent defection to a third party At the same time, I also expect center-right parties to liberalize precisely because extreme individuals on the far Right have *already* likely had the option of joining a far-right party in a multiparty context. The timing of liberalization is really what sets the cases apart, though. When lesbian and gay rights issues first emerge in a national political dialogue, attitude change is not yet likely to have occurred, or at least not broadly, and there is not likely to be an existing, viable pro-gay party. The median voter may well be disapproving of homosexuality. Thus, in multiparty context, a center-left party should be more averse to losing left-wing voters before attitude change has occurred, especially if it is easy for such a pro-gay third party to become viable. The party likely already have these more liberal voters in their electoral coalitions prior to attitude change. For example, many lesbian and gay voters in the 1970s were still Democrats, despite the fact that neither American major party supported gay rights consistently.

A center-right party, on the other hand, has to face a long-standing tradition of far-right parties already forming and running candidates in most developed countries. More extreme right-wing voters have already defected to these parties based on issues such as immigration or abortion policy. In a two-party system, where far-right social conservatives are active in a center-right party, it may be more difficult for the center-right party to shift its position in response to changing voter preferences. But in a multiparty context, where more far-right activists and voters have already formed and joined a viable far-right party, a center-right party may be freed up to reorient itself after attitude change has occurred and to liberalize on gay rights. Thus right-leaning voters in multiparty systems may be more liberal on gay rights because the leadership of the center-right party can move left on gay rights in response to constituency attitude change. Just such a scenario may have occurred in the United Kingdom, where a Conservative prime minister pushed same-sex marriage through Parliament, aided by the fact that the most right-wing voters has likely defected to the United Kingdom Independent Party (UKIP).

The important thing to remember is that those who are extremely pro-gay or extremely anti-gay generally have more power to get their views across in a multiparty context. Intense minority viewpoints are what generally drive third parties. At the same time, center-left and center-right parties care about majorities and winning moderate voters.

A very specific measure exists for the number of effective political parties a country has. The problem is that not all political parties are equal. When we say the American system is a two-party system, this does not mean there are only two parties across the country. However, for all intents and purposes, in the United States only the Democrats and Republicans really compete for power nationally.

The number of effective parties measure that I employ involves parliamentary seat shares and election results as a basis. From these, a number is obtained for each party. When a party is in close competition for the national majority, the number is very close to 1. Smaller parties, which compete regionally or which attract few voters, receive smaller values. The sum of these values over every party in a country then becomes the number of effective parties within a nation's party system. Values of the number of effective parties in the United States are very close to 2. Values in Canada, where there are two very large major parties, range from 2.5 to about 3.5. The United Kingdom has historically had a number close to 2, but the value has moved closer to 2.5 as the Liberal Democrats have become competitive. Many nations consistently have numbers over 4 or 5, such as Chile, the Czech Republic, and Finland.

A second factor, one specific to proportional representation systems, may also measure how viable third parties that take a pro-gay (or extremely anti-gay) position are in political systems. That variable is the electoral threshold necessary for a party to win seats in a parliament. In proportional representation systems, this is the percentage of the votes that a party must win nationally to get any seats in a parliament. It generally exists to discourage those with very extreme viewpoints from winning seats in a country's parliament with very few votes. This percentage threshold can range from 0 percent to 10 percent, with 3 percent, 4 percent, and 5 percent being the most common values. The lower the threshold, the easier it is for third parties to form and win seats. Once this happens, as is usual in proportional representation systems, they can gain power by entering into a governing coalition, often with a center-left or center-right counterpart.

If the electoral context makes it easier for lesbian and gay activists to persuade a center-left party to support their rights, I expect left-leaning individuals to believe that homosexuality is more justifiable in order to be consistent with the stances of the center-left party. I expect a similar result for right-leaning individuals, as a preexisting far-right third party would make it easier for a center-right party to take pro-gay positions after the majority of the public becomes pro-gay, causing additional attitude change on the Right. In figures 8.7 and 8.8, I break down the relationships between year of birth and the justifiability of homosexuality by ideological placement and the two measures relating to a nation's party system discussed earlier. In figure 8.7, I show the relationships for party systems with more or fewer than 2.5 effective parties, which is used as a measure of whether a country has a two-party system or a multiparty system. Figure 8.8 shows the corresponding relationship in nations with electoral thresholds below and above the value of 3.2 percent. The gay and lesbian population, at least in the United States, is often estimated to be between 3 and 5 percent of the population, making this an appropriate threshold. The first thing to note is that the relationships are much less robust when compared with the analyses of media systems earlier in this chapter. This is largely because there are far fewer surveys from countries with competitive party systems available for the analysis.

The results are mixed. Right-leaning voters in two-party systems (or near two-party systems) do appear to find homosexuality less justifiable as compared to those in multiparty systems. Recall this was because

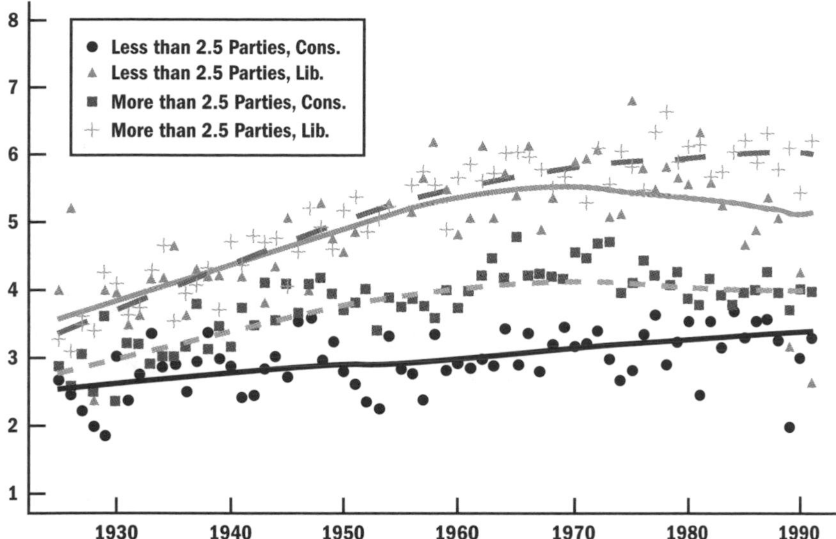

Figure 8.7. Justifiability of Homosexuality Respondents' by Year of Birth, Ideological Placement, and Number of Political Parties.

This figure illustrates differences in respondents' answers to the question involving the justifiability of homosexuality by year of birth, left-right placement, and the number of effective political parties in a country. We might suspect that more liberalization would take place among left-wing voters, or more polarization may be experienced, in a two party-system based on the American experience. Right-wing identified voters do appear to be more conservative in a system with less than 2.5 effective parties, but left-wing voters do not appear to be more liberal.

center-right parties in two-party contexts must maintain anti-gay positions in order to cater to far-right voters. But only among the youngest voters do we see a similar gap emerge among left-leaning voters, as predicted because center-left parties must liberalize on gay rights faster to prevent the defection of lesbian and gay voters to left-wing parties in multiparty contexts. The findings do show that those in multiparty systems appear to be more liberal on the justifiability of homosexuality, especially among conservatives.

As even fewer countries have electoral thresholds, the results in figure 8.8 are less robust than those in figure 8.7, but they do appear to be somewhat clearer when it comes to the findings. There appears to be no differences in right-leaning voters' views on the justifiability of

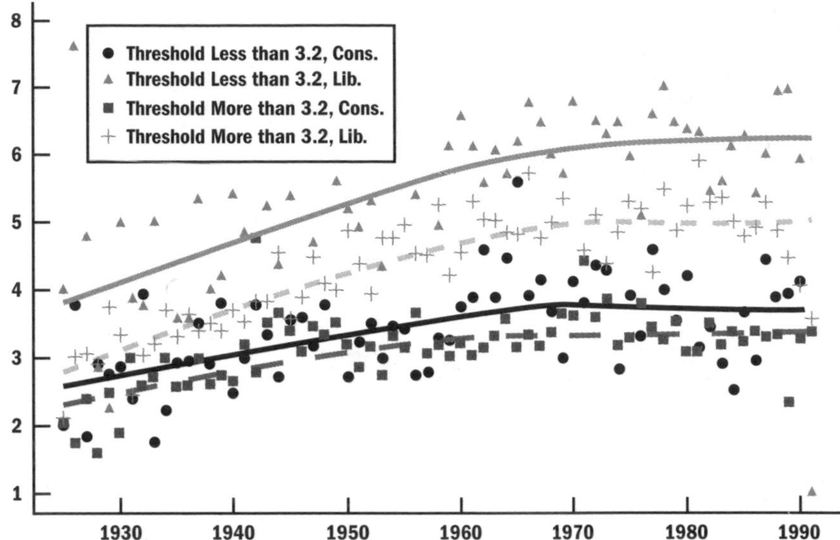

Figure 8.8. Justifiability of Homosexuality Respondents' by Ideological Placement, Year of Birth, and Vote Threshold for Winning Seats in a Country's Parliament.

homosexuality based on differences on the electoral threshold. However, left-leaning voters appear to be about 1 point more liberal when the electoral threshold is below 3.2.

Taken together, the following story about party system dynamics and attitudes toward homosexuality emerges: when it is easy to create a third party (a lower electoral threshold), left-leaning voters are 1 point more liberal on homosexuality in terms of the justifiability question; when there are already many third parties (and likely a far-right party), right-leaning voters also appear to be more liberal on homosexuality.

Several other important points emerge, too. In figure 8.7, which includes a larger sample, younger left-leaning and younger right-leaning voters are generally more divided on homosexuality. Another finding is that year-of-birth effects appear to be stronger for left-leaning respondents as compared to right-leaning respondents. This makes sense if younger left-leaning voters have been more receptive to change. Finally, it is worth noting that attitudes among right-leaning individuals in countries with competitive party systems generally average a response of between 2.5 and 3.5 regardless of age. Mirroring the shifts in the feeling thermometer in the United States among conservatives in the late 1990s, right-leaning voters in democratic countries can, on average, imagine some situations in which homosexuality can be justified in recent years. This may be influenced by interpersonal interactions without lesbians or gays in a free society or messages from free media. As previous figures show, this is not the case for those in countries without a free or pervasive media system, who nearly universally hold anti-gay views.

Conclusion

This chapter has generally found that the gulf between Liberal and illiberal countries on gay rights is much larger than the gulf between social liberals and conservatives in the West. This is crucial for understanding how lesbian and gay issues may be used in internationally politics in coming years.

Because most countries that have higher levels of tolerance for homosexuality are culturally Liberal and Western, and tolerance of homosexuality itself is caused by one of the defining characteristics of these liberal Western countries—freedom of expression and the press—homosexuality and lesbians and gays themselves will likely increasingly become symbolic of the West in general.

That is a terrifying prospect for LGBTQ people in non-Western countries because as a result, individuals who are members of sexual and gender minorities will stand an *increasing chance of being targets for domestic oppression or violence* among those who dislike the West due to this growing symbolism, independent of any local tradition a country may have of disapproving of homosexuality. For local political leaders, especially those whose mass supporters have been subject to Western power and imperialism, explicitly targeting homosexuals or lesbians and gays (or those considered to be lesbian or gay) is a relatively easy way to symbolically fight Western powers, on which their governments may be dependent for aid, *without aggrieving these Western powers directly*.

Westerners and Western leaders need to be aware that sexual and gender minorities, specifically, will be increasingly (and irrationally) held to account for the past sins of the West in the postcolonial or post-Soviet world. International organizations and those in power to provide aid *must* be made aware of this over the coming decades so they can counter such LGBTQ scapegoating and provide badly needed resources to those marginalized and disempowered.

9

Social Change in Liberal Democracies

The single most important thing you can do politically for gay rights is to come out. Not to write a letter to your congressman but to come out.
—Representative Barney Frank (D-MA)

In this chapter, I explore the general conclusions that can be draw from this study. After a brief recap of the historical narrative that has formed the core of this book, I discuss what my findings mean for the future of LGBTQ rights support and for LGBTQ rights activists in the United States and in other Western nations, as well as how these findings may provide some tentative guidance for sexual minority activists outside of Liberal democracies. Lastly, given that the process of affective liberalization arises from (mostly) subconscious processes, rather than an active, deliberative reevaluation of prior beliefs, I discuss what the findings of this study mean for democracy more generally.

The conclusions I present are rather optimistic.[1] This is due to my focus on mass attitudinal change. I think this optimism is warranted given that Millennials generally have positive affect toward LGBTQs, and as prior chapters have made clear, this affect is "sticky," in the sense that it is difficult to change once formed. I am considerably less optimistic when it comes to policy advances on LGBTQ rights in the short term, as a majority of elected officials still remain opposed to LGBTQ rights in the United States. Moreover, the 2016 election of Donald Trump as president, with his attempts to undermine the national press by calling it "fake news," suggests that a free and fair media can no longer be taken for granted in the United States. Although it still seems highly unlikely, if freedom of the press is curtailed in the United States, future generations may end up decidedly less tolerant of lesbians and gays compared to those who have come of age since the mid-1990s.

One conclusion drawn from this research is particularly important and worth stating at the onset: it is that the elites who hold the levers of power can be encouraged to support the political rights of disliked or minority social groups, but they will only do so in response to the sustained activism of members of the general public.

The Historical Sequence of Social Change: A Summary

Before the 1969 Stonewall riots, LGBT activists existed only in small numbers and had little effect on mass opinion or public policy. Indeed, it would be fair to say that the American LGBT movement in these earlier times was politically ineffective. The basic reality of the situation for gay rights prior to 1969 was that these activists lacked a sizable constituency that identified as LGBT, the necessary condition to affect the political calculations of democratic politicians dependent on mass elections for the source of their power. This left even highly strategic and persuasive activists, like Frank Kameny of the Washington, DC Mattachine Society, with little leverage when trying to advocate for policy changes. Occasionally, a reporter could be persuaded to print a sympathetic story in a magazine or similar medium, but little systematic debate of the treatment of homosexuals in American society occurred prior to the 1970s.

Figure 9.1 summarizes many of the key elements of lesbian and gay political history presented in the previous chapters. At the bottom of

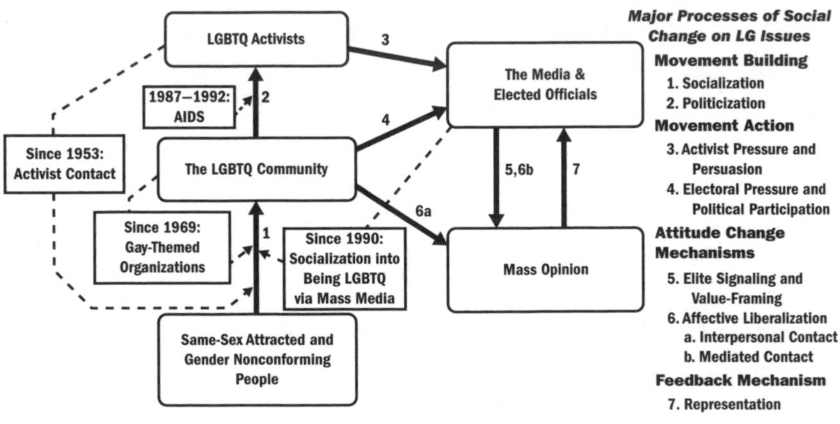

Figure 9.1. Overview of Social Change and Lesbian and Gay Rights.

the chart are same-sex attracted and gender nonconforming people who could comprise a LGBTQ constituency if some psychological identification with other LGBTQ people, or a social identity, developed. While this group was sizable in the 1950s, according to the Kinsey studies, at that time it lacked the necessary sense of a linked fate.[2]

What initially made some early activists politically effective (in limited geographic areas) was the massive expansive of an LGBTQ-identified community that occurred as LGBTQ-centered cultures developed in urban areas in the aftermath of Stonewall. The LGBTQ-identified community expanded with the development first of gay liberation organizations in the 1970s and then of gay-themed organizations in the mid-1970s and 1980s. The larger the LGBTQ community became in these urban areas, due mostly to the development of a shared culture and social identity, the more LGBTQ organizations formed and became visible. As this occurred, the anti-gay climate in these urban areas began to dissipate compared to what it had been in the 1950s and 1960s. This, in turn, led to the development of more organizations encouraging LGBTQ-identification.

As this LGBTQ community grew, it naturally included a substantial number of people who could potentially join the activist cohort. For their part, non-activist LGBTQs could vote for pro-LGBTQ candidates, donate to supportive candidates, or engage in economic boycotts, which could be initiated and publicized by the smaller group of LGBTQ political activists. This feedback process continued until an LGBTQ constituency, which controlled enough votes, donations, or political volunteers to be of note to some local political elites (or potential political elites), existed.

Once a shared, collective identity was established through socialization (mechanism 1 in figure 9.1), the activist cohort (and also liberal non-LGBTQ politicians) could more easily sway the nascent LGBTQ community into political participation, reinforcing the activists' efforts at pressuring decision-makers to take pro-LGBT actions in urban communities where LGBT-identified people were concentrated at that time. A new level of liberal, urban political support for gay rights was thus reached in the late 1970s. The LGBT community developed some political effectiveness, although only in urban areas and only among some liberal politicians. Endorsements of gay rights among liberal political leaders in these areas became common, but nowhere near universal. At a national level, negative public opinion was still enough incentive for mainstream Democrats to hold back support for lesbian and gay rights.

What upset the status quo of the 1970s and early 1980s was AIDS, which provided the necessary circumstances for formerly apolitical LGBTQs to become political activists. AIDS both socialized and politicized a large segment of the public, including those who did not initially identify as LGBTQ. As the ranks of activists grew dramatically, LGBT activism rose to levels rarely seen in other stigmatized minority groups in American politics. ACT-UP heavily assaulted the media status quo regarding the lack of AIDS coverage and a general inattention to other lesbian and gay issues. Moreover, ACT-UP was willing to work with decision-makers ranging from news anchors like Brian Williams to presidential candidates like Bill Clinton in helping them to achieve their goals, whether producing "good" news for journalists, or dramatic events that reinforced their campaign themes. Media coverage of LGBTQ issues exploded in 1990–1993. Moderate members of the Democratic Party from rural and suburban areas then started to routinely endorse lesbian and gay rights.

With the national media and a more diverse group of elected officials becoming sympathetic to the positions of LGBT people, the well-known elite-signaling and value-framing mechanisms of attitude change began to operate in 1992 and 1993 (mechanism 5 in figure 9–1). But while these mechanisms likely helped persuade a small proportion of the public to rethink anti-gay positions, they cannot explain the magnitude of the change in attitudes on gay rights or the rise of youth liberalism on the issue in the mid-1990s.

Media coverage of AIDS and gay rights issues from 1990 to 1993 also had a broader effect on LGBT and same-sex attracted people outside of the nation's urban centers. Evidence of this comes in the form of the swift rise in the percentage of the American population that reported direct interpersonal contact with lesbians and gays across the course of the 1990s. By creating a national dialogue on lesbian and gay issues, media coverage encouraged lesbians and gays across the country to reveal their sexual identities to their friends and family members if they had not already done so. As demonstrated in chapter 6, this interpersonal contact, along with a rise in lesbian and gay representation in popular culture, caused attitude change on gay rights and concentrated it among younger people. Cross-national evidence presented in chapter 8 demonstrates that these cohort effects have emerged only in countries with free and pervasive national media like the United States. This strongly suggests that changes in media in the 1990s, spurred by ACT-UP and other forms of anti-AIDS activism, were what inspired this wave of coming out and transformed mass opinion.

The Future of Gay Rights in the United States

Many in the media have bemoaned the fact that, with the notable exception of the election of Barack Obama in 2008, racial progress is occurring more slowly in recent years than had occurred from the 1940s to the 1980s. In those years, support for interracial marriage, interracial dating, and school desegregation all liberalized swiftly.[3] However, trends on these issues have largely stalled since the 1990s. Little attitude change on racial issues has taken place since then.[4] Furthermore, new forms of anti-minority bias have developed, including racial resentment based on the belief that racial minorities are less inclined to be hardworking or intelligent as compared to whites.[5] For instance, majorities still hold the view that if African Americans "just worked harder they would be as well off as whites," all social science evidence to the contrary notwithstanding.[6] These views are linked to opposition to affirmative action and other policies that combat racial discrimination.

One of the reasons why progress on race has been so difficult of late stems from the increasing overlap between that issue and socioeconomic inequality, which, like race, tends to strongly divide the Democratic and Republican Parties. Beginning in the 1970s, views on race and views on government programs to fight economic inequality became tightly intertwined,[7] partly in response to news stories that portrayed racial minorities as disproportionately benefiting from antipoverty programs.[8] As African Americans became stereotyped in that way, the overlap between opposition to redistribution programs and negative attitudes toward African Americans increased.

Because support for more liberal or more conservative antipoverty and redistributive policies form the core of the ideological division between Democrats and Republicans in the mass public, this has led to a growing division between the parties on race. Republicans have become less supportive of policies that advance racial equality, and Democrats have become more supportive since the 1960s. In a related development, the Republican Party took positions against government programs that would benefit African Americans, leading white southerners to switch to the Republican Party in increasing numbers and further reinforcing the racial division between the parties.[9]

As of the 2010s, Americans' views on race now largely overlap with views on the size and scope of government. It seems unlikely that views either for (or against) government redistribution will die out on the political Left (or Right). This suggests that as long as a sizable number of people view those on government programs as lazy or unmotivated (or as "moochers," to use Mitt Romney's phrase) and as long as racial minorities must disproportionately take advantage of government programs in order to make ends meet, then these people will continue to believe that racial minorities lack the work ethic of Caucasian or Asian Americans. Our current political era is characterized by conservative beliefs in smaller government, the notion that the United States is a meritocracy, and the idea that anyone who tries hard enough should be able to get ahead. Thus, conservatives will continue to oppose programs that reduce poverty, believing them unnecessary, and attribute the fact that African Americans are less well off than whites to common racist stereotypes of African Americans as being less hard-working or intelligent. It may take an economic collapse similar to that of the 1930s, causing a spike in levels of poverty among all racial groups, to dislodge such firmly held linked views.

When it comes to lesbians and gays, however, there are several reasons to believe that attitudes toward them will not follow the same perilous path as attitudes on race. The first involves the nature of intergroup contact. Residential segregation based both on socioeconomic differences between whites and racial minorities and on white racial attitudes has persisted since the 1960s. Naturally, this has led to less intergroup contact between racial groups. Furthermore, television programming has become increasingly segregated since the early 1990s, with shows featuring African American casts moving from the "Big 3" networks to newer networks like UPN and the WB.[10]

When it comes to sexual minorities, residential segregation is much less extensive. Since most lesbians and gays are born into non-gay families, cross-group contact based on sexual orientation and gender identity is facilitated. People from all socioeconomic groups are more likely to have contact with lesbian or gay people as compared to racial out-groups. Furthermore, because of the more diverse background of sexual and gender minorities, they are more likely to share interests, hobbies, and professions with non-sexual and gender minorities as compared to racial minorities, who are disproportionately likely to be found in lower socioeconomic classes in the United States. Shared traits facilitate attitude change in the face of contact, and whites' perception of not sharing traits with racial minorities may be why intergroup contact does not have the clear positive effects it does when heterosexuals interact with sexual minorities.

The fact that lesbians and gays are born integrated into non-gay families, which was originally a hindrance to the LGBT movement by impeding the spread of an in-group LGBT identity, now appears to be a substantive advantage for maintaining social change on lesbian and gay issues. That sexual minorities are not stereotypically linked with lower socioeconomic status, as racial minorities have been, is significant to the trajectory of gay rights support in the United States. In fact, many individuals falsely associate lesbians and gays with having higher than average incomes.[11] This is contradicted by research that has found LGBTQs to have lower incomes on average than heterosexuals. Nonetheless, because sexual orientation and gender identity seem unlikely to become as interrelated with class differences in the United States as race has, the liberalizing trend on gay rights is much less likely to stall.

Political opposition from conservatives active in politics and religious-based opposition from socially conservative denominations may, however, impede further progress on gay rights. Still, insofar as gays and lesbians are likely to be born into both Democratic and Republican families, political conservatives could quite possibly have more meaningful contact with lesbians and gays in the coming years. Motivated reasoning may continue to limit contact effects among politically active conservatives, but young people, even those who may grow to become conservative activists in the future, are much less likely to have developed the strong ideological views necessary to trigger motivated reasoning and negate the liberalizing effects of contact. Even among political conservatives, contact and exposure are likely to have liberalizing effects, though more on the attitudes of future generations of conservatives than those who are politically active today.

This leaves opposition from religious groups as the one trend that is likely to persist into the next, post-millennial generation. To the extent that Republicans need the active support of religious conservatives to win party primaries, anti-gay views will remain dominant within the Republican Party at the elite level. However, anti-gay positions, once a boon to the GOP,[12] have become a political liability for GOP candidates in general elections[13], and this is only likely to intensify as time passes. For instance, Governor Pat McCrory (R) of North Carolina is widely believed to have lost his bid for reelection in 2016 due to his embrace of an anti-LGBTQ "bathroom bill" in that state. At some point, Republican candidates, particularly outside of the South, may have to "evolve," as older Americans who developed anti-gay views prior to the 1990s leave the electorate. That anti-gay views in the Republican Party outside the South have persisted for so long after strong majorities of the public have endorsed lesbian and gay rights is largely a testament to the low saliency of gay rights as an issue. Indeed, although Donald Trump actively disparaged multiple groups of marginalized individuals during his run for the presidency in 2016, ranging from Latinas/os, to Muslims, to war veterans and their families, the one marginalized group he largely left out was lesbians and gays. Trump declared same-sex marriage "settled law" after his election victory, although he promised to appoint socially conservative justices who would likely strike down same-sex marriage to the Supreme Court. He also appointed an attorney general who directed the Justice Department to stop advocating for interpretations of existing law benefitting sexual and gender minorities and announced a ban on transgender troops serving in the US military. What is more dangerous in terms of mass opinion on gay rights are any restrictions on freedom of the press that maybe associated with Mr. Trump's agenda or the agenda of those he appoints to high office.

What about events like the Pulse nightclub shootings in Orlando, Florida, in 2016? Even if they discouraged some from coming out, the positive response and media coverage of this event, which depicted the predominantly Hispanic LGBTQ victims in sympathetic ways (which likely resulted is some positive attitudinal change among those who saw the coverage) is more a sign of positive change than anything else.

Contrast this with the complete lack of media coverage of the firebombing of the Upstairs Lounge in New Orleans in 1973, which killed thirty-two.

The prognosis for further advances for the rights of sexual minorities is thus good, although events like the Pulse shootings and the election of Donald Trump mean that such progress will not be uncontested and must not be taken for granted. But the degree of social stigma needed to convince lesbians and gays to return to the shadows is not likely to be reached, and with mediated and interpersonal contact with LGBT people continuing to work their effects on mass attitudes, future generations are likely to continue to develop pro-gay attitudes.

Lessons for US and Western Activism

Can the process of social change vis-à-vis lesbian and gay issues be used in other avenues where such change is badly needed? The lessons for social groups seeking to improve mass tolerance toward their groups are rather straightforward: media coverage matters but not necessarily to affect mass attitudes in any durable way. Media coverage matters because it is, and continues to be, the most important means by which movement leaders and activists communicate with members of their social group, strengthen the bonds of attachment, and encourage them to take actions to help the group as a whole. However, as social media slowly replaces the ways in which group leaders can connect with more distant members of their social groups, the national news media will likely become less important.

Social media is currently becoming the predominant means for movement leaders to spread a shared sense of group identity and encourage their followers to act on it. However, social media is unlikely to provide much of a platform for activists to communicate with those opposed to their rights. This is because social media has fostered selective exposure—the tendency of information or news to be shared with *only* those already supportive of the message in the first place. Unless social media changes from its current form, media "bubbles" will render cross-group dialogue nearly impossible.

However, portrayals in films and on television shows are and will remain a key medium through which marginalized groups can tell their stories and create effective, positive intergroup contact. While still suffering from some selective exposure, films and television shows are more likely than social media to be seen by those disagreeing with any embedded message. Organizations representing marginalized groups such as atheists and the non-religious, Muslims, and undocumented immigrants (among others) should devote significant resources into lobbying Hollywood and the entertainment industry into promulgating positive and multifaceted portrayals of their members, rather than just reacting to negative and stereotypical portrayals. Tokenism does not work. No one can *connect emotionally* with a token. In order to effect change, portrayals must humanize members of other social groups, be sustained, and stress the commonalities between those portrayed and those viewing the films and shows.

Another obvious takeaway is that when representatives of marginalized groups appear in the media, they can encourage others to disclose their marginalized status as well, although it is also the case that disclosure of an identity risks opening individuals up to very real forms of discrimination ranging from deportation to unemployment and hate crimes. Some combined strategy of lobbying and leveraging support from elected officials to push for new legal protections from such discrimination is advisable. Such new legal protection will tangibly reduce fear of disclosure among the stigmatized, thereby reducing stigma, encouraging more disclosure, and so on, as has occurred with LGBTQs.

Could the theory of affective liberalization be applicable to other issues like healthcare, education, or criminal justice policy? Without a shared demographic or social identity to unite a group of people and spur them into collective action, the answer would appear to be no. Here, the political psychology of the attitudinal change process on gay rights, and likely civil rights and women's rights in the past, suggests limited applicability to other such contexts. However, that conclusion maybe premature. For example, attitudes toward the legal use of marijuana may have shifted in ways similar to gay rights.

At first brush, there is nothing in common about federal policy toward marijuana and gay rights. One involves the use of a drug, the other involves discrimination and intolerance against a group of people. However, the parallels in terms of attitude change are astounding. In 1995, only one in four people supported the legalization of marijuana. By 2016, support for legalization had skyrocketed to 60 percent.[14] This makes it the only issue, unrelated to expanding tolerance toward social groups, which has experienced marked opinion change. Furthermore, younger people have changed more quickly. Between 2005 and 2016, support among Americans aged fifty-five and older increased from 26 percent to 45 percent overall. At the same time, support among those aged eighteen to thirty-five increased from 33 percent to an astounding 77 percent overall.[15]

Marijuana users are not a distinct social group, although the marijuana legalization movement is a well-organized and strategic political movement. So what accounts for attitude change? Contact may still be operating here, but not in the same psychological way that it does with regard to lesbian and gay rights. Individuals may be seeing marijuana use among their friends or discussing the issue with them in informal settings, learning that the negative effects of the drug emphasized by the government and other official sources of information are likely false, and updating their impressions of the drug in a fashion that may approximate *affective liberalization*. These discussions and experiences with marijuana use among friends may then be responsible for changing attitudes, just as interpersonal contact with lesbians and gays affected attitudes toward gay rights.

Some evidence for this comes from the Gallup poll. If this hypothesis is correct, younger people should be using marijuana more than older people, despite the ubiquity of discussions about the benefits of medical marijuana for pain associated with aging or end of life issues and the use of the drug among now older baby boomers. Gallup asked people if they used the drug somewhat regularly in 2016. Among those over age sixty-five, use was reported at only 3 percent. However, among those under age thirty, reported use was at 19 percent—over *six times* the level of reported use of older individuals.[16] Remember, younger people don't follow news reports at anywhere close to the level of older individuals. That younger people are the most liberal on marijuana, and that younger people have the greatest rate of use (although still small in over percentage terms), suggests that personal experience with users of marijuana is likely driving attitude change. Contact, albeit in a form that is very different from that operating on gay rights issues, is highly likely to be responsible for the shift. Something else of note: Gallup reported that the overall rate of usage was 13 percent—more than double the highest estimated size of the LGBTQ population[17] Affective liberalization, liberalization through individual contact, appears to work on issues that do not involve the rights of discrete social groups.

Lessons for International Activism

To a significant degree, the background conditions in which activists must operate structure the key points that international activists should take away from this study. Largely hidden in the American context, these relevant factors emerged from the cross-sectional analysis in chapter 8. The prerequisites for a successful LGBTQ movement include economic development, media infrastructure, and freedom of the press. Education also tends to correlate with individual commitments to political freedoms, making it an additional prerequisite for attitude change.[18]

Since economic development and an educated populace are associated with increasing levels of tolerance,[19] anything limiting the pace of economic development is detrimental to advancing gay rights. Increasing economic security and expanding higher education from the 1950s to the 1990s likely allowed the LGBTQ movement in the West to develop and accomplish its goals without much public backlash. As individuals become more educated, they exhibit greater levels of support for the speech and assembly rights of unpopular groups.[20] Thus greater levels of education, in conjunction with legal protections for assembly and free speech, may have been instrumental in preventing (or at least limiting) police investigations and arrests of LGBTQ activists in the United States prior to the 1980s. An absence of such state-sponsored backlash is something that activists in many countries cannot take for granted, since legal provisions guaranteeing speech and assembly rights can often easily be ignored with impunity if political leaders oppose LGBTQ activism. A lack of education and economic security in much of the world likely limits the effectiveness of local sexual minority movements by forcing them to operate below the radar. Naturally, this drastically limits their ability to advocate for themselves and affect change through intergroup contact.

Given the link between economic development and gay rights, the suggestion that donor countries should reduce or limit foreign aid to countries that pass anti-gay legislation is likely to hurt gay rights in the long-run. In countries like Nigeria or Uganda reducing foreign aid will probably make it more difficult for those countries to invest in education or communications infrastructure. This would lead to a less tolerant society disadvantaging LGBTQ activism.

For countries that have reached higher levels of economic development, however, different factors are limiting opinion change. For instance, it is probable that what is holding back mass support for gay rights in developed nations like the Russian Federation is an inability for local LGBTQ movements to initiate a national dialogue on gay rights in the same way that American anti-AIDS activists did in the late 1980s. State regulation of the media in illiberal countries makes the job of LGBTQ activists much more difficult. Because the state has a vested interest in maintaining the status quo, the viewpoints of dissident minorities, including sexual minorities, are unlikely to find their way onto the airwaves or into print. Without a free media independent of state control, the muffling of unpopular viewpoints makes large-scale attitudinal change nearly impossible.

New technology, including some forms of social media, may eventually help LGBTQ activists to bypass national media. For instance, smartphones allow members of sexual minorities to network in ways impossible just a few years ago. On the Internet, images of lesbians and gays can bypass state control, at least for those savvy enough to get around filters put in place by authoritarian governments.

Without substantive national media attention to gay rights, however, it still seems unlikely that a wave of coming out, initiated by a discussion of gay rights, would develop under an authoritarian regime. While social media are important, they lack the broadness of coverage associated with traditional mass media and especially so in regional contexts where global economic disparities put new technology out of reach. Finding ways to encourage a free and fair media everywhere and to provide universal access to that media for unpopular groups may be a crucial goal on which international LGBTQ activists can focus their efforts. From the perspective of those in the West watching events in the third world and wanting to help marginalized sexual minorities, encouraging those in their own governments to focus specifically on aid that benefits the development of and support for free media and universal education is a prudent focus.

For activists within illiberal countries, developing relationships with political and social leaders, especially while these leaders are still in their formative years, may be a crucial step in the social change process. Several LGBTQ allies discussed in this book, like Evelyn Hooker and Bill Clinton, had extensive contact with LGBTQ people during their early careers, even if, as in Bill Clinton's case, they did not know it at the time. Over time, the LGBTQ community would find these individuals more receptive to supporting LGBTQ rights, especially in contexts where LGBTQ activists could incentivize pro-gay behavior.

Crucially, LGBTQ activists must focus on encouraging the development of a larger LGBTQ constituency through socialization. Cultural identity can be fostered by community-based organizations, *below and above ground*, as well as by cultural transmission via mass media. This gives activists an almost unlimited range of possibilities to develop a self-identified community that can be tailored to local conditions. A common cultural identity need not be based on a Westernized definition of what constitutes being lesbian, gay, bisexual, or transgender; it can just as easily be based on an indigenous or queer interpretation of what it means to be a sexual or gender minority. Local identities are likely to be more effective, as they are less susceptible to being framed as an encroachment of Western culture by political opponents.

The last item that international LGBTQ activists should be aware of, and focus on exploiting, is the role that media presence has in LGBTQ-movement development. When events occur that can encourage media coverage of LGBTQ people and LGBTQ issues, media coverage must be maximized in order to encourage as large an impact as possible on LGBTQ community development. Media coverage of LGBTQ issues can embolden additional people to consciously think of themselves as members of a larger group of sexual minorities and frame collective action like coming out as key to a better life, thereby allowing activists to more effectively lobby political leaders. ACT-UP's gains regarding AIDS funding, Clinton's endorsement of gay rights, the sizable numbers of liberal and Democratic elites endorsing LGBTQ rights in the 1990s, and the growing cultural representation of lesbians and gays in the mid-1990s came to be widely covered in the United States, and many young LGBTQ people learned what is was to be LGBTQ at that time. If coverage nurtures coming out, as well as attitude change, then maximizing this coverage will help both by growing the community and affecting the mass public.

Mass Opinion, Activism, and Democracy

This study presents evidence that affective liberalization, involving *subconscious* mechanisms rather than a *conscious* reevaluation of prejudicial attitudes, caused public opinion toward gays and lesbians. In other words, I argue that most people did not change their attitudes on gay rights by rationally evaluating the pros and cons or by applying democratic values like liberty or equality to the case of sexual minorities. Rather, they arrived at pro-gay positions because they have developed more positive gut reactions to lesbians and gays than in the past through *affective liberalization*.

This is not to suggest that that attitude change on gay rights has not been *real* however. How much people like and dislike other social groups, implicitly and explicitly, is as important and central to prejudice and tolerance as attitudes and values that maybe adopted through rational deliberation or formal education.

The theory of affective liberalization is also consistent with some of the initial findings in the public opinion literature, including those in the tradition of Phil Converse's early work on mass opinion. Roughly fifty years ago, Converse demonstrated that large segments of the public lacked standing positions on prominent political issues and constrained attitudes consistent with either a liberal or conservative political ideology and that they were generally unaware of the finer points of these ideologies.[21] Group-based attitudes, specifically those relating to race and the political parties, were an exception and generally gave structure to people's policy positions. Members of the mass public rarely deliberated over any given issue, but rather use cues and group attachments to form opinions on the fly on specific policies. Indeed, when individuals do consider all the pros and cons of a given position, they can actually be *less* likely to give a response in a manner consistent with their stated preferences and interests.[22]

The theory of affective liberalization may initially be interpreted as assuming a passive and unsophisticated mass public, one susceptible to elite domination consistent with the findings of Converse, yet there are two very important reasons why this would interpretation would be incomplete.

First, the ability of the public to change their attitudes toward social groups subconsciously (or via a system 1 process, as described in chapter 2) rather than through conscious deliberation (or via a system 2 process) is not necessarily detrimental to the character of the mass public. In fact, if anything, the possibility of an alternative mechanism through which positive attitude change can occur, on top of conscious deliberation, should be viewed as a net positive for those who wish to affect public opinion.

System 2, or logical deliberation, can be mentally taxing. Anyone in a math class may attest to this. Combine the low salience of gay rights for most people, as compared to issues like healthcare or taxation, and we would expect little motivation for citizens to actively think about gay rights or the rights of any minority group they are not a part of. This is not to say that some citizens do not do so, but merely that they are unlikely to expend the mental effort without a very powerful incentive. To expect them to engage in such deliberation in the absence of such an incentive, when they are unlikely to engage in deliberation on very salient issues related to their own self-interest like healthcare or taxation, is unrealistic.

That such a small action, such as watching a television show with a gay character can durably change attitudes involving gay rights, is definitely a boon to those who wish to reduce prejudicial attitudes. LGBTQ people need not drone on about the benefits of ENDA or of same-sex marriage in an extended conversation to effect change. They need only be themselves and to identify as LGBTQ to increase support for such measures in their friends and family. If that is most of what is strictly necessary to affect change in mass opinion, then I think this reflects well on the mass public.

Second, a (mostly) passive public in a democracy is a problem only if it results in domination by elites in the media or in government. The larger story of increased support for gay rights upends the notion of a passive public completely. The political activation and participation of the lesbian and gay community from the 1940s to the AIDS crisis was the driving force of attitudinal change. Despite the intense pressure to remain hidden and the fact that they were politically powerless, many LGBTQ people participated in politics in order to encourage social change. From Evelyn Hooker to Bill Clinton, interaction with LGBTQ people affected the attitudes of future elites, reducing prejudice. This later predisposed many to see LGBTQ people not as a deviant group corrupting the morals of others, but as "a community of our nation's gifted people," as Clinton said in his 1992 speech on gay rights. When AIDS forced a much larger portion of the gay community to become politically active or face death, the LGBTQ community and nonprejudiced elites could partner together to effect changes on a larger scale, using the activism of LGBTQ people as political currency. Change was limited at first, but cascaded into greater progress starting later in the 1990s and 2000s.

While a passive public can be dominated by elites, the changes that the lesbian and gay community have inspired, both at the elite and mass levels, suggest that even the most unpopular of groups can affect both the course of national politics and mass opinion in the long term. The key is sustained, intensive political activism from the powerless. If those at the lower rungs of society or in minority groups are willing to participate in a Liberal, democratic system that protects the rights of all individuals to organize and advocate without a violent backlash, they can affect the attitudes and positions of political elites. Crucially, activism on behalf of those at the bottom can thus instill in elites *values supportive of individual rights*, even in the presence of countervailing political and social pressures.

In a true Liberal democracy, participation in politics *matters* regardless of the social standing of those participating. Activism among minority segments of society can increase political tolerance among both the nation's political leadership and the mass public. Tolerance triumphs when people disregard the cynical viewpoint that they are powerless to change their world and begin to strategically advocate for, and persuade others of, the possibility of a better world in the future. The psychological forces that instill notions of powerlessness in oppressed and stigmatized people are powerful, but as this study has demonstrated, if these psychological barriers are removed, the prospect of a better, transformed world is within reach.

APPENDIX 1

Additional Information on Statistical Methods

Interpreting Logit and Other Statistical Models

We cannot use a traditional linear regression, like the one discussed at the end of chapter 2, when predicting whether an event occurs or does not occur, such as when a member of Congress co-sponsors a bill. The event can be represented mathematically by assigning a value of 1 to a member if he or she co-sponsored the legislation and a value of 0 if he or she did not co-sponsor the legislation. This variable is not smooth; it naturally clumps at the values of 0 and 1. It turns out, we can get a more accurate model, if we model the probability of a member of Congress being a 0 or 1 on this variable (i.e., co-sponsoring or not co-sponsoring the legislation), rather than the actual 0's and 1's. This is exactly what a logit, or alternatively, a probit model does.

Contrasting the logit, or probit, model with the linear regression model better illustrate the difference. The effect of a causal variable estimated in the latter model represented something akin to the gap in feelings toward lesbians and gays associated with the highest and lowest values of a demographic variable. The highest and lowest values of the demographic variables were coded as 0's and 1's. For instance, the estimated coefficient in a regression table of the effect of religiosity on lesbian and gay feelings was akin to the difference in lesbian and gay feelings reported by someone who never attends religious services and someone who attends religious services weekly (the minimum and maximum values on religiosity).

Logit models are similar: instead of estimating the actual difference in the variable of interest, they estimate the general propensity that an observation will be a 0 or 1 based on different values of the variables. Based on the different values of the causal variables, which were all demographics in the model discussed in chapter 2, we can estimate that propensity for any given set of values. The key aspect of logit models is that they are associated with the logit function y = log (x/(1− x)). When the numeric value of the propensity associated with some combination of the causal variables is plugged into the inverse of the logit function (y = 1 / (1 + exp(-x))), it supplies a predicted probability of the event occuring. In my logit model of co-sponsorship, these are the propensity that a member co-sponsored the legislation and the probability that a member co-sponsored the legislation.

There are other models, called ordered logit and ordered probit models, which use different functions when there are more than two outcomes for an event. I use such models later in this book. They work the same way they. They estimate the propensity of a certain event occurring based on some combination of the casual variables, and then that propensity can be transformed into a set of predicted probabilities of the various events when plugged into mathematical function associated with the specific type of model. The effects given in these ordered models are interpreted in the same way as those in a linear regression model, except they correspond to the gaps in the propensity instead of the actual variable. The propensity, of course, is imaginary until it is changed into a predicted probability by the model's associated function. The statistical significance of differences in the propensity can be interpreted in a way similar to the effects of a linear regression.

In this book, I generally map likelihoods in such statistical models into predicted probabilities in order to make it easier to interpret the results. For the more mathematically inclined readers though, I also report the estimated models for the propensities.

Estimation of Lesbian and Gay Policy Support for Members of Congress (Chapter 4)

In order to estimate policy support scores from both co-sponsorship information and roll-call votes, I begin with the Bayesian Markov Chain Monte Carlo (MCMC) method outlined by Clinton, Jackman, and Rivers.[1] If a member is liberal and a bill is liberal, we should expect a relatively high probability that that member will co-sponsor that bill and vice-versa for conservative members and bills. In order to estimate the model, I use the number of days from the introduction of a bill to when a specific member co-sponsors a bill as my dependent variable and model it as an event history:

$$\#\text{Days} \sim \exp(\text{Propensity})$$
$$\text{Propensity} = \gamma_h{*}(\text{Bill Liberalism}{*}\text{Member Liberalism} + \text{Bill Conservativism}{*}\text{Member Conservativism}),$$

where "exp" is the exponential distribution, and γ_h is a parameter measuring the nonideological factors specific to a bill leading a member to co-sponsor. The exponential distribution is used for count data where each time period has an equal probability of a co-sposorship, in this case days. The majority of co-sponsorships occur on the first day a bill is introduced, meaning this affects the ideal point estimates derived only slightly.

By defining Bill Liberalism ≡ [1 - Bill Conservatism] and Member Liberalism ≡ [2μ - Member Conservativism], we can estimate this model easily using the Bayesian Markov Chain Monte Carlo algorithm. μ is a number close to the mean of the ideal points chosen to keep all the terms positive for use in the exponential distribution. (This function cannot take negative arguments mathematically.)

More formally, the model for co-sponsorship data along with my specification for the Bayesian priors is:

$$\#\text{Days}_{ih} \sim \exp(P_{ih})$$
$$P_{ih} = \gamma_h{*}((L_h{*}x_i) + (1-L_h){*}(200-x_i))$$
$$x_i \sim \text{normal}(100,1)$$
$$L_h \sim \text{uniform}(0,1)$$
$$\gamma_h \sim \text{uniform}(0,1)$$

i signifies legislators, *h* signifies bills to co-sponsor

L_h and γ_h are parameters specific to the bill relating to its propensity to be co-sponsored in a partisan and nonpartisan manner respectively. P_{ih} is the propensity of the ith legislator to co-sponsor the hth bill. They are both given a uniform prior distribution. The x_i are the bill points for the legislature and are given a normal prior distribution. This model was coded into the BUGS language used by the program WinBUGS for estimation, and this code was inserted into the preexisting model published by Clinton, Jackman, and Rivers for the estimation of an ideal point model based on roll-call data. The ideal points based on the two types of data were then estimated based on my exponential model for co-sponsorship and Clinton, Jackman, and River's logit model for roll-call votes simultaneously. I estimated 20,000 MCMC iterations (with 1,000 burn-in) in WinBUGS for the four time periods.

Finally, in order to bridge between Congresses, I assume that Representative John Conyers, a liberal Democrat from Detroit, had a policy support score of 105 in every time period. Likewise I assumed that Representative Phil Crane, a strong conservative and opponent of gay rights, had a score of 95. Thus, the ideal point estimates ranged from approximately 95 to 105, with larger values being more liberal. However, point estimates for each legislator can range outside of 95 and 105, as Crane and Conyers are simply used as baselines by which to estimate a comparable scale over time and across legislators, and the model may estimate that some legislators are to the right or left of Crane and Conyers on gay rights. These values of 95 and 105 are akin to the poles of +1 and −1 used in other ideal-point models.[2]

This allows for a weak comparison of the scores over time, as long as these two members did not shift their positions sharply on gay rights. They may have, which is why one should be reluctant to compare scores in different time periods. However, the estimates of support are a more valid measure than interest group scores, such as those from the Human Rights Campaign, and the ordering of members within a specific Congress should still be comparable across various years.[3]

Treatment and Control Conditions for the "Ellen" Experiment (Chapter 7)

"Obama" Treatment

Television has become the medium through which most citizens learn about politics. We would like to show you a picture and a short transcript of an interview that took place on television a few months ago about the 2008 presidential election. The interviewer here is Ellen DeGeneres, who is married to Portia De Rossi and known for her role on a sitcom in the mid-1990s. She interviews Barack Obama, one of the candidates for president in 2008.

Figure A1.1. Image Used in "Obama" Condition.

Obama Talks Politics on Ellen

ELLEN: I'd like to welcome our very special guest today, Barack Obama. He's come a very long way to talk to us about the 2008 presidential election. <Applause>

OBAMA: I'm glad to be here, Ellen. Thank you so much for having me. After all this is one of the most important elections we've had in decades. A lot is riding on it.

ELLEN: What do you think has been the most important issue in this election so far?

OBAMA: Well, I think a lot of people in Middle America today are suffering because of the way things are going in this country. One of the most important things we can do is provide relief to people. We have to fix the mess that has developed over the years in Washington.

What do you think is the most important problem facing the country today?

1. The Economy
2. Healthcare
3. Terrorism
4. Iraq and Afghanistan

5. Social Issues such as Abortion and Gay Rights
6. Energy
7. Something Else
8. Haven't Thought Much about It

"McCain" Treatment

Television has become the medium through which most citizens learn about politics. We would like to show you a picture and a short transcript of an interview that took place on television a few months ago about the 2008 presidential election. The interviewer here is Ellen DeGeneres, who is married to Portia De Rossi and known for her role on a sitcom in the mid-1990s. She interviews John McCain, one of the candidates for president in 2008.

McCain Talks Politics on Ellen

ELLEN: I'd like to welcome our very special guest today, John McCain. He's come a very long way to talk to us about the 2008 presidential election. <Applause>

Figure A1.2. Image Used in "McCain" Condition.

McCain: I'm glad to be here, Ellen. Thank you so much for having me. After all this is one of the most important elections we've had in decades. A lot is riding on it.

Ellen: What do you think has been the most important issue in this election so far?

McCain: Well, I think a lot of people in Middle America today are suffering because of the way things are going in this country. One of the most important things we can do is provide relief to people. We have to fix the mess that has developed over the years in Washington.

What do you think is the most important problem facing the country today?

1. The Economy
2. Healthcare
3. Terrorism
4. Iraq and Afghanistan
5. Social Issues such as Abortion and Gay Rights
6. Energy
7. Something Else
8. Haven't Thought Much about It

"Brokaw" Treatment

Television has become the medium through which most citizens learn about politics. We would like to show you a picture and a short transcript of an interview that took place on television a few months ago about the 2008 presidential election. The interviewer here is Ellen DeGeneres, who is married to Portia De Rossi and known for her role on a sitcom in the mid-1990s. She interviews Tom Brokaw, an anchor for a major television news channel.

Brokaw Talks Politics on Ellen

Ellen: I'd like to welcome our very special guest today, Tom Brokaw. He's come a very long way to talk to us about the 2008 presidential election. <Applause>

Figure A1.3. Image Used in "Brokaw" Condition.

BROKAW: I'm glad to be here, Ellen. Thank you so much for having me. After all this is one of the most important elections we've had in decades. A lot is riding on it.

ELLEN: What do you think has been the most important issue in this election so far?

BROKAW: Well, I think a lot of people in Middle America today are suffering because of the way things are going in this country. One of the most important things we can do is provide relief to people. We have to fix the mess that has developed over the years in Washington.

What do you think is the most important problem facing the country today?

1. The Economy
2. Healthcare
3. Terrorism
4. Iraq and Afghanistan
5. Social Issues such as Abortion and Gay Rights
6. Energy
7. Something Else
8. Haven't Thought Much about It

Control Condition

Television has become the medium through which most citizens learn about politics. We'd like to show you a picture and a short transcript of an interview that took on television a few months ago about the 2008 presidential election. The interviewer here is David Letterman, who is married to Regina Lasko and known for his role on a late-night comedy show. He interviews Tom Brokaw, an anchor for a major television news channel.

Brokaw Talks Politics on Letterman

LETTERMAN: I'd like to welcome our very special guest today, Tom Brokaw. He's come a very long way to talk to us about the 2008 presidential election. <Applause>

BROKAW: I'm glad to be here, Dave. Thank you so much for having me. After all this is one of the most important elections we've had in decades. A lot is riding on it.

LETTERMAN: What do you think has been the most important issue in this election so far?

Figure A1.4. Image Used in Control Condition.

BROKAW: Well, I think a lot of people in Middle America today are suffering because of the way things are going in this country. One of the most important things we can do is provide relief to people. We have to fix the mess that has developed over the years in Washington.

What do you think is the most important problem facing the country today?

1. The Economy
2. Healthcare
3. Terrorism
4. Iraq and Afghanistan
5. Social Issues Such as Abortion and Gay Rights
6. Energy
7. Something Else
8. Haven't Thought Much about It

Question Wording for Lesbian and Gay Rights Scale in the "Ellen" Experiment (Chapter 7)

A. Should same-sex couples be allowed to marry, or do you think they should not be allowed to marry?
   1. Should be allowed
   2. Should not be allowed
B. How strongly do you feel about your position on same-sex marriage?
   1. Strongly
   2. Not Strongly
C. Do you think gay or lesbian couples, in other words, homosexual couples, should be legally permitted to adopt children?
   1. Should be allowed
   2. Should not be allowed
D. How strongly do you feel about your position on same-sex couples adopting?
   1. Strongly
   2. Not Strongly

E. Should same-sex couples be allowed to form civil unions, or do you think they should not be allowed to form civil unions?
   1. Should be allowed
   2. Should not be allowed

F. How strongly do you feel about your position on same-sex civil unions?
   1. Strongly
   2. Not Strongly

G. Do you favor or oppose laws to protect homosexuals against job discrimination?
   1. Favor
   2. Oppose

H. Do you favor or oppose such laws strongly or not strongly?
   1. Strongly
   2. Not Strongly

I. Do you think homosexuals should be allowed to serve in the United States Armed Forces or don't you think so?
   1. Homosexuals should be allowed to serve
   2. Homosexuals should not be allowed to serve

J. Do you feel strongly or not strongly that homosexuals should be allowed or should not be allowed to serve?
   1. Strongly
   2. Not Strongly

APPENDIX 2

Additional Information on Data and Variable Coding

Details for Regression Analyses of the ANES Feeling Thermometer for Gays in Chapter 2

For analysis of change in causes of pro-gay affect, all of the variables are coded to range from 0 to 1. Religiosity is coded to range from no church attendance (0) to weekly attendance (1). Party ranges from strong Republican (0) to strong Democrat (1). Ideology ranges from very conservative (0) to very liberal (1). Gender takes on the value 1 if a respondent is female and 0 otherwise. Race takes on the value 1 if the respondent is black or African American and 0 otherwise. Education ranges from no high school degree (0) to those with a postgraduate degree (1). Finally, year of birth is the actual year of birth of the respondent in the combined ANES dataset rescaled to range from 0 to 1. Younger people thus get higher values on this variable. The model is included in Table A2.1.

Details for Logistic Regression Analysis of Annual Support for the Gay Rights Bill in Chapter 4

In this analysis, I measure district urbanicity as the percentage of a district's population that is classified as urban by the US Census Bureau. Some other factors that may also be important and are included in my model are the percentage of a member's district that is college-educated and the median income of a district (measured in $1000s). I leave these in their natural units, as I report predicted probabilities in the analysis in the chapter. As members of the Congressional Black Caucus have also traditionally been more supportive of nondiscrimination measures, especially those relating to lesbian and gay rights, I also include a variable equaling "1" if a member is African American and "0" otherwise. Newer members may be more inclined to support the bill than older

TABLE A2.1. Changing Year Demographic Effects on Feelings toward Lesbians and Gays on the ANES (Chapter 2)

Variable	Intercept	*Relig.*	Party	Ideology	Gender	Black	Educ.	Year of Birth
Baseline Effect (in 1984)	1.60 *(4.67)*	**-9.58***** ***(1.81)***	**5.48**** ***(2.11)***	**20.93***** ***(3.26)***	**8.24***** ***(1.36)***	0.25 *(1.87)*	**17.90***** ***(2.34)***	**9.64@** ***(5.79)***
* 1988	1.47 *(6.83)*	1.03 *(2.65)*	0.21 *(3.10)*	5.23 *(4.72)*	**−3.36@** ***(1.96)***	−1.24 *(2.64)*	**7.66*** ***(3.32)***	−10.06 *(8.27)*
* 1992	6.23 *(6.40)*	0.64 *(2.40)*	**4.98@** ***(2.92)***	6.26 *(4.32)*	−0.17 *(1.83)*	−3.84 *(2.45)*	−0.29 *(3.11)*	−1.31 *(7.72)*
* 1994	**−14.30*** ***(6.77)***	−2.81 *(2.48)*	3.98 *(3.08)*	**15.62**** ***(4.81)***	1.74 *(1.91)*	2.43 *(2.55)*	1.68 *(3.30)*	12.91 *(8.05)*
* 1996	−1.70 *(6.89)*	1.59 *(2.60)*	3.16 *(3.26)*	**12.97*** ***(5.08)***	−0.56 *(1.97)*	−1.74 *(2.64)*	−1.04 *(3.30)*	7.48 *(8.33)*
* 1998	0.39 *(7.75)*	−0.11 *(2.78)*	−2.95 *(3.43)*	**10.62*** ***(5.23)***	**4.66*** ***(2.09)***	−2.30 *(2.72)*	−1.45 *(3.59)*	13.93 *(8.76)*
* 2000	2.71 *(9.54)*	−0.92 *(3.30)*	5.35 *(4.14)*	1.65 *(6.15)*	0.65 *(2.52)*	3.16 *(3.32)*	5.73 *(4.58)*	1.41 *(10.94)*
* 2002	9.39 *(7.63)*	−0.56 *(2.70)*	2.96 *(3.36)*	-6.09 *(4.91)*	2.53 *(2.03)*	−0.49 *(2.75)*	2.52 *(3.60)*	6.82 *(8.87)*
* 2004	1.56 *(8.24)*	3.16 *(2.92)*	0.42 *(3.71)*	0.90 *(5.61)*	−0.25 *(2.19)*	3.29 *(2.80)*	2.40 *(3.82)*	11.98 *(9.65)*
* 2008	−2.16 *(6.97)*	2.18 *(2.51)*	−0.25 *(3.14)*	−1.17 *(4.45)*	**3.29@** ***(1.88)***	−0.78 *(3.39)*	−1.36 *(3.31)*	**23.64**** ***(7.98)***
Adj. R^2	0.261							
N	11284							
σ^2	575							

*** ~ p < .001, ** ~ p <. 01, * ~ p <. 05, @ ~ p < .1 (two-tailed tests)

members. I include a variable equaling the number of years a member has served called "seniority." Also included is a variable measuring general support for civil rights. The civil rights support variable ranges from 0 to 100, with larger values indicating greater support for civil rights legislation. This variable comes from the Leadership Conference on Civil and Human Rights (LCCR), a coalition of interest groups supportive of civil rights.[1] The group uses this measure to rate members on how supportive they are of civil rights, based on their voting record in Congress.

The exact estimated regression models by year are included in table A2.2.

TABLE A2.2. Determinants of Support for the Gay Rights Bill

	Intercept		District % Urban		Black Representative		Democratic Representative	
Congress	Param.	S.E	Param	S.E.	Param.	S.E	Param	S.E.
94th	−11.82	3.083***	0.074	0.027**	−0.985	0.851	0.984	1.253
95th	−16.98	3.592***	0.06	0.027*	1.017	0.81	0.012	1.083
96th	−11.05	2.607***	0.039	0.014**	1.201	0.826	−1.238	0.808
97th	−11.98	2.182***	0.046	0.016*	2.274	0.988*	2.2	0.957*
98th	−13.14	2.493***	0.033	0.011*	0.842	0.72	0.595	0.909
99th	−12.29	1.803***	0.025	0.011*	0.241	0.804	3.114	0.795***
100th	−13.64	2.046***	0.02	0.01*	−0.263	0.759	2.095	0.92*
101st	−13.39	2.103***	0.012	0.01	−0.021	0.734	0.694	0.696
102nd	−17.31	2.11***	0.025	0.01*	−1.45	0.857@	3.525	0.705***

	Democratic Presidential Vote		District Education		District Income		LCCR Score (Civil Rights Support)	
Congress	Param.	S.E	Param	S.E.	Param.	S.E	Param	S.E.
94th	0.047	0.022*	0.235	0.064**	−0.537	0.193**	0.038	0.02@
95th	0.057	0.029*	0.141	0.057*	−0.001	0.191	0.058	0.021**
96th	0.016	0.023	0.077	0.053	−0.141	0.172	0.086	0.18***
97th	0.006	0.022	0.209	0.056***	−0.159	0.162	0.044	0.011***
98th	0.054	0.029@	0.154	0.039***	−0.075	0.071	0.058	0.014***
99th	0.073	0.021***	0.147	0.039***	−0.008	0.066	0.009	0.004*
100th	0.069	0.021***	0.151	0.038***	−0.062	0.064	0.053	0.016***
101st	0.074	0.023***	0.119	0.038**	−0.038	0.067	0.064	0.015***
102nd	0.151	0.025***	0.188	0.041***	0.073	0.067	0.002	0.005

	Seniority		Cox and Snell	Percent Correctly	Years
Congress	Param.	S.E.	R^2	Predicted	
94th	−0.109	0.041*	94.9%	94.9%	75–76
95th	−0.035	0.031	0.236	92.5%	77–78
96th	−0.035	0.028	0.302	90.0%	79–80
97th	−0.006	0.024	0.327	90.2%	81–82
98th	−0.02	0.022	0.343	87.3%	83–84
99th	−0.019	0.021	0.335	87.6%	85–86
100th	−0.008	0.019	0.341	86.8%	87–88
101st	0.005	0.019	0.363	87.6%	89–90
102nd	−0.071	0.22	0.449	87.2%	91–92

Statistical Details of Regression Analyses for Chapter 5

To determine if any specific groups shifted more in their support from 1988 to 1992, employment protections and the feeling thermometer were first independently modeled as a function of these demographics directly (with all demographics coded on scales from 0 to 1), along with interaction terms created by multiplying them with a 1992 dummy indicator variable. This indicator takes on the value of "1" for those surveyed in 1992 and "0" for those surveyed in 1988. As a reminder, these interaction terms measure changes in the support among these various demographic groups from 1988 to 1992. Strengthening relationships will be indicated by positive interaction effects (which are the terms in the model that are multiplied times the demographic variables). Drops in the strength of the relationship will be indicated by negative interactions effects. I also include the feeling thermometer score in the model predicting responses to the employment protections question. Theoretically, feelings involving gays and lesbians should affect gay rights support, as discussed in chapter 2. For reasons of clarity, after initially estimating these models, I then estimated the same models, but removed interaction terms in the new model for variables that the initial models indicated did not change in their effects from 1988 to 1992. This creates simpler, yet equally accurate models of changing attitudes in these years. These second models are displayed in table 5.2 (for employment protections) and table 5.4 (for lesbian and gay feelings).

Additional Details on Regression Analyses for Chapter 6

Coding for Grace under Fire Analysis (Table 6.1)

Included are a number of demographic controls asked on the 1994 ANES wave, all coded from 0 to 1. These include ideology (7 points, higher = more liberal), party identification (7 points, higher = more Democratic), biblical interpretation (3 points, higher = Bible is the word of God), religious attendance (4 points, higher = greater attendance), age (higher = younger), education (5 points, higher = more educated), race (1= African American), and gender (1= female).

Coding for Analysis of Media Polls of Contact (Table 6.2)

To examine how both interpersonal contact and mediated contact have changed attitudes, I model a respondent's support for employment protections on these surveys using a multilevel logistic regression, the interpretation of which is very similar to the interpretation of logistic regression or "logit" discussed earlier in appendix 1. A multilevel model is generally appropriate when some variables are measured at an aggregate level. This is important, because I include my variable measuring the number of lesbian and gay television characters in each year in this analysis as a contextual measure of the amount of mediated exposure taking place in that year. Year is the "aggregate level" here. The way a multilevel model is different from a regular logit in this context, is that it can more accurately control for slightly different effect sizes in different years (or on different surveys) than a traditional logit. The LGBTQ television characters measure is low in the 1980s and high after 1995 (see figure 6.1). I also include all of the demographics variables listed above in this multilevel logistic regression, including contact with lesbians and gays and views on the origins of homosexuality. This last variable is measured as a dummy variable taking on the value of 1 if a respondent believes that gays are born gay and 0 otherwise. All others have been rescaled to range from 0 to 1, with the exception of television news. Younger cohorts take on higher values of age.

Coding for the Analysis of the GSS and Television Viewing (Table 6.3)

I use a multilevel logistic model in table 6.3 similar to the model in table 6.2. A more complicated ordered probit model, using all response categories in addition to "not wrong at all," works just as well in this context and gives nearly identical results.

I created a set of eight regional dummy variables to use as controls. All take a value of 1 if a respondent lives in that region and 0 otherwise. These represent those who live in the South Atlantic, North Central, South Central, Mountain, Pacific, and Mid-Atlantic regions. Religion is controlled for via a set of dummy variables equaling 1 if a respondent identifies as either Jewish, Catholic, a liberal or moderate Protestant, or an evangelical/fundamentalist Protestant and 0 otherwise. I also control for ideology (7 points, more conservative), party identification (7 points, more Republican), church attendance (5 points), the belief that the Bible is to be interpreted literally (literal Biblical interpretation = 1), race (African American = 1 and other = 1), gender (female =1), residing in a rural area at age 16 (rural childhood = 1), and attitudes in support of premarital sex (1–4, more supportive), extramarital sex (1–4, more supportive), and interracial marriage (oppose a legal ban = 1). On the GSS, self-reported daily hours of television consumption can take on any value from 0 to 24. A few respondents (43 over the history of the GSS) indicated that they consumed over 18 hours of TV a day on average and were coded as 18 hours. This top-coding does not affect the results of the analysis.

Results for the Analysis of the Cumulative ANES in Chapter 6

TABLE A2.3. Changing Year-of-Birth Effects on the Feelings toward Lesbians and Gays Thermometer in the ANES (Chapter 6)

Variable	Intercept	Religiosity	Party	Ideology	Gender	Black	Education	Year of Birth	Year of Birth^2
Baseline Effect (in 1984)	−14.61	**−9.52*****	**5.35***	**21.15*****	**8.25*****	0.22	**17.61*****	65.34	−45.53
	(17.23)	***(1.81)***	***(2.11)***	***(3.26)***	***(1.35)***	*(1.86)*	***(2.36)***	*(57.27)*	*(46.59)*
Δ in 1988	19.03	0.98	0.35	5.01	**−3.37@**	−1.22	**7.99***	−70.37	49.23
	(24.12)	*(2.65)*	*(3.10)*	*(4.72)*	***(1.96)***	*(2.64)*	***(3.36)***	*(79.68)*	*(64.12)*
Δ in 1992	2.21	0.51	**5.02@**	6.21	−0.11	−3.75	−0.52	8.29	−4.52
	(24.05)	*(2.40)*	***(2.93)***	*(4.43)*	*(1.83)*	*(2.45)*	*(3.16)*	*(77.70)*	*(61.44)*
Δ in 1994	−7.07	−2.91	4.12	**15.40****	1.76	2.45	1.83	−14.38	24.14
	(25.70)	*(2.49)*	*(3.08)*	***(4.81)***	*(1.90)*	*(2.55)*	*(3.32)*	*(81.88)*	*(64.00)*
Δ in 1996	7.56	1.50	3.27	**12.78***	−0.52	−1.70	−0.84	−26.57	29.36
	(26.1)	*(2.60)*	*(3.27)*	***(5.08)***	*(1.98)*	*(2.64)*	*(3.33)*	*(82.52)*	*(64.20)*
Δ in 1998	**58.45***	−0.11	−2.66	**10.04@**	**4.68***	−2.47	−0.27	**−166.28@**	**134.35***
	(28.68)	*(.442)*	*(3.43)*	***(5.23)***	***(2.09)***	*(2.72)*	*(3.64)*	***(87.38)***	***(66.06)***
Δ in 2000	**68.00@**	−1.15	5.54	0.55	0.50	3.11	6.75	**−198.17@**	**148.11@**
	(37.32)	*(3.30)*	*(4.15)*	*(6.18)*	*(2.43)*	*(3.32)*	*(4.58)*	***(110.44)***	***(81.60)***

(*continued*)

TABLE A2.3. Changing Year-of-Birth Effects on the Feelings toward Lesbians and Gays Thermometer in the ANES (Chapter 6) (*continued*)

Variable	Intercept	Religiosity	Party	Ideology	Gender	Black	Education	Year of Birth	Year of Birth²
Δ in 2002	38.04 *(30.61)*	−0.67 *(2.70)*	3.14 *(3.36)*	−6.38 *(4.91)*	2.50 *(2.03)*	−0.43 *(2.75)*	2.94 *(3.62)*	−85.17 *(92.02)*	71.18 *(68.83)*
Δ in 2004	−15.73 *(33.97)*	3.25 *(2.92)*	0.67 *(3.71)*	1.14 *(5.62)*	−0.26 *(2.19)*	3.38 *(2.80)*	2.07 *(3.87)*	48.93 *(97.65)*	−16.66 *(70.47)*
Δ in 2008	−6.15 *(28.68)*	2.21 *(2.51)*	−0.21 *(3.14)*	−1.26 *(4.46)*	**3.29**@ ***(1.88)***	−0.67 *(3.39)*	−1.41 *(3.34)*	22.00 *(82.94)*	10.51 *(60.58)*
Adj. R^2	0.261								
N	11284								
σ^2	574								

*** ~ p < .001, ** ~ p <. 01, * ~ p <. 05, @ ~ p < .1 (two-tailed tests)

Additional Details for Regression Analyses in Chapter 7

Coding for Analysis in Table 7.4

I use the same variable coding as Dyck and Pearson-Merkowitz except as noted.[2] That study included dummy and control variables ranging from 0 to 1 for women, blacks, Latinas/os, members of other non-white races, education, age, identification as a born-again Christian, income, party identification, and approval of George W. Bush's job as president. Because the variable of interest, same-sex marriage support, can take on 4 values, I used an "ordered probit" model.

Coding of the Ellen Experiment

In addition to lesbian and gay rights questions, questions concerning ideological self-placement, party identification, and some demographics were asked on the survey. Political knowledge was assessed by the number of correct responses to nine standard questions: control of the House and Senate, who appoints Supreme Court justices, the branch of government that interprets law, and identification of the offices held by Nancy Pelosi,

Harry Reid, Robert Gates, John Roberts, and Gordon Brown. The number of correct responses was rescaled to range between 0 and 1. The exact question wordings for the dependent variable (gay rights) are in appendix 1.

As would be expected of a sample consisting of highly educated young people in 2009, the sample was very supportive of Barack Obama and unsupportive of John McCain even controlling for ideology and partisan identification. Most of the potential biases of the student sample in terms of age, education, income, ideology, party, and the general level of support for lesbian and gay rights create a strong bias *against* finding positive results. In fact, gay rights support was generally so high that many individuals clustered at the uppermost point (10) suggesting the scale may be truncated at higher levels. In order to adjust for this, I use tobit regression models, which correct for truncation at a maximum or minimum value. To clarify the findings, which are contingent on political knowledge, ideological self-placement, and treatment, I present the results by ideological group, but report a combined analysis below.

The sample consisted of 87 self-identified liberals, 55 conservatives, and 125 moderates. I control for racial groups, gender, party identification (using a traditional 7-point scale), and religion including identification as a born-again or evangelical Christian. Racial groups, gender, and religion were all controlled for by using dummy variables equaling 1 if the respondent was Asian, black, Latina/o, Protestant, Catholic, born-again or evangelical, Muslim, or male, and 0 otherwise respectively. Party was coded to range from 0 to 1.

Alternative Triple-Interaction Model of Experimental Results from Chapter 7

TABLE A2.4. Experimental Results: Fully Specified Interactive Censored Regression Model (Tobit)

(Dependent Variable = Lesbian/Gay Rights Support Scale)

	All Respondents	
	Coef. Est.	*S.E*
Intercept 1	8.76	*0.69****
Intercept 2	−0.01	*0.05*

(*continued*)

TABLE A2.4. Experimental Results: Fully Specified Interactive Censored Regression Model (Tobit) (*continued*)

(Dependent Variable = Lesbian/Gay Rights Support Scale)

	All Respondents	
	Coef. Est.	*S.E*
Party (Republican)	−1.80	*0.30****
Sex (Male)	−0.65	*0.14****
Asian	−1.05	*0.30****
Black	−0.71	*0.25***
Latino	0.31	*0.32*
Born-Again/Evangelical	−0.63	*0.19***
Protestant	−0.11	*0.17*
Catholic	−0.16	*0.19*
Muslim	0.38	*0.80*
Political Knowledge	2.06	*1.03**
Ideology (Liberalism)	2.19	*0.98**
Knowledge * Liberalism	−2.54	*1.51*
Ellen-Obama Treatment	2.84	*0.97***
Ellen-Obama * Knowledge	−3.73	*1.52**
Ellen-Obama * Liberalism	−4.22	*1.50***
Ellen-Obama * Knowledge * Liberalism	6.02	*2.33**
Ellen-McCain Treatment	2.30	*0.89**
Ellen-McCain * Knowledge	−3.56	*1.52**
Ellen-McCain * Liberalism	−3.87	*1.34***
Ellen-McCain * Knowledge * Liberalism	5.73	*2.11***
Ellen-Brokaw Treatment	1.11	*0.96*
Ellen-Brokaw * Knowledge	−1.91	*1.48*
Ellen-Brokaw * Liberalism	−3.88	*1.61**
Ellen-Brokaw * Knowledge * Liberalism	1.72	*2.37*
Log-Likelihood	−323.0	
N	267	

*** ~ p < .001, ** ~ p < .01, * ~ p < .05 (two-tailed tests)

NOTES

CHAPTER 1. A TRANSFORMED SOCIETY

1 Generally, when referencing lesbian, gay, bisexual, and transgender activists, organization, or movements, I will use the common acronyms "LGBT" or "LGBTQ" for economy. At the same time, it should be acknowledged that this is an imperfect shorthand for describing who may or may not fit under that acronym, that the use of these labels is highly policed and contested (especially in academia), and that the accepted usage tends to shift overtime. An example of this is the ever-changing name of the National LGBTQ taskforce, which was renamed from the National Gay and Lesbian Taskforce (or NGLTF), as this study was being written. That said, in many situations throughout this book, I discuss polling and trend data that surveys the public's support for either "gay rights" or, at most, "lesbian and gay rights." In an effort to be as accurate as possible, I will generally use "lesbian and gay" (or gay, for stylistic reasons) when referring to social and political changes documented by polling and other data, since most of these sources omit bisexuals and transgender people or other forms of gender and sexual diversity. This, rather unfortunately, includes nearly all polling data on LGBT rights from the period under study in this book. Additional research on public support for bisexual and transgender rights is badly needed, especially from national polling firms, which regularly poll on lesbian and gay rights only.

2 Generally, this is an empirical study. As such, it tries to keep normative stances (in support of LGBTQ rights) to a minimum in this text. However, doing so on such an emotionally charged issue is next to impossible, and normative statements will make their way into the text from time to time. Tolerance of minority groups is key to a functioning modern liberal democracy, and as a majority of the Supreme Court has agreed, the arguments against support for lesbian and gay rights are generally unpersuasive for people who lack a strong religious or conservative identity, or as this study makes clear, who have preexisting negative affect toward lesbians and gays. For those readers who disagree with my normative stance, I invite you to read through the text in order to gain an empirically based understanding of how and why the nation has shifted in the last three decades in favor of LGBTQ rights. Skipping the third and last chapters should help the reader avoid most normative statements. I would like to state that the data and empirical analyses presented in this book were generated independently of any normative stance of the author, and as such, should generally be independent of such a stance whenever normative language crops up. Indeed, several of the

surveys discussed in this book were taken before the author was even born, which ensures that that data is, at the very least, generally independent of the author.

3 Tom W. Smith, Peter Marsden, Micheal Hout, and Jibum Kim, *General Social Surveys, 1972–2016*, Sponsored by the National Science Foundation (Chicago: NORC at the University of Chicago [producer]; Storrs, CT: The Roper Center for Public Opinion Research, University of Connecticut [distributor], 2016).

4 Calculation by the author using the University of California at Berkeley's website for analysis of survey data, sda.berkeley.edu. Subsequent numbers from the GSS in this chapter were also calculated using this resource.

5 Pew, "Changing Attitudes on Gay Marriage," 2016, www.pewforum.org.

6 Edward Alwood, *Straight News: Gays, Lesbians, and the News Media* (New York: Columbia University Press, 1996).

7 David K. Johnson, *The Lavender Scare: The Cold War Persecution of Gays and Lesbians in the Federal Government* (Chicago: University of Chicago Press, 2004).

8 Dudley Clendinen and Adam Nagourney, *Out for Good: The Struggle to Build a Gay Rights Movement in America* (New York: Simon and Shuster, 1999).

9 Stephen Tropiano, *The Prime Time Closet: A History of Gays and Lesbians on TV* (New York: Applause Theatre and Cinema, 2002); Larry Gross, *Up From Invisibility: Lesbians, Gay Men, and the Media in America* (New York: Columbia University Press, 2001).

10 Gallup.com, "Lesbian and Gay Rights," 2016, www.gallup.com.

11 Gerald N. Rosenberg, *The Hollow Hope: Can Courts Bring Social Change?*, 2nd ed. (Chicago: University of Chicago Press, 2008); Ron Becker, *Gay TV and Straight America* (New Brunswick, NJ: Rutgers University Press, 2006).

12 Gregory M. Herek and John P. Capitanio, "'Some of My Best Friends': Intergroup Contact, Concealable Stigma, and Heterosexuals' Attitudes toward Gay Men and Lesbians," *Personality and Social Psychology Bulletin* 22, no. 3 (1996): 412–24.

13 Gary Mucciaroni, *Same-Sex, Different Politics: Success and Failure in the Struggles over Gay Rights* (Chicago: University of Chicago Press, 2008); Paul R. Brewer, *Value War: Public Opinion and the Politics of Gay Rights* (Lanham, MD: Rowman and Littlefield, 2008); Gregory Lewis, "The Friends and Family Plan: Contact with Gays and Support for Gay Rights," *Policy Studies Journal* 39, no. 2 (2011): 217–38; Edward Schiappa, Peter B. Gregg, and Dean E. Hewes, "Can One TV Show Make a Difference? *Will and Grace* and the Parasocial Contact Hypothesis," *Journal of Homosexuality* 51, no. 4 (2006): 15–37.

14 Shanto Iyengar and Donald Kinder, *News That Matters: Television and American Opinion* (Chicago: University of Chicago Press, 1989); Edward Carmines and James Stimson, *Issue Evolution: Race and the Transformation of American Politics* (Princeton, NJ: Princeton University Press, 1989).

15 Many of the public opinion trends depicted in this chapter are taken from Karlyn Bowman and Adam Foster, "Attitudes about Homosexuality and Gay Marriage," *American Enterprise Institute Studies in Public Opinion*, 2008, www.aei.org.

16 Smith et al., *General Social Surveys, 1972–2016*.

17 Bowman and Foster, "Attitudes about Homosexuality and Gay Marriage."
18 Mucciaroni, *Same-Sex, Different Politics.*
19 Bowman and Foster, "Attitudes about Homosexuality and Gay Marriage."
20 Margot Canaday, *The Straight State: Sexuality and Citizenship in Twentieth-Century America* (Princeton, NJ: Princeton University Press, 2009).
21 Patrick Egan, Nathaniel Persily, and Kevin Wallsten, "Gay Rights," in *Public Opinion and Constitutional Controversy*, ed. Nathaniel Persily, Jack Citrin, and Patrick J. Egan (New York: Oxford University Press, 2008).
22 Ibid.
23 Ibid.
24 Andrew Flores, "Examining Variation in Surveying Attitudes on Same-Sex Marriage: A Meta-Analysis," *Public Opinion Quarterly* 72, no. 2 (2015): 580–93.
25 Mucciaroni, *Same-Sex, Different Politics.*
26 Ibid.
27 Laura E. Durso and Gary J. Gates, *Serving Our Youth: Findings from a National Survey of Service Providers Working with Lesbian, Gay, Bisexual, and Transgender Youth Who Are Homeless or At Risk of Becoming Homeless* (The Williams Institute, UCLA, 2012), williamsinstitute.law.ucla.edu.
28 Joanne DiPlacido, "Minority Stress among Lesbians, Gay Men, and Bisexuals: A Consequence of Heterosexism, Homophobia, and Stigmatization," in *Stigma and Sexual Orientation: Understanding Prejudice against Lesbians, Gay Men, and Bisexuals*, ed. Gregory M. Herek (Los Angeles: Sage, 1998); Anthony D'Augelli, "Developmental Implications of Victimization of Lesbian, Gay, and Bisexual Youths," in *Stigma and Sexual Orientation: Understanding Prejudice against Lesbians, Gay Men, and Bisexuals*, ed. Gregory M. Herek (Los Angeles: Sage, 1998).
29 American National Election Studies, and Stanford University, *ANES Times Series Cumulative Data File (1948–2012)*, ICPSR08475-v15, (Ann Arbor, MI: Inter-University Consortium for Political and Social Research [distributor], 2015), doi.org/10.3886/ICPSR08475.v15.
30 Ibid.
31 This may be the case because the ANES may have changed the format of its "thermometer" picture in 2012.
32 Milton Lodge and Charles S. Taber, *The Rationalizing Voter* (New York: Cambridge University Press, 2013).
33 Cynthia Burack, *Sin, Sex, and Democracy: Antigay Rhetoric and the Christian Right* (Albany: State University of New York Press, 2008); Tina Fetner, *How the Religious Right Shaped Lesbian and Gay Activism* (Minneapolis: University of Minnesota Press, 2008).
34 Brewer, *Value War*; Paul R. Brewer, "Values, Political Knowledge, and Public Opinion about Gay Rights: A Framing-Based Account," *Public Opinion Quarterly*, no. 2 67 (2003): 173–201; Paul R. Brewer, "The Shifting Foundations of Public Opinion about Gay Rights," *Journal of Politics* 6, no. 4 (2003): 1208–20; Clyde Wilcox and Robin Wolpert, "President Clinton, Public Opinion, and Gays in the

Military," in *Gay Rights, Military Wrongs: Political Perspectives on Lesbian and Gays in the Military*, ed. Craig Rimmerman (New York: Garland Press, 1996); Clyde Wilcox and Robin Wolpert, "Gay Rights in the Public Sphere: Public Opinion on Gay and Lesbian Equality," in *The Politics of Gay Rights*, ed. Craig Rimmerman, Kenneth D. Wald, and Clyde Wilcox (Chicago: University of Chicago Press, 2000); Jeremiah J. Garretson, "Exposure to the Lives of Lesbians and Gays and the Origin of Young People's Greater Support for Gay Rights," *International Journal of Public Opinion Research* 27, no. 2 (2014): 277–88.

35 For instance, see Efren O. Perez, *Unspoken Politics: Implicit Attitudes and Political Thinking* (New York: Cambridge University Press, 2016).

36 Lodge and Taber, *The Rationalizing Voter*; Amos Tversky and Daniel Kahneman, "Judgement under Uncertainty: Heuristics and Biases," *Science* 185, no. 4 (1974): 1124–31; Daniel Kahneman, *Thinking Fast and Slow* (New York: Farrar, Straus, and Giroux, 2011).

37 Brewer, *Value War*; Wilcox and Wolpert, "Gay Rights in the Public Sphere"; Scott L. Althaus, *Collective Preferences in Democratic Politics: Opinion Surveys and the Will of the People* (New York: Cambridge University Press, 2003).

38 Gordon Allport, *The Nature of Prejudice* (New York: Addison-Wiley, 1954); Miles Hewstone and Hermann Swart, "Fifty-Odd Years of Inter-Group Contact: From Hypothesis to Integrated Theory," *British Journal of Social Psychology* 50, no. 3 (2011): 374–86.

39 Althaus, *Collective Preferences in Democratic Politics*.

40 Lodge and Taber, *The Rationalizing Voter*.

41 Brewer, *Value War*.

42 Lewis, "The Friends and Family Plan"; Amy Becker and Dietram A. Scheufele, "New Voters, New Outlook? Predispositions, Social Networks, and the Changing Politics of Gay Civil Rights," *Social Science Quarterly* 92, no. 2 (2011): 324–45.

43 Elias Dinas, "Opening 'Openness to Change': Political Events and the Increased Sensitivity of Young Adults," *Political Research Quarterly* 66, no. 4 (2013): 868–95.

44 Susan MacManus, *Young V. Old: Generational Combat in the 21st Century* (Boulder, CO: Westview Press, 1995).

45 Johnson, *The Lavender Scare*.

46 See Benjamin Page and Robert Shapiro, *The Rational Public* (Chicago: University of Chicago Press, 1992).

47 See Dennis Altman, *Homosexual Oppression and Liberation* (New York: New York University Press, 1971), for an example.

48 David Dodge, *The Right's Marriage Message: Talking Tolerance, Marketing Inequality* (Somerville, MA: Political Research Associates, 2013); The Third Way, "Why Marriage Matters: The Research behind the Message," n.d., content.thirdway.org.

49 Dodge, *The Right's Marriage Message*.

50 John Zaller, *The Nature and Origin of Mass Opinion* (New York: Cambridge University Press, 1992).

51 Ibid., 322.

52 Ibid., 324.
53 John D'Emilio, *Sexual Politics, Sexual Communities: The Making of a Homosexual Minority in the United States, 1940–1970*, 2nd ed. (Chicago: University of Chicago Press, 1998).
54 Ibid., 73–74.

CHAPTER 2. UNDERSTANDING AFFECTIVE LIBERALIZATION

1 Edward Carmines and James Stimson, *Issue Evolution: Race and the Transformation of American Politics* (Princeton, NJ: Princeton University Press, 1989); Michael Bailey, Lee Sigelman, and Clyde Wilcox, "Presidential Persuasion on Social Issues: A Two-Way Street?," *Political Research Quarterly* 56, no. 1 (2003): 49–58.
2 Paul R. Brewer, *Value War: Public Opinion and the Politics of Gay Rights* (Lanham, MD: Rowman and Littlefield, 2008).
3 Donald P. Haider-Markel and Mark R. Joslyn, "Beliefs about the Origins of Homosexuality and Support for Gay Rights: An Empirical Test of Attribution Theory," *Public Opinion Quarterly* 72, no. 2 (2008): 291–310.
4 Andrew R. Flores and Scott Barclay, "Backlash, Consensus, or Naturalization: The Impact of Policy Shift on Subsequent Public Opinion Levels," presented at the April 2014 Meeting of the Western Political Science Association, Seattle, WA.
5 Brewer, *Value War*.
6 John L. Sullivan, Jason Pierson, and George E. Marcus, *Political Tolerance and American Democracy* (Chicago: University of Chicago Press, 1982).
7 Gregory M. Herek, "Gender Gaps in Public Opinion about Lesbian and Gay Men," *Public Opinion Quarterly* 66, no. 1 (2002): 40–66; Gregory M. Herek, "Heterosexuals' Attitudes toward Lesbians and Gay Men: Correlates and Gender Differences," *Journal of Sex Research* 25, no. 4 (1988): 451–77.
8 Gregory Lewis, "Black-White Differences in Attitudes toward Homosexuality and Gay Rights," *Public Opinion Quarterly* 67, no. 1 (2003): 59–78; Gregory Lewis, "The Friends and Family Plan: Contact with Gays and Support for Gay Rights," *Policy Studies Journal* 39, no. 2 (2011): 217–38.
9 Jeni Loftus, "America's Liberalization in Attitudes toward Homosexuality, 1973 to 1998," *American Sociological Review* 66, no. 5 (2001): 762–82; Brewer, *Value War*; Alan Yang, *From Wrongs to Rights, 1973 to 1999: Public Opinion on Gay and Lesbian Americans Moves toward Equality* (New York: National Gay and Lesbian Task Force Policy Institute, 1999).
10 Bailey, Sigelman, and Wilcox, "Presidential Persuasion on Social Issues"; Brewer, *Value War*; Yang, *From Wrongs to Rights*.
11 Yang, *From Wrongs to Rights*.
12 Jeremiah J. Garretson, *Changing Media, Changing Minds: The Lesbian and Gay Movement, Television, and Public Opinion*, PhD diss. (Nashville, TN: Vanderbilt University, 2009).
13 Loftus, "America's Liberalization."

14 Laura Olsen, Wendy Cage, and James T. Harrison, "Religion and Public Opinion about Same-Sex Marriage," *Social Science Quarterly* 87, no. 2 (2006): 340–60; Clyde Wilcox and Barbara Norrander, "Of Moods and Morals: The Dynamics of Public Opinion on Abortion and Gay Rights," in *Understanding Public Opinion*, 2nd ed., ed. Barbara Norrander and Clyde Wilcox (Washington, DC: CQ Press, 2002); Clyde Wilcox and Robin Wolpert, "Gay Rights in the Public Sphere: Public Opinion on Gay and Lesbian Equality," in *The Politics of Gay Rights*, ed. Craig Rimmerman, Kenneth D. Wald, and Clyde Wilcox (Chicago: University of Chicago Press, 2000).
15 See sources cited in the previous note.
16 Robert Anderson and Tina Fetner, "Cohort Difference in Tolerance of Homosexuality: Attitudinal Change in Canada and the United States, 1981–2000," *Public Opinion Quarterly* 72, no. 2 (2008): 311–30; Wilcox and Wolpert "Gay Rights in the Public Sphere"; Wilcox and Norrander, "Of Moods and Morals."
17 Wilcox and Wolpert "Gay Rights in the Public Sphere."
18 Ibid.
19 Ibid.
20 Loftus, "America's Liberalization."
21 Bailey, Sigelman, and Wilcox, "Presidential Persuasion."
22 Carmines and Stimson, *Issue Evolution*.
23 Ibid.; Christina Wolbrecht, *The Politics of Women's Rights: Parties, Positions, and Change* (Princeton, NJ: Princeton University Press, 2000).
24 K. Lindaman and D. P. Haider-Markel, "Issue Evolution, Political Parties, and the Culture Wars," *Political Research Quarterly* 55, no. 1 (2002): 91–110.
25 Tina Fetner, *How the Religious Right Shaped Lesbian and Gay Activism* (Minneapolis: University of Minnesota Press, 2008); Cynthia Burack, *Sin, Sex, and Democracy: Antigay Rhetoric and the Christian Right* (Albany: State University of New York Press, 2008).
26 Brewer, *Value War*.
27 Ibid.
28 Ibid.
29 Shanto Iyengar and Donald Kinder, *News That Matters: Television and American Opinion* (Chicago: University of Chicago Press, 1989); Thomas E. Nelson, Rosalee A. Clausen, and Zoe M. Oxley, "Media Framing of a Civil Liberties Conflict and Its Effect on Tolerance," *American Political Science Review* 91, no. 3 (1997): 567–83.
30 Brewer, *Value War*.
31 Rosalee A. Clausen and Zoe M. Oxley, *Public Opinion: Democratic Ideals* (Washington, DC: CQ Press, 2012), chap. 6.
32 Many political scientists argue that this is a superior measure of news consumption because of social desirability.
33 James W. Stoutenborough, Donald P. Haider-Markel, and Mahalley D. Allen, "Reassessing the Impact of Supreme Court Decisions on Public Opinion: Gay Civil Rights Cases," *Political Research Quarterly* 59, no. 1 (2006): 419–33.

34 B. G. Bishin, T. J. Hayes, M. B. Incantalupo, and C. A. Smith, "Opinion Backlash and Public Attitudes: Are Political Advances in Gay Rights Counterproductive?," *American Journal of Political Science* 60, no. 3 (2016), doi: 10.1111/ajps/12.181.

35 Ibid.

36 Andrew R. Flores and Scott Barclay, "Backlash, Consensus, Legitimacy, or Polarization: The Effect of Same-Sex Marriage Policy on Mass Attitudes," *Political Research Quarterly* 69, no. 1 (2015): 43–56.

37 Flores and Barclay, "Backlash, Consensus, or Naturalization" (2014 version).

38 See Donald P. Haider-Markel and Mark Joslyn, "Politicizing Biology: Social Movements, Parties, and the Case of Homosexuality," *Social Science Journal* 50, no. 4 (2013): 603–15; Andrew L. Whitehouse, "Politics, Religion, Attribution Theory, and Attitudes toward Same-Sex Unions," *Social Science Quarterly* 95, no. 3 (2014): 701–718.

39 Haider-Markel and Joslyn, "Beliefs about the Origins of Homosexuality."

40 Ibid.; Gregory Lewis, "Does Believing Homosexuality Is Innate Increase Support for Gay Rights?," *Policy Studies Journal* 37, no. 4 (2009): 669–93.

41 Elizabeth Suhay and Jeremiah J. Garretson, "Science, Sexuality, and Civil Rights: Does Research on the Causes of Homosexuality Have a Political Impact?," *Journal of Politics*, forthcoming. We use an experimental design to show that reading scientific information about a link between biology and homosexuality has no effect on support for gay rights. It appears that liberals and conservatives respond to information on the origin of homosexuality in ways that reinforce their political ideology, rather than in an objective fashion.

42 Gordon Allport, *The Nature of Prejudice* (New York: Addison-Wiley, 1954).

43 Thomas F. Pettigrew and Linda R. Tropp, "A Meta-Analytic Test of Intergroup Contact Theory," *Journal of Personality and Social Psychology* 90, no. 5 (2006): 751–83.

44 Lewis, "The Friends and Family Plan.

45 Brittany Bramlett, "The Cross-Pressures of Religion and Contact with Gays and Lesbians, and Their Impact on Same-Sex Marriage Opinion," *Politics and Policy* 40, no. 1 (2012): 13–42; Sue Ann Skipworth, Andrew Garner, and Bryan J. Dettrey, "Limitations of the Contact Hypothesis: Heterogeneity in the Contact Effects on Attitudes toward Gay Rights," *Politics and Policy* 37, no. 5 (2010): 31–50; Joshua J. Dyck and Shuanna Pearson-Merkowitz, "To Know You Is Not Necessarily to Love You: The Partisan Mediators of Intergroup Contact," *Political Behavior* 36, no. 3 (2013): 553–80.

46 Interestingly enough, it is typically only on lesbian and gay issues where this concern has been so vocally raised by critics.

47 Selection effects occur when social scientists hypothesize that a value of variable A causes a specific value of variable B, and a statistical correlation to that effect is found. But in reality, the correlation is due to variable A taking on a specific value in a direct response to variable B's value. Variable A does not directly cause

variable B to be high; the preexisting value of B is really causing the value of A. B is gay rights support in this example. A is contact with lesbians and gays.

48 Patrick Egan and Kenneth Sherrill, "'Coming Out' and American's Attitudes on Gay Rights," unpublished working paper (2007).

49 Bob Altemeyer, "Change in Attitudes toward Homosexuals," *Journal of Homosexuality* 42, no. 2 (2001): 63–75.

50 Ibid.

51 Altemeyer also found that, among those who were very authoritarian (a trait often found in the highly religious and very conservative people), his teaching assessments were much lower for those in the class he came out to when compared to the same group in the "control" class.

52 Edward Schiappa, Peter B. Gregg, and Dean E. Hewes, "Can One TV Show Make a Difference? *Will and Grace* and the Parasocial Contact Hypothesis," *Journal of Homosexuality* 51, no. 4 (2006): 15–37.

53 Ellen B. D. Riggle, Alan L. Ellis, and Anne M. Crawford, "The Impact of 'Media Contact' on Attitudes toward Gay Men," *Journal of Homosexuality* 31, no. 3 (1996): 55–69.

54 Lau Holning, Charles Q. Lau, and Kelley Loper, "Public Opinion in Hong Kong about Gays and Lesbians: The Impact of Interpersonal and Imagined Contact," *International Journal of Public Opinion Research* 26, no. 3 (2014): 301–22.

55 R. Brown and M. Hewstone, "An Integrated Theory of Intergroup Contact," in *Advances in Experimental Social Psychology*, ed. M. Zanna (San Diego, CA: Academic Press, 2005).

56 Ibid.

57 Brian Harrison and Melissa Michelson, *Listen, We Need to Talk* (New York: Oxford University Press, 2017).

58 Richard J. Crisp and Rhiannon N. Turner, "Can Imagined Interactions Produce Positive Perceptions?: Reducing Prejudice through Stimulated Social Contact," *American Psychologist* 64, no. 4 (2009): 231–40.

59 Miles Hewstone and Hermann Swart, "Fifty-Odd Years of Inter-Group Contact: From Hypothesis to Integrated Theory," *British Journal of Social Psychology* 50, no. 3 (2011): 374–86.

60 Ibid.

61 Milton Lodge and Charles S. Taber, *The Rationalizing Voter* (New York: Cambridge University Press, 2013).

62 Ibid.

63 Daniel Kahneman, *Thinking Fast and Slow* (New York: Farrar, Straus, and Giroux, 2011).

64 Ibid.

65 Lodge and Taber, *The Rationalizing Voter*, 3.

66 Ibid.

67 Ibid., 51.

68 Of course, this is only an assumption of the model, and its validity should be open to testing.
69 Flores and Barclay, "Backlash, Consensus, or Naturalization" (2014 and 2015 versions).
70 Ibid.
71 Rebecca J. Kreitzer, Allison J. Hamilton, and Caroline J. Tolbert, "Does Policy Adoption Change Attitudes on Minority Rights? The Effects of Legalizing Same-Sex Marriage," *Political Research Quarterly* 67, no. 4 (2014): 795–808.
72 See Loftus, "America's Liberalization"; Brewer, "The Shifting Foundations"; Anderson and Fetner, "Cohort Difference in Tolerance of Homosexuality"; Dawn Michelle Baunach, "Changing Same-Sex Marriage Attitudes in America from 1988 through 2010," *Public Opinion Quarterly* 76, no. 2 (2012): 364–78; Richard Seltzer, "AIDS, Homosexuality, Public Opinion, and Changing Correlates over Time," *Journal of Homosexuality* 26, no. 1 (1999): 85–97, for exceptions.
73 See chapter 1 for a discussion of the American National Elections Study and General Social Survey. The Worlds and European Values Studies are discussed further in chapter 8.
74 Flores and Barclay, "Backlash, Consensus, or Naturalization" (2015 version).

CHAPTER 3. THE SPREAD AND INTENSIFICATION OF GAY AND LESBIAN IDENTITIES

1 The US Holocaust Memorial Museum has the entire English translation of the text of paragraph 175 of the German criminal code on its website as of early 2017; see www.ushmm.org. The full historical code in German can be found at lexetius.com.
2 Annemarie Jagose, *Queer Theory: An Introduction* (New York: New York University Press, 1996).
3 Ibid.; Michel Foucault, *The History of Sexuality*, vol. 1 (New York: Vintage, 1978).
4 Foucault, *The History of Sexuality*.
5 Havelock Ellis, *Studies in the Psychology of Sex* (New York: Random House, 1942).
6 Ibid., 70.
7 Foucault, *The History of Sexuality*.
8 Margot Canaday, *The Straight State: Sexuality and Citizenship in Twentieth-Century America* (Princeton, NJ: Princeton University Press, 2009).
9 Ibid.
10 George Chauncey, *Gay New York: Gender, Urban Culture, and the Gay Male World, 1890–1940* (New York: Basic Books, 1994).
11 Deborah B. Gould, *Moving Politics: Emotion and ACT-UP's Fight against AIDS* (Chicago: University of Chicago Press, 2009).
12 Canaday, *The Straight State*.
13 David K. Johnson, *The Lavender Scare: The Cold War Persecution of Gays and Lesbians in the Federal Government* (Chicago: University of Chicago Press, 2004).
14 Ibid.
15 Ibid., 3.

16 Ibid., 18.
17 John D'Emilio, *Sexual Politics, Sexual Communities: The Making of a Homosexual Minority in the United States, 1940–1970*, 2nd ed. (Chicago: University of Chicago Press, 1998).
18 Ibid, 22.
19 Ibid.
20 John Scagliotti, Greta Schiller, and Robert Rosenberg, dirs., *Before Stonewall: The Making of a Gay and Lesbian Community* (N.p.: First Run Features Studio, Before Stonewall, 1984), DVD, 87 mins.
21 Eric Marcus, *Making Gay History: The Half Century Fight for Lesbian and Gay Equal Rights* (New York: Perennial, 2002).
22 Ibid.
23 Franklin Kameny, "Civil Rights: A Progress Report," 1964, reprinted in *Great Speeches in Gay Rights*, ed. James Daley, Ed. (Mineola, NY: Dover, 2010), 33–34.
24 Alfred Kinsey, Wardell B. Pomeroy, and Clyde E. Martin, *Sexual Behavior in the Human Male* (Philadephia: W. B. Saunders, 1949).
25 Alfred Kinsey, Wardell B. Pomeroy, Clyde E. Martin, and Paul H. Gebhard, *Sexual Behavior in the Human Female* (Philadelphia: W. B. Saunders, 1953).
26 Simon Levay, *Queer Science: The Use and Abuse of Research into Homosexuality* (New York: Cambridge University Press, 1996).
27 Kinsey, Pomeroy, and Martin, *Sexual Behavior in the Human Male*, p. 660.
28 Ibid., 666.
29 Quoted in Marcus, *Making Gay History.*
30 D'Emilio, *Sexual Politics, Sexual Communities.*
31 Ibid.; Scagliotti, Schiller, and Rosenberg, *Before Stonewall*; Stephen M. Engel, *The Unfinished Revolution: Social Movement Theory and the Gay and Lesbian Movement* (New York: Cambridge University Press, 2001).
32 D'Emilio, *Sexual Politics, Sexual Communities.*
33 Jagose, *Queer Theory.*
34 D'Emilio, *Sexual Politics, Sexual Communities*; Dudley Clendinen and Adam Nagourney, *Out for Good: The Struggle to Build a Gay Rights Movement in America* (New York: Simon and Shuster, 1999).
35 D'Emilio, *Sexual Politics, Sexual Communities.*
36 Ibid.
37 Ibid.; Craig A. Rimmerman, *From Identity to Politics: The Lesbian and Gay Movement in the United States* (Philadelphia, PA: Temple University Press, 2002).
38 Johnson, *The Lavender Scare.*
39 Scagliotti, Schiller, and Rosenberg, *Before Stonewall* (1985).
40 Engel, *The Unfinished Revolution*; Johnson, *The Lavender Scare.*
41 Clendinen and Nagourney (1999).
42 H. Taijfel and J. C. Turner, "The Social Identity Theory of Intergroup Behavior," in *Psychology of Intergroup Relations*, ed. S. Worchell and W. G. Austin (Chicago: Nelson-Hall, 1986).

43 Ibid.

44 Ibid.

45 Marilynn B. Brewer, "The Psychology of Prejudice: Ingroup Love or Outgroup Hate?," *Journal of Social Issues* 55, no. 3 (1999): 173–201.

46 Ibid.

47 Kameny, "Civil Rights: A Progress Report."

48 Clendinen and Nagourney, *Out for Good*; Martin Duberman, *Stonewall* (New York: Penguin, 1993).

49 See Elizabeth A. Armstrong, *Forging Gay Identities: Organizing Sexuality in San Francisco, 1950–1994* (Chicago: University of Chicago Press, 2002). See also Clendinen and Nagourney, *Out for Good*; D'Emilio, *Sexual Politics, Sexual Communities*; Marcus, *Making Gay History*.

50 Ibid.

51 Armstrong, *Forging Gay Identities*; Clendinen and Nagourney, *Out for Good*; D'Emilio, *Sexual Politics, Sexual Communities*; Marcus, *Making Gay History*.

52 Harvey Milk, "The Hope Speech," 1978, repr. in *Great Speeches in Gay Rights*, ed. James Daley (Mineola, NY: Dover, 2010).

53 John Zaller, *The Nature and Origin of Mass Opinion* (New York: Cambridge University Press, 1992).

54 Lawrence K. Altman, "Rare Cancer Seen in 41 Homosexuals," *New York Times*, July 3, 1981.

55 Randy Shilts, quoted in Marcus, *Making Gay History*.

56 Larry Kramer, quoted in ibid.

57 Clendinen and Nagourney, *Out for Good*, 517.

58 Gould, *Moving Politics*.

59 Kristen Luker, *Abortion and the Politics of Motherhood* (Oakland: University of California Press, 1984).

60 Gould, *Moving Politics*.

61 Larry Kramer, Interview with Sarah Schulman for the ACT-UP Oral History Project, 2003, www.actuporalhistory.org.

62 Michelangelo Signorile, Interview with Sarah Schulman for the ACT-UP Oral History Project, 2003, www.actuporalhistory.org.

63 Edward Alwood, *Straight News: Gays, Lesbians, and the News Media* (New York: Columbia University Press, 1996).

64 Signorile, Interview.

65 Kramer, Interview.

66 After that year, coverage of AIDS largely shifts to the epidemic in Africa and other continents.

67 See Scott L. Althaus, *Collective Preferences in Democratic Politics: Opinion Surveys and the Will of the People* (New York: Cambridge University Press, 2003), for more details on the construction of the series on lesbian and gay issues.

68 Gould, *Moving Politics*.

69 Alwood, *Straight News*.

70 Ibid.
71 Ibid.
72 See Tim Walker, "School's Out," *Teaching Tolerance* 21 (2002), https://www.tolerance.org.
73 For additional studies on the distinctiveness of this collective sense of linked fate among LGBTQ people and its effects on political behavior, see Gregory B. Lewis, Marc A. Rodgers, and Kenneth Sherrill, "Lesbian, Gay, and Bisexual Voters in the 2000 U.S. Presidential Elections," *Politics and Policy* 39, no. 5 (2011): 655–77; Joe Rollins and Harry N. Hirsh, "Sexual Identities and Political Engagement: A Queer Survey," *Social Politics* 10, no. 3 (2003): 290–313; Brian Schaffner and Nenad Senic, "Rights or Benefits? Explaining the Sexual Identity Gap in American Political Behavior," *Political Research Quarterly* 59, no. 1 (2006): 123–32.

CHAPTER 4. THE CAPTURE OF THE DEMOCRATIC PARTY AND THE CLINTON VICTORY

1 Benjamin G. Bishin, *Tyranny of the Minority: The Subconstituency Politics Theory of Representation* (Philadelphia: Temple University Press, 2009); Benjamin G. Bishin and Charles A. Smith, "When Do Legislators Defy Popular Sovereignty? Testing Theories of Representation Using DOMA," *Political Research Quarterly* 66, no. 4 (2013): 794–803.
2 Bishin, *Tyranny of the Minority*.
3 Ibid., 29–20.
4 David Karol, *Party Position Change in American Politics: Coalition Management* (New York: Cambridge University Press, 2009).
5 Ibid., 19–20, emphasis added.
6 David Karol, "How Does Party Position Change Happen? The Case of Gay Rights in the U.S. Congress," unpublished working paper, 2013, University of Maryland.
7 John D'Emilio, *Sexual Politics, Sexual Communities: The Making of a Homosexual Minority in the United States, 1940–1970*, 2nd ed. (Chicago: University of Chicago Press, 1998).
8 Elizabeth A. Armstrong, *Forging Gay Identities: Organizing Sexuality in San Francisco, 1950–1994* (Chicago: University of Chicago Press, 2002); Robert W. Bailey, *Gay Politics, Urban Politics: Identity and Economic in the Urban Setting* (New York: Columbia University Press, 1999).
9 Dudley Clendinen and Adam Nagourney, *Out for Good: The Struggle to Build a Gay Rights Movement in America* (New York: Simon and Shuster, 1999).
10 This political dilution was a contributing factor in the carving out of West Los Angeles from Los Angeles in the 1980s.
11 Chai Feldblum, "The Federal Gay Rights Bill: From Bella to Enda," in *Creating Change: Sexuality, Public Policy, and Civil Rights*, ed. John D'Emilio, William B Turner, and Urvashi Vaid (New York: St. Martin's Press, 2000).
12 Steve Endean and Vicki Lynn Eaklor, *Bringing Gay Rights into the Mainstream: Twenty Years of Progress* (New York: Routledge, 2006).

13 Ibid.

14 Ibid.

15 Sasha Gregory-Lewis, "The Republicans: Embracing Homophobes and Gay Rights Backers—A Fresh Look at the Grand Old Party," *Advocate*, 1976, repr. in *Witness to the Revolution: The Advocate Reports on Gay and Lesbian Politics, 1967–1999*, ed. Chris Bull (Los Angeles: Alyson Press, 1999).

16 Ibid.

17 Kenneth Sherrill, "On Gay People as a Politically Powerless Group," in *Gays in the Military: Joseph Steffan versus the United States*, ed. Marc Wolinsky and Kenneth Sherrill (Princeton, NJ: Princeton University Press, 1993).

18 All other factors are set to their mean values in that specific year, so these predicted probabilities assume that members otherwise have identical districts in terms of their demographics.

19 Ibid.

20 Karol, "How Does Party Position Change Happen?"

21 Bishin, *Tyranny of the Minority*.

22 Eric R. Hansen and Sarah Treul, "The Symbolic and Substantive Representation of LGB Americans in the U.S. House," *Journal of Politics* 77, no. 4 (2015): 955–67. This study uses data from 2005–2011 when estimates of district level LGBTQ constituencies were available.

23 Clendinen and Nagourney, *Out for Good*.

24 Unfortunately, space prevents a full discussion of the Gay and Lesbian Victory Fund, which provides starter campaign funds and training to LGBTQ-identified candidates for public office in the United States and has been crucial in increasing LGBTQ representation among elected officials. Since the Victory Fund does not engage in direct lobbying of elected officials, I omit a full discussion here, although the Victory Fund may influence support for LGBTQ rights by positioning LGBTQ-identified individuals to lobby other elected officials once elected to office. See Kathleen DeBold, *Out for Office: Campaigning in the Gay Nineties* (Washington, DC: Gay and Lesbian Victory Fund, 1994) for more on the Victory Fund. See Andrew Reynolds, "Representation and Rights: The Impact of LGBT Legislators in Comparative Perspective," *American Political Science Review* 107, no. 2 (2013): 259–74, and Donald P. Haider-Markel, *Out and Running: Gay and Lesbian Candidates, Elections, and Policy Representation* (Washington, DC: Georgetown University Press, 2010), for more on the role of LGBTQ elected officials.

25 Endean and Eaklor, *Bringing Gay Rights into the Mainstream*.

26 "Human Rights Campaign," n.d., www.opensecrets.org, accessed July 23, 2009.

27 Donald P. Haider-Markel, "Redistributing Values in Congress: Interest Group Influence under Sub-Optimal Conditions," *Political Research Quarterly* 52, no. 1 (1999): 113–44.

28 Gregory-Lewis, "The Republicans."

29 Guy Charles, "Ted Kennedy Says He's for Gay Rights," *Advocate*, 1971, repr. in *Witness to the Revolution: The Advocate Reports on Gay and Lesbian Politics, 1967–1999*, ed. Chris Bull (Los Angeles: Alyson Press, 1999).
30 Jean O'Leary, "From Agitator to Insider: Fighting for Inclusion in the Democratic Party," in *Creating Change: Sexuality, Public Policy, and Civil Rights*, John D'Emilio, William B Turner, and Urvashi Vaid, Eds. (New York, NY: St. Martin's Press, 2000).
31 O'Leary, "From Agitator to Insider."
32 Ibid.
33 Ibid.
34 Clendinen and Nagourney, *Out for Good*.
35 David Mixner, *Stranger among Friends* (New York: Bantam Books, 1996).
36 Ibid.
37 Quoted in Charles Kaiser, *The Gay Metropolis* (New York: Grove Press, 1997).
38 Mixner, *Stranger among Friends*, 204.
39 Ibid., p 207.
40 See http://www.actupny.org for a transcript of the confrontation..
41 Ibid.
42 Ibid.
43 Quoted in Mixner, *Stranger among Friends*.
44 Kaiser, *The Gay Metropolis*.
45 William Jefferson Clinton, "1992 Nomination Speech to the Democratic National Convention," repr. in the *New York Times*, July 17, 1992, www.nytimes.com.
46 Bishin and Smith, "When Do Legislators Defy Popular Sovereignty?"
47 Keith Poole and Howard Rosenthal, *Ideology and Congress* (New Brunswick, NJ: Transaction Publishers, 2007); Keith Poole, *Spatial Models of Parliamentary Voting* (New York, NY: Cambridge University Press, 2005).
48 Donald P. Haider-Markel, "Morality, Policy, and Individual-Level Political Behavior: The Case of Legislative Voting on Lesbian and Gay Issues," *Policy Studies Journal* 27, no. 4 (1999): 735–749.
49 Other factors included healthcare, the budget bill, and so on.
50 Charles Antony Smith, "The Electoral Capture of Gay and Lesbian Americans: Evidence and Implications from the 2004 Election," *Studies in Law, Politics, and Society* 40 (2007): 103–121.

CHAPTER 5. ISSUE EVOLUTION?

1 David K. Johnson, *The Lavender Scare: The Cold War Persecution of Gays and Lesbians in the Federal Government* (Chicago: University of Chicago Press, 2004).
2 Edward Carmines and James Stimson, *Issue Evolution: Race and the Transformation of American Politics* (Princeton, NJ: Princeton University Press, 1989); John Zaller, *The Nature and Origin of Mass Opinion* (New York: Cambridge University Press, 1992).

3 Carmines and Stimson, *Issue Evolution*; Marc J. Hetherington, "Resurgent Mass Partisanship: The Role of Elite Polarization," *American Political Science Review* 95, no. 3 (2001): 619–31.
4 Changes in question wording may cast some doubt on this.
5 Samuel Stouffer, *Communism, Conformity, and Civil Liberties* (New York: Doubleday, 1955).
6 Paul M. Sniderman, Richard A. Brody, and Philip E. Tetlock, *Reasoning and Choice: Explorations in Political Psychology* (New York: Cambridge University Press, 1991).
7 David Rayside, "The Perils of Congressional Politics," in *Gay Rights, Military Wrongs: Political Perspectives on Lesbians and Gays in the Military*, ed. Craig Rimmerman (New York: Garland Press, 1996).
8 Ibid.
9 Nathaniel Frank, *Unfriendly Fire: How the Gay Ban Undermines the Military and Weakens America* (New York: Thomas Duane, 2009).
10 Ibid.
11 Rayside, "The Perils of Congressional Politics."
12 David Mixner, *Stranger among Friends* (New York: Bantam Books, 1996).
13 Rayside, "The Perils of Congressional Politics."
14 Ibid.
15 Mixner, *Stranger among Friends.*
16 Because the 1992–1993–1994–1996 ANES panel had a limited number of respondents and I expected respondents to be polarize based on ideology, I have restricted the sample to non–African American respondents, a common practice in American public opinion research. This is because "liberal" identification likely signifies somewhat different concepts for African American respondents than for white respondents. See Michael C. Dawson, *Black Visions: The Roots of Contemporary African-American Political Ideologies* (Chicago: University of Chicago Press, 2001). Socially conservative African Americans are more likely to define themselves as "liberal" than whites for instance. This would have the effect of attenuating any effect of ideological placement. Furthermore, African Americans seem to use different considerations than Whites in assessing support for gay rights. See Gregory Lewis, "Black-White Differences in Attitudes toward Homosexuality and Gay Rights," *Public Opinion Quarterly* 67, no. 1 (2003): 59–78.
17 Readers familiar with the academic literature will notice that, while I include egalitarianism as a predictor, I do not include "moral traditionalism." I find, in a separate analysis, that the standard measure of moral traditionalism on the ANES panel appears to be strongly affected by changes in gay rights support in this time period. Generally, I find that the effect of gay rights in previous time periods on moral traditionalism in the current time period increases strongly on the 1992–1994–1996 ANES panel. This suggests that those who score high in moral traditionalism are increasingly doing so only *because* they oppose gay rights and interpret the moral traditionalism questions as referring to lesbians and gays

specifically. Including moral traditionalism as a predictor of change in gays rights support would thus introduce endogeneity into the model. "Endogeneity" is a term meaning that the cause and the effect specified in the model are incorrectly reversed: thus, what we thought was the effect is actually the causal variable and vice versa. A similar analysis suggested that egalitarianism was independent of gay rights support.

18 Ceiling (or floor) effects occur when public support for some position is so high (or low) that it is difficult for it to go much higher (or lower), leading to a difficulty in detecting changes in support caused by some other variable.

19 John R. Hibbing, Kevin B. Smith, and John R. Alford, *Predisposed: Liberals, Conservatives, and the Biology of Political Differences* (New York: Taylor and Francis, 2013).

20 Jeremiah J. Garretson and Elizabeth Suhay, "Scientific Communication about Biological Influences on Homosexuality and the Politics of Gay Rights," *Political Research Quarterly* 69, no. 1 (2016): 17–29.

21 Ibid.

22 Elizabeth Suhay and Jeremiah J. Garretson, "Science, Sexuality, and Civil Rights: Does Research on the Causes of Homosexuality Have a Political Impact?," *Journal of Politics*, forthcoming.

CHAPTER 6. COMING OUT, ENTERTAINMENT TELEVISION, AND THE YOUTH REVOLT

1 John Zaller, *The Nature and Origin of Mass Opinion* (New York: Cambridge University Press, 1992).

2 Michael X. Delli Carpini and Scott Keeter, *What Americans Know about Politics and Why It Matters* (New Haven, CT: Yale University Press, 1996).

3 Craig A. Rimmerman, "Beyond Political Mainstreaming: Reflections on the Lesbian and Gay Organizations and the Grassroots" in *The Politics of Gay Rights*, ed. Craig A. Rimmerman, Kenneth Wald, and Clyde Wilcox (Chicago: University of Chicago Press, 2000); John D'Emilio, "Cycles of Change, Questions of Strategy: The Gay and Lesbian Movement after Fifty Years," in *The Politics of Gay Rights*, ed. Craig A. Rimmerman, Kenneth Wald, and Clyde Wilcox (Chicago: University of Chicago Press, 2000).

4 Quoted in Deborah B. Gould, *Moving Politics: Emotion and ACT-UP's Fight against AIDS* (Chicago: University of Chicago Press, 2009).

5 Larry Kramer, *Reports from the Holocaust: The Making of an AIDS Activist* (New York: Penguin, 1989).

6 Gould, *Moving Politics*.

7 Ibid.

8 Gregory M. Herek, "Why Tell If You're Not Asked? Self-Disclosure, Intergroup Contact, and Heterosexuals' Attitudes toward Lesbians and Gay Men," *Psychology Perspectives on Lesbian, Gay, and Bisexual Experiences*, 2nd ed., ed. Linda D. Garnets and Douglas C. Kimmel (New York: Columbia University Press, 2003).

9 Gregory Lewis, "The Friends and Family Plan: Contact with Gays and Support for Gay Rights," *Policy Studies Journal* 39, no. 2 (2011): 217–38.

10 Gordon Allport, *The Nature of Prejudice* (New York: Addison-Wiley, 1954); Thomas F. Pettigrew and Linda R. Tropp, "A Meta-Analytic Test of Intergroup Contact Theory," *Journal of Personality and Social Psychology* 90, no. 5 (2006): 751–83.

11 Breaking down respondents by partisan groups gives identical results.

12 Stephen Tropiano, *The Prime Time Closet: A History of Gays and Lesbians on TV* (New York: Applause Theatre and Cinema, 2002); Vito Russo, *The Celluloid Closet: Homosexuality in the Movies, Revised Edition* (New York: Harper and Row, 1987).

13 Leezel Tanglao, "Study Finds Republicans Favor Popular 'Non-Conservative' TV Shows," ABCnews.com, 2010, www.abcnews.go.com.

14 Tropiano, *The Prime Time Closet.*

15 Ibid.; Ron Becker, *Gay TV and Straight America* (New Brunswick, NJ: Rutgers University Press, 2006); Larry Gross, *Up From Invisibility: Lesbians, Gay Men, and the Media in America* (New York: Columbia University Press, 2001); Steven Capsuto, *Alternate Channels: The Uncensored Story of Gay and Lesbian Images on Radio and Television* (New York: Ballantine Books, 2000); Suzanna Walters, *All the Rage: The Story of Gay Visibility in America* (Chicago: University of Chicago Press, 2001).

16 Jeremiah J. Garretson, "Does Change in Minority and Women's Representation on Television Matter?: A Thirty-Year Study of Television and Social Tolerance," *Politics, Groups, and Identities* 3, no. 4 (2015): 615–32.

17 Milton Lodge and Charles S. Taber, *The Rationalizing Voter* (New York: Cambridge University Press, 2013).

18 James Uleman and John Bargh, *Unintended Thought* (New York, NY: Guilford, 1989).

19 Elias Dinas, "Opening 'Openness to Change': Political Events and the Increased Sensitivity of Young Adults," *Political Research Quarterly* 66, no. 4 (2013): 868–95.

20 Pettigrew and Tropp, "A Meta-Analytic Test of Intergroup Contact Theory."

21 Edward Schiappa, M. Allen, and Peter B. Gregg, "Parasocial Relationships and Television: A Meta-Analysis of the Effects," in *Mass Media Research: Advances through Meta-Analysis*, ed. R. Preiss, B. Gayle, N Burrell, M. Allen, and J. Bryant (Mahwah, NJ: Lawrence Erlbaum, 2006).

22 Edmon W. Tucker and Miriam Potocky-Tripodi, "Changing Heterosexuals' Attitudes toward Homosexuals: A Systematic Review of the Empirical Literature," *Research on Social Work Practice* 16, no. 2 (2006): 176–90.

23 Tropiano, *The Prime Time Closet.*

24 Elsewhere, I have shown that affective feelings are indeed involved in the relationship between exposure and gay rights support using more sophisticated statistical techniques beyond the scope of this book. See Jeremiah J. Garretson, "Exposure

to the Lives of Lesbians and Gays and the Origin of Young People's Greater Support for Gay Rights," *International Journal of Public Opinion Research* 27, no. 2 (2014): 277–88.

25 Ibid.

26 Garretson, "Exposure to the Lives of Lesbians and Gays."

27 Jeni Loftus, "America's Liberalization in Attitudes toward Homosexuality, 1973 to 1998," *American Sociological Review* 66, no. 5 (2001): 762–82.

CHAPTER 7. THE PERSISTENCE OF POLITICAL CONFLICT OVER GAY RIGHTS

1 Pew, "Vast Majority of Americans Know Someone Who Is Gay, Fewer Know Someone Who Is Transgender," September 28, 2016, www.pewforum.org.

2 Jeffrey R. Lax and Justin Phillips, "Gay Rights in the States: Public Opinion and Policy Responsiveness," *American Political Science Review* 103, no. 3 (2009): 367–86.

3 The Williams Institute, UCLA, "Majority of Americans in Every Congressional District Support Law to Protect against Sexual Orientation Discrimination," 2013, williamsinstitute.law.ucla.edu.

4 These, along with Pennsylvania, are the two states that Donald Trump surprisingly won in 2016, delivering him the presidency. It may not be coincidence. The GOP has controlled the government in each of these states over much of the Obama years, meaning that Republicans could refuse to adopt more liberal policy advances on LGBTQ rights (not imposed by federal courts), while at the same time implementing more restrictive voting rules discouraging young people and minorities from voting, in spite of slight Democratic majorities in these states.

5 Milton Lodge and Charles S. Taber, *The Rationalizing Voter* (New York: Cambridge University Press, 2013); Charles S. Taber and Milton Lodge, "Motivated Skepticism in the Evaluation of Political Beliefs," *American Journal of Political Science* 50, no. 3 (2006): 755–69; David Redlawsk, Andrew J.W. Civettini, and Karen E. Emmerson, "The Affective Tipping Point: Do Motivated Reasoners Ever Get It?," *Political Psychology* 31, no. 4 (2010): 563–93; Jennifer Jerit and Jason Barabas, "Partisan Perceptual Bias and the Information Environment," *Journal of Politics* 74, no. 3 (2012): 672–84.

6 James N. Druckman, Erik Peterson, and Rune Slothuus, "How Elite Polarization Affects Public Opinion Formations," *American Political Science Review* 107, no. 1 (2013): 57–79.

7 Gordon Allport, *The Nature of Prejudice* (New York: Addison-Wiley, 1954).

8 Data for this figure is available at Pew's website at www.pewforum.org.

9 Karlyn Bowman and Adam Foster, "Attitudes about Homosexuality and Gay Marriage," *American Enterprise Institute Studies in Public Opinion*, 2008, www.aei.org.

10 Ibid.

11 Ed O'Keefe, "Support for Same-Sex Marriage Jumps among Lawmakers," *Washington Post*, October 9, 2014, www.washingtonpost.com; other figures compiled by the author from various *Human Rights Campaign Scorecards* in various years.
12 Taber and Lodge, "Motivated Skepticism"; Druckman, Peterson, and Slothuus, "How Elite Polarization Affects Public Opinion Formations"; Matthew Levendusky, "Clearer Cues, More Consistent Voters," *Political Behavior* 32, no. 1 (2010): 111–31.
13 Taber and Lodge, "Motivated Skepticism"; Redlawsk, Civettini, and Emmerson, "The Affective Tipping Point."
14 Joshua J. Dyck and Shuanna Pearson-Merkowitz, "To Know You Is Not Necessarily to Love You: The Partisan Mediators of Intergroup Contact," *Political Behavior* 36, no. 3 (2013): 553–80.
15 Paul M. Sniderman, Richard A. Brody, and Philip E. Tetlock, *Reasoning and Choice: Explorations in Political Psychology* (New York: Cambridge University Press, 1991).
16 John R. Hibbing, Kevin B. Smith, and John R. Alford, *Predisposed: Liberals, Conservatives, and the Biology of Political Differences* (New York: Taylor and Francis, 2013).
17 Ibid.
18 See also Lodge and Taber, *The Rationalizing Voter*.
19 Sue Ann Skipworth, Andrew Garner, and Bryan J. Dettrey, "Limitations of the Contact Hypothesis: Heterogeneity in the Contact Effects on Attitudes toward Gay Rights," *Politics and Policy* 37, no. 5 (2010): 31–50; Brittany Bramlett, "The Cross-Pressures of Religion and Contact with Gays and Lesbians, and Their Impact on Same-Sex Marriage Opinion," *Politics and Policy* 40, no. 1 (2012): 13–42. See also John Zaller, *The Nature and Origin of Mass Opinion* (New York: Cambridge University Press, 1992).
20 Stephen Ansolabehere, "Cooperative Congressional Election Study, 2006," ICPSR30141-v1 (Ann Arbor, MI: Inter-University Consortium for Political and Social Research, 2012-03-26), doi.org/10.3886/ICPSR30141.v1.
21 Dyck and Pearson-Merkowitz, "To Know You Is Not Necessarily to Love You."
22 Cindy D. Kam and Robert J. Franzese, *Modeling and Interpretation of Interactive Hypotheses in Regression Analysis* (Ann Arbor: University of Michigan Press, 2007).
23 Phillip E. Converse, "The Nature of Belief Systems in Mass Publics," in *Ideology and Discontent*, ed. David Apter (New York: Free Press, 1964); Michael X. Delli Carpini and Scott Keeter, *What Americans Know about Politics and Why It Matters* (New Haven, CT: Yale University Press, 1996).
24 Y. Amir, "The Role of Intergroup Contact Theory in Change of Prejudice and Race Relations," in *Towards the Elimination of Racism*, ed. P. A. Katz (New York: Pergamon, 1976).

25 Charles S. Taber, Damon Cann, and Simona Kucsova, "The Motivated Processing of Political Arguments" *Political Behavior* 31, no. 2 (2009): 137–55.
26 Kam and Franzese, *Modeling and Interpretation*.
27 Paul R. Brewer, "The Shifting Foundations of Public Opinion about Gay Rights," *Journal of Politics* 6, no. 4 (2003): 1208–1220.

CHAPTER 8. THE GLOBAL SHIFT IN ATTITUDES TOWARD HOMOSEXUALITY

1 European Values Study 1981–2008, Longitudinal Data File, GESIS Data Archive, Cologne, Germany, ZA4804 Data File Version 2.0.0 (2011–12–30), doi:10.4232/1.11005, 2011; World Value Survey 1981–2014 Longitudinal Aggregate v.20150418, 2015, World Values Survey Association,www.worldvaluessurvey.org
2 Robert Anderson and Tina Fetner, "Economic Inequality and Intolerance: Attitudes toward Homosexuality in 35 Democracies," *American Journal of Political Science* 52, no. 4 (2008): 942–58.
3 Ibid.
4 Phil Ayoub and Jeremiah J. Garretson, "Getting the Message Out: Media Context and Global Changes on Attitudes Involving Homosexuality," *Comparative Political Studies* 50, no. 8 (2017): *1055–85*.

CHAPTER 9. SOCIAL CHANGE IN LIBERAL DEMOCRACIES

1 Please note that I will continue to take a normative stance that attitude change in favor greater support of LGBTQ rights is beneficial for a society. See my note on chapter 1 explaining this stance. That said, given the broader problematic state of American politics as of the writing of this book—political polarization, the return of authoritarianism and populism, and congressional gridlock—and that I am generally pessimistic about politics and policy change in the short term, it should be noted that such optimism is, in reality, out of character.
2 Michael C. Dawson, *Behind the Mule: Race and Class in African-American Politics* (Princeton, NJ: Princeton University Press, 1994).
3 Howard Schuman, Charlotte Steeh, Lawrence Bobo, and Maria Kryson, *Racial Attitudes in America: Trends and Interpretations* (Cambridge, MA: Harvard University Press, 1997).
4 Kinder and Sanders, *Divided by Color*.
5 Ibid.
6 Ibid.
7 Paul R. Kellstedt, *The Mass Media and the Dynamics of American Racial Attitudes* (New York: Cambridge University Press, 2003).
8 Martin Gilens, *Why Americans Hate Welfare: Race, Media, and the Politics of Antipoverty Policy* (Chicago: University of Chicago Press, 1999).
9 Edward Carmines and James Stimson, *Issue Evolution: Race and the Transformation of American Politics* (Princeton, NJ: Princeton University Press, 1989).

10 Jeremiah J. Garretson, "Does Change in Minority and Women's Representation on Television Matter?: A Thirty-Year Study of Television and Social Tolerance," *Politics, Groups, and Identities* 3, no. 4 (2015): 615–32.
11 The Williams Institute, UCLA, "Myth: 'Gays Make More Money than Non-Gays,'" 2012, williamsinstitute.law.ucla.edu.
12 Daniel C. Lewis, *Direct Democracy and Minority Rights: A Critical Assessment of the Tyranny of the Majority in the American States* (New York: Routledge, 2013).
13 Jeremiah J. Garretson, "Changing with the Times: The Spillover Effect of Same-Sex Marriage Ballot Measures on Presidential Elections," *Political Research Quarterly* 67, no. 2 (2014): 280–92.
14 Gallup.com, "Support for Legal Marijuana Use Up to 60% in the U.S.," 2016, www.gallup.com.
15 Ibid.
16 Gallup, "One in Eight U.S. Adults Say They Smoke Marijuana," 2016, www.gallup.com.
17 Ibid.
18 Robert Anderson and Tina Fetner, "Economic Inequality and Intolerance: Attitudes toward Homosexuality in 35 Democracies," *American Journal of Political Science* 52, no. 8 (2008): 942–58.
19 Ibid.
20 Samuel Stouffer, *Communism, Conformity, and Civil Liberties* (New York: Doubleday, 1955).
21 Phillip E. Converse, "The Nature of Belief Systems in Mass Publics," in *Ideology and Discontent*, ed. David Apter (New York: Free Press, 1964).
22 Richard R. Lau and David P. Redlawsk, *How Voters Decide: Information Processing During Election Campaigns* (New York: Cambridge University Press, 2006).

APPENDIX 1

1 Joshua Clinton, Simon Jackman, and Douglas Rivers, "The Statistical Analysis of Roll Call Data," *American Political Science Review* 98, no. 2 (2004): 355–70.
2 Keith Poole and Howard Rosenthal, *Ideology and Congress* (New Brunswick, NJ: Transaction, 2007).
3 Keith Poole, *Spatial Models of Parliamentary Voting* (New York: Cambridge University Press, 2005).

APPENDIX 2

1 The demographic data came from E. Scott Adler's website: sobek.colorado.edu. Presidential election data was coded from various editions of *The Almanac of American Politics.*
2 Joshua J. Dyck and Shuanna Pearson-Merkowitz, "To Know You Is Not Necessarily to Love You: The Partisan Mediators of Intergroup Contact," *Political Behavior* 36, no. 3 (2013): 553–80.

INDEX

ABOUT THE AUTHOR

Jeremiah J. Garretson is Assistant Professor of Political Science at California State University—East Bay. He is the winner of the 2009–2011 Best Dissertation Award from the Sexuality and Politics Section of the American Political Science Association and has published articles on LGBTQ politics and social change in academic journals, including the *Journal of Politics*, *Comparative Political Studies*, and *Political Research Quarterly*.